OLD TESTAMENT
AND ANCIENT EGYPT
TEACHER'S MANUAL

by Laurie Detweiler

Designed by
Ned Bustard

www.VeritasPress.com
800-922-5082

Second Edition 2004

Veritas Press

Copyright ©2004 Veritas Press
www.VeritasPress.com
800-922-5082

ISBN 1-932168-28-1

Printed in the United States of America.

OLD TESTAMENT AND ANCIENT EGYPT
How to use this Manual

We hope this guide will be helpful as you study Old Testament and Ancient Egypt this year. You are about to take a journey through the past where you can see God's providence on a daily basis. Imagine being Noah as he labored over his ark for years, or Moses as he led God's people out of bondage. The Israelites were able to see God crush an entire civilization as He destroyed the Egyptians with plagues. God was faithful to His people through the years just as He is today. What a joy it is for young children to come to realize God's faithfulness as they learn from the past.

CUSTOMIZE IT

There are 32 events/people featured in the cards in each of the Veritas Press History Sets. That is approximately one per week. A few of the cards have extra projects which may spread into the following week. Before you begin, also familiarize yourself with the materials in the Appendix. Many of these projects may be used throughout the year. All the projects in this manual are only suggestions, so use your imagination and have fun with your group. You will note that the projects vary in appeal to different ages. You may choose the ones you think are appropriate for your group. The projects are marked in the answer key to indicate if the project is better suited for younger students or older (grades fourth and higher) students. If you are using this series for second grade or below, you may need to do some of it orally for the first six weeks; after that three times a week is usually enough. Remember, the reason for the Old Testament and Ancient Egypt History Song is to help memorize the chronology of the events. It is also good, after the song has been memorized, to have the children recite events in proper order, rather that singing them.

SAMPLE SCHOOL WEEK

Monday: Sing the Old Testament and Ancient Egypt Memory Song (page 335). You may want to have a student come to the front of the room and hold up the flashcards as the class sings. Present the new card. Read the synopsis on the back and discuss it with the class. Allow different students to read it out loud if you can. The allow the students to answer questions on the corresponding worksheet. The questions are based on information found on the cards. If you are working with second grade or below, they may need to be asked to do this orally for the first part of the year.

Tuesday: Sing the song. Orally review questions from this card's worksheet and from previous events. Obviously, you cannot review every question every day, so do a sampling. Assign different children different sources from the Priority 1 Resources listed on the card and allow them to look up the information and share it with the class.

Wednesday: Sing the song. Orally review questions from the worksheet. Do one of the projects.

Thursday: Sing the song. Orally review from this week and previous weeks. Discuss how this card relates to those before it. Do another project, if there is one.

Friday: Give test. Use remaining time for class instruction and drill.

ENJOYING HISTORY

Having fun makes it easy to learn. Using the cards for games is one way. Ask the children to shuffle them and then see who can get their cards in order the fastest. Or have four to six students mix up their cards and then play Go Fish. This allows them to get familiar with the titles. Or you can get in a large room and see who can use their cards to make their own timeline the fastest. A good way to drill questions in a classroom is to divide the children into two teams and ask questions in order. Teams receive a point for each right answer.

"ONE RING TO BIND THEM . . ."

We have found one of the best ways to file the cards is to laminate them, punch a hole in the top right corner, and keep them on a large ring. The children can add the newest card and also have the previous cards handy. Another idea is to laminate them, put a Velcro strip on the card and on the wall, and start a timeline that children can put up and take down over and over again. An extra set of cards mounted at the other end of the room for a reference timeline is a good idea too.

LITERATURE KIT

To truly send students' imaginations flying, we recommend having the students read historical fiction pertaining to the cards they are studying. The books we find work the best are listed in our catalog as a Literature Kit, following the Priority 1 Resources. In order to encourage children to read books related to classroom work, we suggest a book chart to show points earned for each book read by each student. After receiving a cer-

tain number of points, the child may receive a reward, such as a special lunch with his teacher. You could have a mom bring in a special lunch or allow the winners to go out.

GRADING

Each worksheet, test, or writing assignment should receive three grades, one each for Content, Grammar and Linguistics (Spelling). See page 466 in the Appendix for a helpful grading chart.

Content: On a scale of 1 to 15, grade for completeness or the correct answer to a question. This grade is applied to their history grade. If your grading scale is different from 1 to 15, use yours.

Grammar: The child should answer the questions in complete sentences, in which he first restates the question.

Example:

Question: What is the scripture reference for Creation?

Answer: The scripture reference for Creation is Genesis 1–2.

Initially in second grade the teacher may want to write a portion of the sentence on the board for the students to copy until they learn to do this correctly on their own (i.e., *The scripture reference for Creation is _____.*). The students would then fill in the rest. As the weeks go by gradually wean them until they are able to do this on their own. Second graders adjust to this in about six weeks. You may want to have the students write on a separate, lined sheet of paper if your student is a young writer. Sentences should begin with a capital letter and end with an appropriate punctuation mark. (Please note that for space considerations, the answers provided in the back of this manual do not restate the question and are not necessarily complete sentences.) As the year progresses you can grade more strictly for grammar. This grade should be applied to an application grade in grammar, but should not affect history content grades. We suggest application at twenty percent of the overall grammar grade.

Linguistics: The children should spell all words correctly. You should deduct for misspelled words once the rule for spelling a particular word has been mastered. For example: "I before e except after c." Once this has been covered, a child's grade would be reduced if they spelled *receive* as *recieve.* If they are using a history card to do their worksheet, they should be taught that those words should be spelled correctly. This grade would be applied towards a linguistics application grade. Again we suggest twenty percent, but not to affect their history grade.

When you look at the tests you will see that there are not the same number of questions on each test or worksheet. We assign five points per question, with the listings of the chronology receiving two points per item listed. Partial credit may be counted because the questions are essay in nature, and they may have portions correct.

Some students may ask why they are receiving three grades on each paper. We believe that it is important for a student to realize that grammar and linguistics matter in history class as well as in grammar class. All three contribute to helping make students understood by others, and are thus intertwined.

FEEDBACK

We welcome your feedback and comments. We hope that his resource will enrich the education of those children entrusted to you, and will help them understand the comprehensive responsibility that God requires of them.

Marlin Detweiler

Laurie Detweiler

OLD TESTAMENT AND ANCIENT EGYPT
Table of Contents

OLD TESTAMENT AND ANCIENT EGYPT
Map

The map shown below can be assembled after copying pages 363–378 in the Appendix. Cut out along the solid black lines and tape together by aligning with the light gray interior lines (the panels will overlap—each side of each page is an extra .25"). If you are able, laminating the entire map may prove useful as it will be used throughout the year. For an even larger map, photocopy each page onto tabloid-sized sheets at 140%.

On the final two pages of the map there are simplified line drawings of the artwork found on the history cards. As a card is introduced, that card's circle should be cut out and attached to the map on its corresponding number. Use the timeline pages starting on page 379.

Colored yarn should be attached to the map along the dotted and dashed lines when discussing those travels.

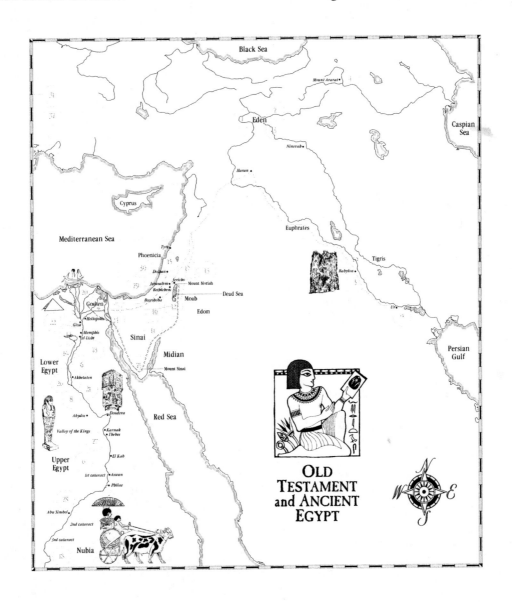

CREATION
Worksheet

1. What book and chapters in the Bible cover the creation of the world?

   _____

   _____

2. How long has God existed?

   _____

   _____

3. Next to each day write what God created.

   Day 1: _____

   _____

   Day 2: _____

   _____

   Day 3: _____

   _____

   Day 4: _____

   _____

   Day 5: _____

   _____

   Day 6: _____

   _____

   Day 7: _____

CREATION
Project 1—Creation Mobile

Materials

paper

brass fasteners

string

colored pencils or markers

scissors

tape

Instructions

Photocopy the artwork below and on the following page (you will need to end up with seven panels) onto stiff paper. On each panel write the day of creation and what was created that day and color it in a solid color, or illustrate what was made. Cut out each day of creation and the voice bubble. Cut a 7" piece of string and tape it to the back of one side of the voice bubble, then fold and fasten the bubble so that it sandwiches the string. Fasten the panels together using the brass fasteners as shown above. Tie one end of the string to the inside top fastener, so the bubble hangs within the globe. Tie another length of string to the top of the top fastener to complete the mobile.

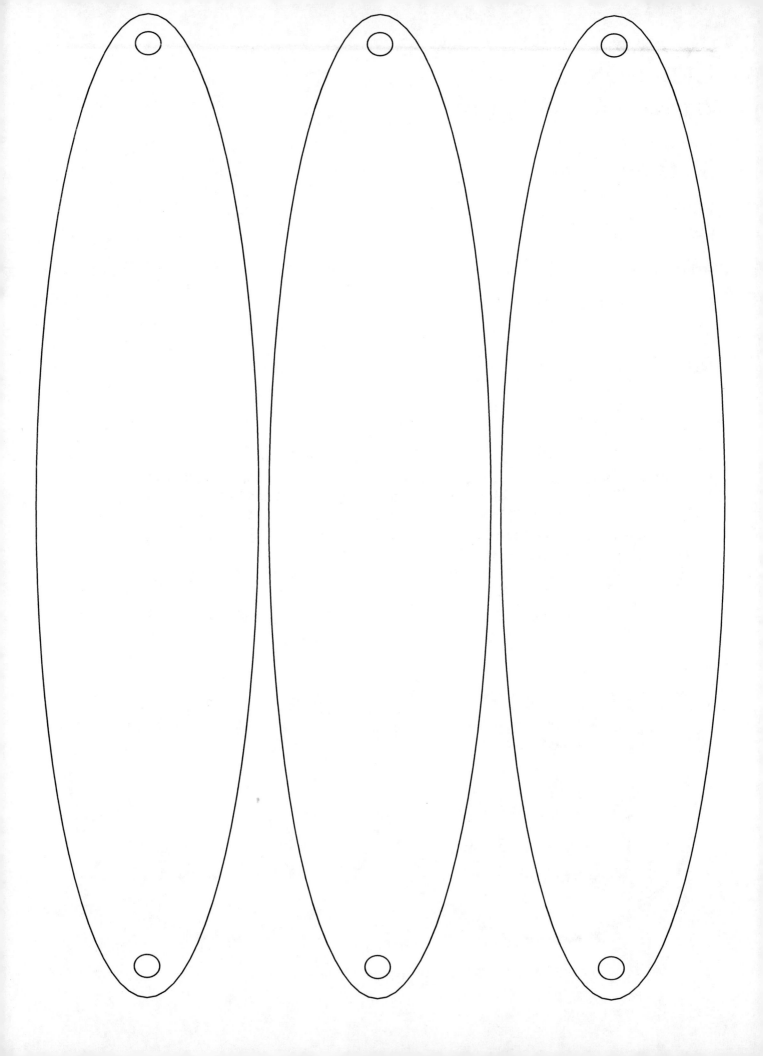

CREATION
Project 2—Creation Myths

Read through the article below then draw a picture of a scene from one of the stories.

The first verse of the Bible says, "In the beginning God created the heavens and the earth." Yet not everyone in the world believes the Bible. Some believe that the description of how everything was made that is found in the Bible is a myth. A myth is a made-up story that explains a belief or natural phenomenon. There are myths all over the world, and though they aren't true like the Bible is, sometimes they have at their root a true idea. It is common to hear from missionaries around the world that isolated tribes often have myths which are similar to the Biblical account of creation. We should not be surprised to hear this, since the Bible says only Noah and his family lived through the Flood—so all their children are the people who have filled the earth. They all tell the same "family history," even if it gets a bit muddled, like it does when you play the game "whisper down the lane."

For example, Indians in southern California tell of Bald Eagle, the chief of the animals, making man of clay and women of a feather while the man was sleeping. The Pima Indians of southern Arizona believe, Earth Maker mixed clay and sweat to make a man and a woman, then breathed life into them. Don't these stories sound familiar?

In Egypt several versions of a creation myth emerged out of their long history. One says that there was a time when nothing had existed, when "the sky had not yet come into being, the earth had not yet come into being, the gods had not yet been born, and death had not yet come into being." Yet, there was the swirling watery chaos from which arose the god Atum, and he created the gods Shu and Tefnut who then gave birth to Geb (earth) and Nut (heaven), who gave birth to Osiris, Isis, Set and Nephthys. People were created from Atum's tears.

CREATION
Test

1. Where can we find the story of Creation in the Bible?

   _____

   _____

2. Who existed before the world began?

   _____

   _____

3. Next to each day write what God created.

   Day 1: _____

   _____

   Day 2: _____

   _____

   Day 3: _____

   _____

   Day 4: _____

   _____

   Day 5: _____

   _____

   Day 6: _____

   _____

   Day 7: _____

   _____

THE FALL IN THE GARDEN
Worksheet

1. Who tempted Eve to eat of the Tree of the Knowledge of Good and Evil?

   _____

   _____

   _____

2. To whom did Eve offer the fruit? Did that person also eat the fruit?

   _____

   _____

   _____

   _____

3. What was the earth like before the fruit was eaten?

   _____

   _____

   _____

4. What did God do when the forbidden fruit was eaten?

   _____

   _____

   _____

   _____

5. What was man's relationship with God like after the fruit was eaten?

   _____

   _____

   _____

The Fall in the Garden
Project 1—Briars and Weeds

Read Genesis 3. Using complete sentences, write a paragraph describing what is happening in the picture below.

_____

_____

_____

_____

_____

_____

_____

_____

_____

_____

THE FALL IN THE GARDEN
Project 2—The Cunning Serpent

Several translations of the Bible say that the serpent was more crafty *than any of the other animals God made. For this project we are going to make a crafty craft serpent!*

Supplies

colored paper

glue

scissors

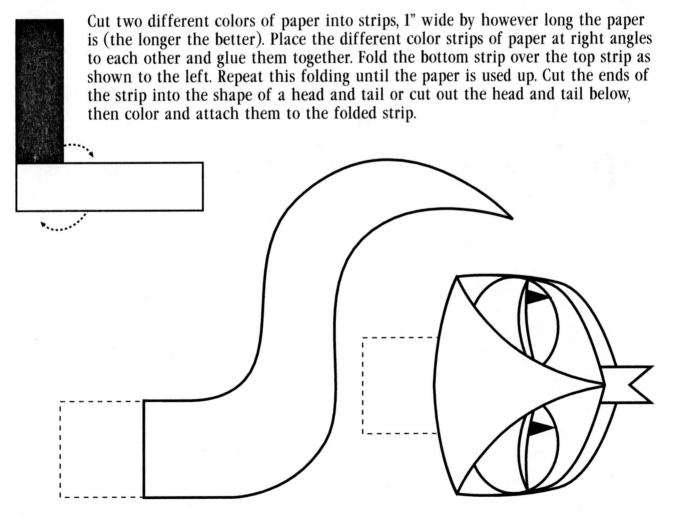

Directions

Cut two different colors of paper into strips, 1" wide by however long the paper is (the longer the better). Place the different color strips of paper at right angles to each other and glue them together. Fold the bottom strip over the top strip as shown to the left. Repeat this folding until the paper is used up. Cut the ends of the strip into the shape of a head and tail or cut out the head and tail below, then color and attach them to the folded strip.

THE FALL IN THE GARDEN
Project 3—Paradise P.I.

You have been called into the Garden of Eden to get to the bottom of what happened at the Tree of the Knowledge of Good and Evil. Your assistant has taken statements from the suspects, and it is your job to makes sense of it all. *Read Genesis 3 (below) then review the suspects' statements on the following page and determine who is telling the truth. Be careful, the suspects are tricky!*

Now the serpent was more cunning than any beast of the field which the LORD God had made. And he said to the woman, "Has God indeed said, 'You shall not eat of every tree of the garden'?" ²And the woman said to the serpent, "We may eat the fruit of the trees of the garden; ³but of the fruit of the tree which is in the midst of the garden, God has said, 'You shall not eat it, nor shall you touch it, lest you die.'" ⁴Then the serpent said to the woman, "You will not surely die. ⁵For God knows that in the day you eat of it your eyes will be opened, and you will be like God, knowing good and evil."

⁶So when the woman saw that the tree was good for food, that it was pleasant to the eyes, and a tree desirable to make one wise, she took of its fruit and ate. She also gave to her husband with her, and he ate. ⁷Then the eyes of both of them were opened, and they knew that they were naked; and they sewed fig leaves together and made themselves coverings.

⁸And they heard the sound of the LORD God walking in the garden in the cool of the day, and Adam and his wife hid themselves from the presence of the LORD God among the trees of the garden. ⁹Then the LORD God called to Adam and said to him, "Where are you?"

¹⁰So he said, "I heard Your voice in the garden, and I was afraid because I was naked; and I hid myself." ¹¹And He said, "Who told you that you were naked? Have you eaten from the tree of which I commanded you that you should not eat?" ¹²Then the man said, "The woman whom You gave to be with me, she gave me of the tree, and I ate."

¹³And the LORD God said to the woman, "What is this you have done?" The woman said, "The serpent deceived me, and I ate."

¹⁴So the LORD God said to the serpent:
"Because you have done this,
You are cursed more than all cattle,
And more than every beast of the field;
On your belly you shall go,
And you shall eat dust
All the days of your life.
¹⁵And I will put enmity
Between you and the woman,
And between your seed and her Seed;
He shall bruise your head,
And you shall bruise His heel."
¹⁶To the woman He said:
"I will greatly multiply your sorrow

THE FALL IN THE GARDEN
Project 3—Paradise P.I., Page 2

and your conception;
In pain you shall bring forth children;
Your desire shall be for your husband,
And he shall rule over you."

[17]Then to Adam He said, "Because you have heeded the voice of your wife, and have eaten from the tree of which I commanded you, saying, 'You shall not eat of it':
"Cursed is the ground for your sake;
In toil you shall eat of it
All the days of your life.
[18]Both thorns and thistles it shall
    bring forth for you,
And you shall eat the herb of the field.
[19]In the sweat of your face you shall eat bread
    Till you return to the ground,
            For out of it you

were taken;
    For dust you are,
    And to dust you shall return."

[20]And Adam called his wife's name Eve, because she was the mother of all living. [21]Also for Adam and his wife the LORD God made tunics of skin, and clothed them.

[22]Then the LORD God said, "Behold, the man has become like one of Us, to know good and evil. And now, lest he put out his hand and take also of the tree of life, and eat, and live forever"—[23]therefore the LORD God sent him out of the garden of Eden to till the ground from which he was taken. [24]So He drove out the man; and He placed cherubim at the east of the garden of Eden, and a flaming sword which turned every
            way, to guard the way to
                the tree of life.

THE FALL IN THE GARDEN
Project 3—Paradise P.I., Page 3

Circle the correct answer.

1. T / F   The serpent spoke.

2. T / F   The woman was told that eating the fruit would make her a god.

3. T / F   The woman was resentful of God's control, so she rebelled against God.

4. T / F   Eve ate the fruit.

5. T / F   Adam and the woman sewed animal skins together to make coverings for themselves.

6. T / F   God walked in the Garden.

7. T / F   Adam and his wife hid from God.

8. T / F   The serpent tricked Adam and the woman into eating the fruit.

9. T / F   God cursed the serpent saying,
"You are cursed more than all cattle, and more than every beast of the field . . ."

10. T / F   Adam told God it was the woman who gave him the fruit to eat.

11. T / F   When the woman was created, God told her that Adam would rule over her.

12. T / F   Adam and Eve made tunics of skin to clothe themselves.

THE FALL IN THE GARDEN
Project 4—Fill in the Blank

Using the history card, fill in the missing blanks. This will help in memorizing the flashcard.

The Lord told Adam not to eat of the _____ of the knowledge of _____ and _____. God's _____ clearly told Adam that he would "surely _____" if he ate of the _____ .

Satan, disguised as a _____ , came and tempted _____ to eat of the tree. Satan twisted God's _____ by making Eve believe that eating the _____ of the tree would "open her _____" and make her "like _____." Instead of trusting God, Eve _____ and ate the _____ . She also _____ the fruit to _____ , and he ate as well.

The _____ of Adam and Eve, our first _____ , had disastrous consequences. Adam was the _____ of all creation, so because of Adam's sin, God _____ the world. As God promised, _____ resulted from _____ transgression. God also punished _____ and _____ by making Adam's work difficult and Eve's pain great when she gave _____ to children. Because Adam stood as our representative, his _____ caused all of us to become _____ before God, too.

Even though Adam sinned and broke God's _____ , God remained gracious and promised that he would send a "_____" that would crush _____ and his kingdom. _____ is that seed.

THE FALL IN THE GARDEN
Test

1. What did the serpent offer Eve?

    _____

    _____

2. What did Adam do when Eve offered him the fruit?

    _____

    _____

3. Why did God curse the ground and make life hard for mankind?

    _____

    _____

    _____

4. How was man's relationship with God changed after he sinned?

    _____

    _____

    _____

Review

1. Write what God created on each day.

    Day 1: _____

    Day 2: _____

    Day 3: _____

    Day 4: _____

    Day 5: _____

    Day 6: _____

    Day 7: _____

CAIN AND ABEL
Worksheet

1. Where is the story of Cain and Abel found in Scripture?

   _____

   _____

2. Who was the first child ever born? Who were his parents?

   _____

   _____

   _____

3. Who was Cain's brother?

   _____

   _____

4. What was the occupation of Cain? Of Abel?

   _____

   _____

   _____

5. What sacrifice did they each bring to God?

   _____

   _____

   _____

6. Who was the world's first murderer? Why did he murder?

   _____

   _____

   _____

   _____

CAIN AND ABEL
Worksheet, Page 2

7. What was God's judgment on Cain?

_____

_____

_____

_____

_____

CAIN AND ABEL
Project 1—Genesis 4 Bible Summary

So the Lord said to Cain, "Why are you angry? And why has your countenance fallen?
If you do well, will you not be accepted? And if you do not do well, sin lies at the door.
And its desire is for you, but you should rule over it." *(Genesis 4:6, 7)*

After discussing the meaning of these verses with your teacher write a paragraph below summarizing their meaning.

CAIN AND ABEL
Project 2—Matching

*Draw lines from the items below to the altar belonging to
the brother who would have sacrificed them.*

CAIN AND ABEL
Test

In your own words write a paragraph retelling the story of Cain and Abel. Be sure to include all the important information.

_____

_____

_____

_____

_____

_____

_____

_____

_____

_____

_____

_____

Review

1. Where in the Bible is the story of Creation?

    _____

2. Who tempted Eve to eat the forbidden fruit?

    _____

3. List the three events covered so far in chronological order.

    _____

    _____

    _____

THE FLOOD
Worksheet

1. Where is the Flood described in the Bible?

   _____

   _____

2. Why was God grieved that He had made man?

   _____

   _____

3. God decided to destroy man. One man found favor in God's sight. Who was that man? And what did God instruct him to do?

   _____

   _____

   _____

4. What did God do to destroy man? For how long?

   _____

   _____

   _____

   _____

5. Define "covenant."

   _____

   _____

   _____

6. What was the purpose of the rainbow God sent after the Flood?

   _____

   _____

THE FLOOD
Project 1—
The Ark's Size

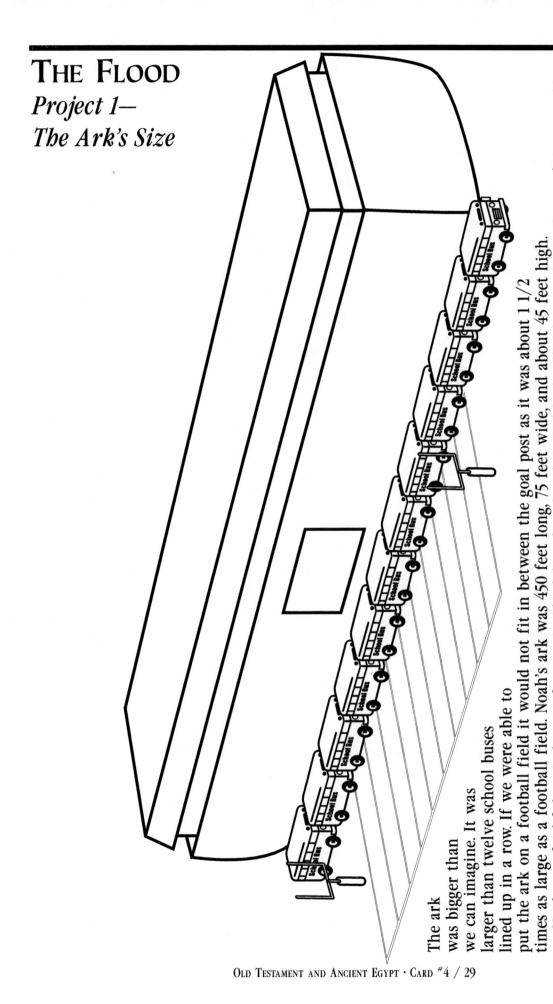

The ark was bigger than we can imagine. It was larger than twelve school buses lined up in a row. If we were able to put the ark on a football field it would not fit in between the goal post as it was about 1 1/2 times as large as a football field. Noah's ark was 450 feet long, 75 feet wide, and about 45 feet high.

Noah was faithful to God year after year as he labored to do what God had called him to do. Noah was 480 years old when God called him to build the ark, and it took him 120 years to complete it. How old would Noah have been? Imagine what it would have been like to work on the ark for 120 years waiting for the flood to come. What lesson can we learn from this as we labor to do God's work in our own lives?

Color this page.

THE FLOOD
Project 2—Mini-Ark Models

Try one of the two projects below to make your own mini ark.

Supplies

cardstock

scissors

tape

markers or colored pencils

Directions

Photocopy the next three pages onto cardstock. Color the parts of the ark in woodtones. Cut away white areas. Tape the the bow and stern of the boat to the midship, overlapping the ends over the midship portion up to the dotted lines. Fold the boat in half along the ridge line of the roof, and then the two lines on either side which indicate the upper and lower edge of the side of the ark. Tape along the bottom of the ark, overlapping the shorter side to the line on the longer edge. Bend both ends and overlap slightly and tape on the inside.

Supplies

two shoe boxes with lids
   (one smaller than the other)

white poster board

brown paint

miscellaneous colors to paint animals

clay that will harden

Directions

1. Glue shoe lids to boxes. (A hot glue gun will speed up the process.)
2. Glue the smaller box centered on top of the larger box.
3. Out of poster board cut a roof for the ark according to the pattern to the right. Glue it to the top of the top (smaller) box.

   width of smaller box

4. Cut a door in one side of the ark.
5. Paint the entire ark brown. (Older children may want to use a dark marker to make the "wood" have a granular look.)

You may wish to use Sculpey™ clay to make Noah, his family, and the animals. (Remember it was not two of every kind of animal. See Genesis 6:19–7:3.) This would also be a good time to distinguish between clean and unclean animals.

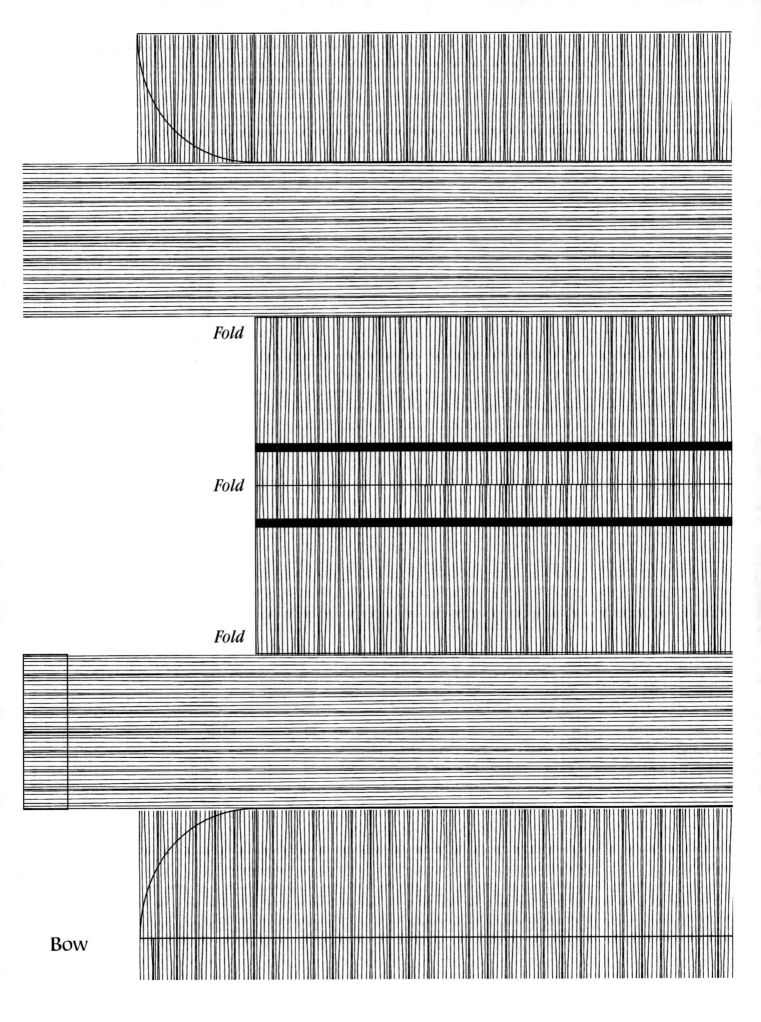

Fold

Fold

Fold

Bow

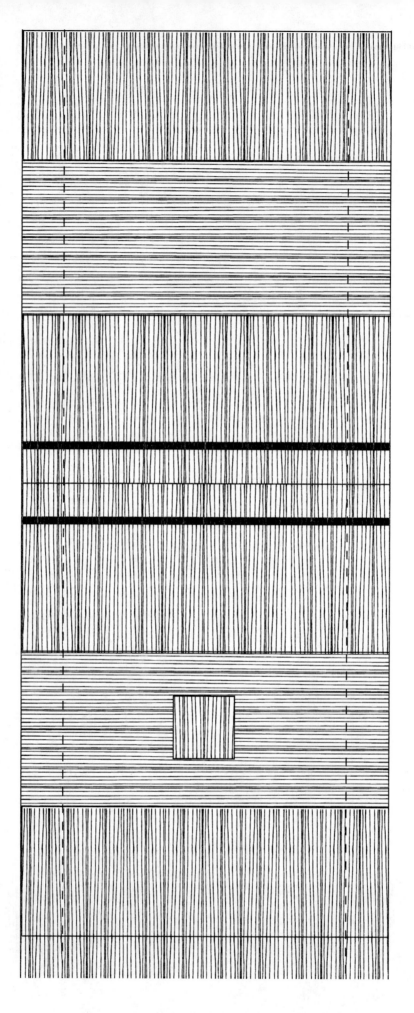

MIDSHIP

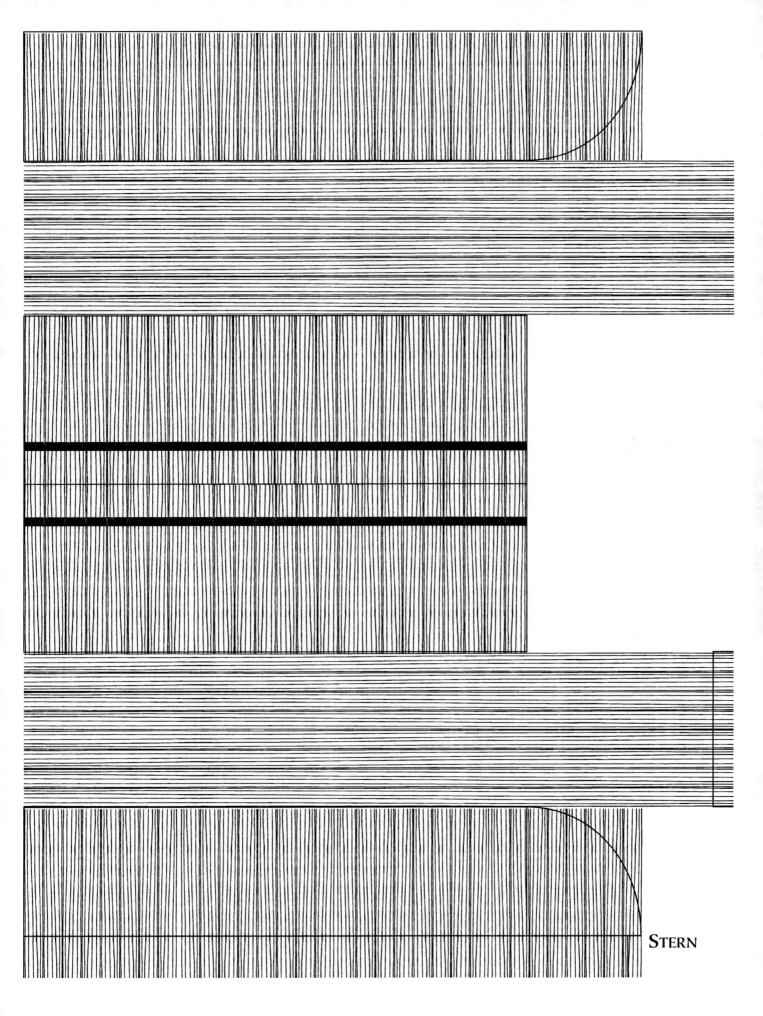

STERN

THE FLOOD
Project 3—Dove Pop-Up Card

Make a book with pop-up greeting card.

Materials

paper

glue

colored pencils

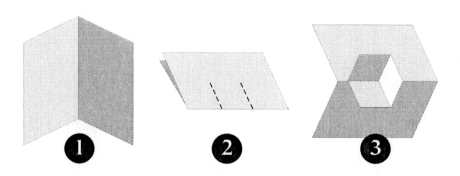

Directions

Photocopy this and the next two pages for each student, with the next two pages backing each other up. Cut out the card and fold in half along the dotted line [1]. Cut two parallel cuts on the folded side, following the solid lines on the card [2]. Open the page. Begin to close the page, but as you do, take your finger and push the cut portion in and crease it inside the page. Now when you open the page halfway, the cut portion pops up and looks like a chair [3]. Color both the happy and sad Noahs. Cut out the dove and glue it on the "leg" of the chair on the inside next to the happy Noah. Write a message on the panel opposite of Noah. For example: *Don't be so blue . . .* (front) / *God keeps His promises to you!* (inside)

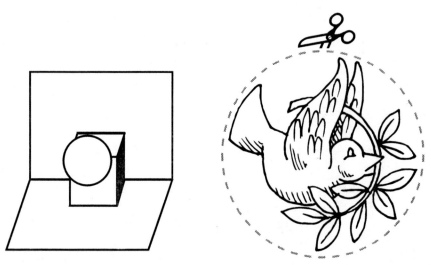

THE FLOOD
Project 3—Dove Pop-Up Card, Page 2

(glue dove here)

THE FLOOD
Project 4—The Logistics of the Ark

Below is a reading and project for older students about the Flood account. Is the Bible wrong about the Ark? Could the Ark carry all the different types of animals? Ark critics have attacked the Bible, denying the Genesis flood account because of this logistical skepticism.

The important creationist book, The Genesis Flood *(1961) by Morris and Whitcomb, contained a detailed analysis. There is now a more detailed and updated study by John Woodmorappe,* Noah's Ark: A Feasibility Study.

HOW MANY TYPES OF ANIMALS
DID NOAH NEED TO TAKE?

WAS THE ARK LARGE ENOUGH TO
HOLD ALL THE REQUIRED ANIMALS?

HOW MANY TYPES OF ANIMALS
DID NOAH NEED TO TAKE?

The texts of scripture that address these questions are Genesis 6:19–20 and 7:2–3.

Genesis 6:19–20: 'And of every living thing of all flesh, two of every sort shalt thou bring into the ark, to keep them alive with thee; they shall be male and female. Of fowls after their kind, and of cattle after their kind, of every creeping thing of the earth after his kind, two of every sort shall come unto thee, to keep them alive.'

Genesis 7:2–3: 'Of every clean beast thou shalt take to thee by sevens, the male and his female: and of beasts that are not clean by two, the male and his female. Of fowls also of the air by sevens, the male and the female; to keep seed alive upon the face of all the earth.'

The Hebrew term for 'beast' and 'cattle' in these passages is the same: *behemah,* and it refers to land animals in general. The word for 'creeping things' is *remes,* which has a number of meanings in scripture, but it probably refers to what we would classify as reptiles. Noah did not need to take sea creatures, of course. But the turbulent and cataclysmic event would cause massive carnage, produc-

ing much of the fossil record. It still appears that the Flood is the best explanation for the massive geological and fossil deposits which attest all over the globe to a world-wide flood. As for other "life," plants could have survived as seeds, and others could have survived on floating mats of vegetation. Insects and other invertebrates were small enough to have survived in a similar manner. What is claimed is that the Flood wiped out all land animals which breathed through nostrils, except those on the Ark (Genesis 7:22).

It is important to note that there is nothing inconsistent about the loss of many species over time and the Biblical teaching. The world is fallen, and death reigns. Many species have become extinct and continue to go extinct. Also, belief in Creation and the Biblical Flood do not require the forced geological time-frames of evolutionary mythology. One should not be surprised when "living fossils" like the Coelacanth are discovered "alive" in 1938. There are now many living examples widely on display. This "early" fish was thought to have been extinct 65 million years ago according to evolutionary dogma.

The text speaks of "clean animals" "by sevens." The term "clean animal" was defined later in the books of Moses. There are actually very few "clean" land animals listed in Leviticus 11 and Deuteronomy 14. The vast majority of animals are not clean and were delivered by only two representatives each.

What is a "kind?" God created different types of animals with capacity for variation within limits. This term, "kind," refers to a larger grouping than what we call species. In most cases, those species descended from a particular original kind would be grouped today within what modern taxonomists (biologists who classify living things) call a *genus* (plural *genera*).

For example, horses, zebras and donkeys are probably descended from an equine (horse-like) kind. Dogs, wolves, coyotes and jackals are probably from a canine (dog-like) kind. We know that tigers and lions can produce hybrids called tigons and ligers, so it is likely that they are descended from the same original kind.

Woodmorappe totals about 8000 genera, including extinct genera, comprising 16,000 animals to be aboard the Ark. The common question arises, "How could you fit all those huge dinosaurs on the Ark?" Of the 668 supposed dinosaur genera, only 106 weighed more than ten tons when fully grown. Contrary to our fine artistic renderings, Noah may have found it easier to transport the young, rather than the fully grown animals. If so, the median size of all animals on the ark would have been squirrel size. Woodmorappe concludes that only about 11% would have been much larger than a sheep.

The Ark measured 300x50x30 cubits (Genesis 6:15) which is about 140x23x13.5 meters or 459x75x44 feet, so its volume was 43,500 m³ (cubic meters) or 1.54 million cubic feet. This is the size of 522 standard railroad boxcars, which can hold 240 sheep per car.

With the animals in pens of an average size of 50x50x30 centimeters (20x20x12 inches), that is 75,000 cm³ (cubic centimeters) or 4800 cubic inches, the 16,000 animals would occupy only 1200m³ (42,000 cubic feet) or 14.4 boxcars!

Beyond that, even if all the insect species in the world were included (probably not),

they would occupy only another 12 boxcars. That would leave about 500 boxcars for food, Noah's family and other space for the animals to play catch. Woodmorappe calculated only 15% of the volume for foodstuffs and 9.4% for drinking water. But of course, there was no absence of water. There would be quite enough room on the Ark for all the animals and other necessary cargo.

What about the dung? This occupies a great deal of the mind of the skeptical inquirer. If you must know, there are many designs which are used today which aid in the dung disposal dilemma: sloped and slatted floors, among them, which would be tidally flushed away or destroyed by vermicomposting (composting by worms). Hibernation is also a realistic possibility for many of the animals, which would reduce many of the logistical requirements even more.

Many Christians believe that the Bible cannot be trusted on scientific matters. Thorough investigation, such as that of Woodmorappe and others, shows otherwise. He devoted seven years to his scholarly, systematic answer to the Ark critics. This summary of his work suggests that the critics' difficulties are not based in scientific or logistical data after all. They are rooted in a denial of the God of scripture and the authority of His Word.

REFERENCES

"How did all the animals fit on Noah's Ark?" Jonathan Sarfati, Creation 19(2):16–19, March–May 1997.

J.C. Whitcomb, and H.M. Morris, *The Genesis Flood*, Phillipsburg, New Jersey, USA, Presbyterian and Reformed Publishing Co., 1961.

A.J. Jones, 'How many animals on the Ark?' Creation Research Society Quarterly 10(2):16–18, 1973.

THE FLOOD

Test

1. Where in the Bible is the story of the Flood found?

   _____

   _____

2. Why did God flood the earth?

   _____

   _____

   _____

3. Who found grace in the eyes of the Lord?

   _____

   _____

4. What did God instruct Noah to do?

   _____

   _____

5. What covenant sign did God send? What did it mean?

   _____

   _____

   _____

Review

1. Why did God curse the ground and make life difficult for man?

   _____

   _____

   _____

   _____

THE FLOOD
Test, Page 2

2. What happened when Cain and Abel brought their sacrifices before the Lord?

_____

_____

_____

_____

3. Why did God curse Cain?

_____

_____

_____

4. List the four events in chronological order covered to date and the scripture references for them.

_____

_____

_____

_____

THE TOWER OF BABEL
Worksheet

1. Where in the Bible do you find the description of the Tower of Babel?

   _____

   _____

2. How many languages were spoken in the world before the Tower of Babel?

   _____

   _____

3. What did God cause to happen while the people built the Tower of Babel?

   _____

   _____

   _____

4. What do some archeologists believe may be the ruins of the Tower of Babel?

   _____

   _____

   _____

   _____

The Tower of Babel
Project 1—Ziggurat Model

The Tower of Babel may have been a ziggurat, also known as a temple tower. The Egyptians may have gotten ideas for their pyramids by copying ziggurats. The tower is built by building small platforms, one on top of the other. They were probably constructed out of bricks which were made from mud and straw. In some instances each level was painted a different color and a shrine was placed at the top.

To see a picture of a ziggurat refer to *The Children's Illustrated Bible*, pages 28 and 29.

You can make a ziggurat model in several ways. You can stack progressively smaller boxes one on top of the other. Or you might construct a small clay model using various colors of clay. Lego or Duplo building bricks make excellent ziggurats as well.

THE TOWER OF BABEL
Project 2—Ziggurat Drawing

Ziggurats were large buildings for worship and ceremonies in Shinar (Genesis 10:10—later, the land of Babylon). The architecture was like the pyramids of the Egyptians, but without smooth sides. They were usually seven stories, with each level getting smaller as it got higher. To reach the top of a ziggurat, you would need to climb stairs or ramps. Two other styles were the "Winding Road" (it consisted of stairs or ramps that wound around the tower) and the four storied style which had three stairways which joined at the top of the first story. Each level of a ziggurat was painted a different color, creating a rainbow effect. They were constructed of mud bricks and asphalt was used to glue them together. The overall stucture was 200-300 feet wide and up to 300 feet high.

Draw one of the three styles of ziggurats below and color it.

THE TOWER OF BABEL
Project 3—Fill in the Blank

Using the history card, fill in the missing blanks. This will help in memorizing the material.
After filling in the blanks, draw a picture how you imagine the towering might have looked.

The whole _____ spoke one _____ at this time. They gathered together to build a _____ into the _____ and became sinfully _____ of their accomplishments. So _____ caused them to speak _____ different languages causing them to _____ abroad _____ the face of the earth.

Some believe the tower is the _____ of _____ at Babylon which stands _____ feet high.

THE TOWER OF BABEL
Test

1. Where in the Bible is the story of the Tower of Babel found?

    _____

    _____

2. How did we come to have many languages spoken in the world?

    _____

    _____

3. What do some archaeologist believe may be the ruins of the Tower of Babel?

    _____

    _____

Review

1. Next to each day write what God created.

    Day 1: _____

    Day 2: _____

    Day 3: _____

    Day 4: _____

    Day 5: _____

    Day 6: _____

    Day 7: _____

THE TOWER OF BABEL
Test, Page 2

2. When did sin enter the world?

_____

_____

3. Who was the first baby born into the world?

_____

_____

4. What was God's covenant with Noah?

_____

_____

5. In sequence write the events studied to date.

_____

_____

_____

_____

_____

_____

UNIFICATION OF UPPER AND LOWER EGYPT
Worksheet

1. Who was the first known pharaoh of Egypt? How old was he when he became pharaoh?

    _____

    _____

    _____

2. What remarkable feat did this pharaoh accomplish?

    _____

    _____

3. What crown did this pharaoh wear? What did it represent?

    _____

    _____

    _____

    _____

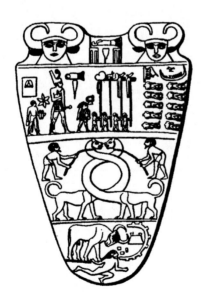

UNIFICATION OF UPPER AND LOWER EGYPT
Project 1—Hunting Expedition

Little is known about Menes. It is known, however, that he was a mighty hunter. Pyramid paintings and reliefs show that he hunted elephants, giraffes, lions and wild oxen with only a bow and arrow. In his little boat he would hunt hippopotami and crocodiles in the Nile River with harpoons and lances. He once chased an antelope over the desert leaving his men behind. He found himself being chased by a pack of half-wild dogs. To escape he dove into a lake and then faced the jaws of crocodiles before reaching safety. *On the panels below, illustrate your own pyramid paintings/reliefs depicting this story.*

UNIFICATION OF UPPER AND LOWER EGYPT
Project 2—The Nile Flood Project

Supplies

3" deep rectangular pan

sand

potting soil

grass seed

foil

rocks and pebbles

toothpicks

glue

air-drying clay (optional)

Directions

Place about 2" of soil on the bottom of the pan (a clean cat litter pan works well). Fold foil into a snakey Y-shape of the river and press into the soil. Place some smooth pebbles in the river to weigh it down. Put a thick layer of sand along the long sides of the pan then fill in the area on either side of the foil river with soil. Press the grass seeds into the soil along each side of the river bed.

Once a week "flood" the river so it over-flows its banks. Enjoy the lush green Nile val-ley for a couple of months.

Label the areas of the living map using labels glued to tooth picks. Rosetta is western branch and Damietta is eastern. Nubia is the land to the south, Red Land is the desert, Tura was a limestone quarry, and Giza is famous for the three pyramids built there. To add another dimension to this project, sculpt small models of the pyramids and the sphinx from air-drying clay and add to the scene. Consult an atlas for placement.

Labels

```
MEMPHIS

NUBIA

ROSETTA BRANCH

DAMIETTA BRANCH

TURA

GIZA

RED LAND
```

UNIFICATION OF UPPER AND LOWER EGYPT
Project 3—Salt Relief Map

Supplies

cardboard box lid (8.5" x 11")

white glue

pencil

two mixing bowls

mixing spoon

measuring cups

flour

salt

water

food coloring

Salt Dough Recipe
(enough to make three maps)

6 cups of salt

6 cups of flour

2–3 cups of water

Combine salt and flour, mix well. Add two cups of water and mix until smooth. Add remaining water as needed. Divide dough in half. Add green food coloring to one portion and blue to the other. Cover and set aside. (This can be mixed the day before and stored in a refrigerator. It may also be frozen to use later.)

Directions

1. Looking at the map on the following page draw the Mediterranean Sea, Red Sea, and Nile River on the inside of the box lid.
2. Using blue dough, cover the bodies of water except the Nile River.
3. Using green dough cover the land areas including the Nile River.
4. Locate Upper and Lower Egypt. Referring to the map on the following page, carve out the Nile River with a pencil.
5. Push blue dough into the Nile River area with a pencil.
6. Allow one week for drying.
7. After drying cut labels out and glue them in the appropriate places.

Labels:

MEDITERRANEAN SEA

RED SEA

LOWER EGYPT

UPPER EGYPT

MEMPHIS

UNIFICATION OF UPPER AND LOWER EGYPT
Project 3, Page 2

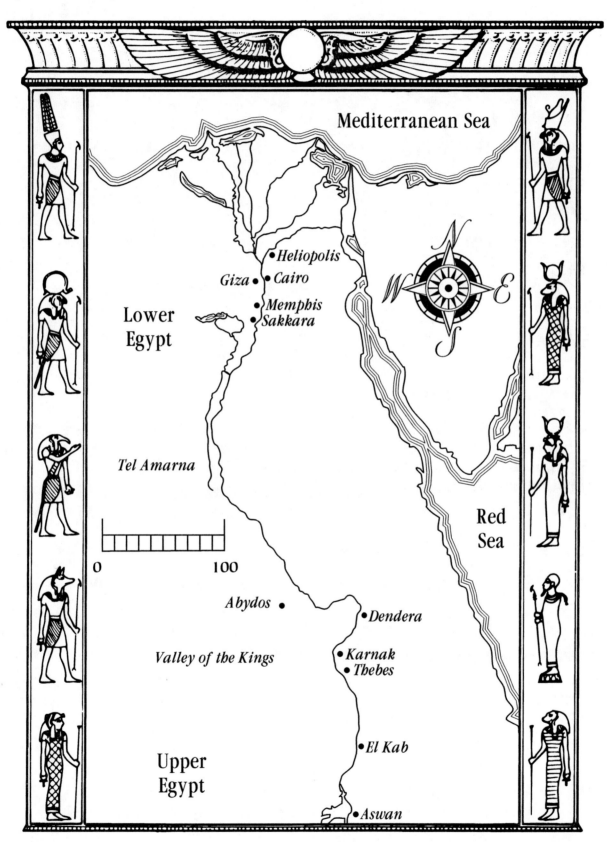

Mediterranean Sea

• *Heliopolis*

Giza •   • *Cairo*

Lower Egypt

• *Memphis*
• *Sakkara*

Tel Amarna

0   100

Red Sea

Abydos •

• *Dendera*

Valley of the Kings

• *Karnak*
• *Thebes*

Upper Egypt

• *El Kab*

• *Aswan*

Unification of Upper and Lower Egypt
Project 4—Crown of Upper and Lower Egypt

Materials

red construction paper (12" x 18")

white construction paper

yellow construction paper

stapler

scotch tape

scissors

poster board

Directions

Trace the patterns on this page and the next onto poster board and cut them out to make a permanent pattern. Place the poster board on the folded edge of red and white paper as noted on this pattern. Trace the pattern and cut out the shape. Use scraps of red, as necessary to size the pattern to fit the child. Staple the red crown so it fits snugly around the head of the child. Staple the white crown inside the front of the red crown. Cut a slit in the center of the red crown to recieve the tab of the yellow serpent. Curl the head of the serpent and glue or tape it in place.

Cut from red construction paper.
Place the right edge on the fold.

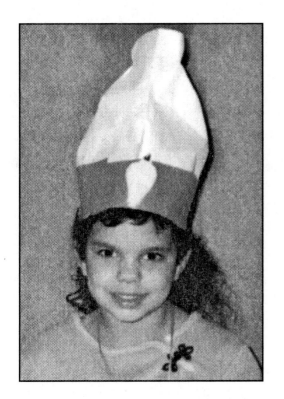

Cut from white construction paper. Place right edge of design on the fold.

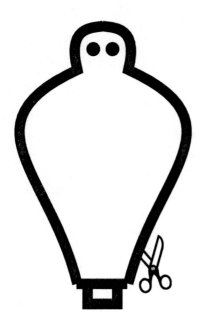

Cut from yellow construction paper.

Unification of Upper and Lower Egypt
Project 5—Flooding of the Nile: A Reading

Egypt's Fascinating Story

A secret is one of the most fascinating things in the entire world. When you have found it out, part of its charm may have flown; but as long as you are kept wondering about it, you are on tiptoe with expectation and excitement. Do you know of a country that has kept shining secrets hidden for centuries? Golden sands, lying smooth and silent beside the stream of a long blue river, gave no sign of brilliant pageants that had long ago passed back and forth there. Rock cliffs stood calm and blank under the blazing sun, never revealing a hint of the treasure they were holding. *Egypt*—the word itself looks cryptic, secretive. The Nile, the ancient sacred river, the very life and heart of the long, narrow land of Egypt, seems to smile like a deep-eyed, beautiful creature always suggesting wonderful things that might be uncovered at any moment.

Beckoned by these gleams of mystery, and guided by a thread of historic truth, scholars have set themselves to learn some of the age-old secrets hidden behind Egypt's strange smile. Patiently they have dug and sifted the sands; persistently they have pierced the doors of the rocks, seeking knowledge of men and events that made up the history of the early centuries of civilized life.

We know that man had learned much in the way of civilization before he invented writing, which provided a way of recording deeds for the benefit of generations that would come after. This was the beginning of written history; and the earliest written history of the land of Egypt that has yet been discovered was probably inscribed more than six thousand years ago.

Six thousand years! It is a long reach of time to try to look back over. You will need the help of imagination's eye. But, while you count your own life-story by days and weeks, we reckon the life-story of old Egypt by stretches of hundreds of years, catching sight of only the higher spots in the long, long prospect.

We have said that the Nile is the life of Egypt, and truly, for without the river there could be no habitable land in that sandy, rainless region. The desert, stretching all across northern Africa, pauses on the threshold of this river valley, whose waters come down from mountains far to the south.

With melting snows upon the mountains and flooding spring rains the waters of the upper river are swollen. Down and down they flow—down and down and down, until the lower valley lays a broad expanse of water dotted here and there with palm groves. Irrigation canals and reservoirs catch the surplus—for the Egyptians learned, ages back, to control this water supply—and the rest spreads over the fields, depositing upon them the rich, black earth which will renew the fruitfulness of the soil. But when the river has shrunk back within its narrower limits, the water must be lifted to the higher fields in order to keep the crops growing. Next to the actual carrying of the precious liquid by hand came a simple primitive device, which had been kept continuously in use until today. This is a sweep, called a *shadoof,* made up of a pole and a bucket. The bucket, dropped into a stream to dip up a load of water, is swung up and around by means of the pole; then the water is poured into an irrigation ditch or into another bucket, to be swung to a still higher level. It groans and creaks as it carries on its steady, necessary work to help provide food for the life of the land. What wonder that the men of Egypt worshiped their river, source of life itself to them?

UNIFICATION OF UPPER AND LOWER EGYPT
Project 5—Flooding of the Nile: A Reading, Page 2

A KING'S TOMB AS HIGH AS A HILL BUILT BY AN ARMY OF MEN

Perhaps the first thing that you would look for if you went to Egypt would be the pyramids—particularly the Pyramids of Giza—built to be the tombs of pharaohs when Egypt was young and the sovereigns lived at Memphis, the city of Menes, who united Upper and Lower Egypt into one nation perhaps about 3400 B.C. and founded the First Dynasty (or family) of rulers. Never have kings or conquerors since had such massive tombs. The Great Pyramid, largest of them all, was made for Khufu, or Cheops, a monarch of the Fourth Dynasty of kings, reigning about 2900 B.C. Its base is a huge square, which was originally 755 feet long on each side, enclosing nearly thirteen acres of ground. With the exception of a few passages and the funeral chamber, the structure was solid, layer upon layer of enormous stone blocks piled one upon another, each layer covering a little smaller square than the one before, until the top stood 482 feet above the ground-level. (It is now only 451 feet high.)

What a scene must have been the building of such a mass, with such a base and such a height, so many centuries ago! You have watched motor trucks carrying bricks and stones for the buildings of today. Not so was the material for the pyramids transported. In the largest one of them there was enough stone to build a middle-sized modern city. Many more than two million limestone blocks, of about forty cubic feet each, were hewn from the hills on the other side of the Nile, floated over the river, and by enormous effort of human labor were drawn, pushed or rolled to their places in that monumental pile. Rollers, levers, pulleys and ropes were the contrivances used; the roadway was oiled; and a mighty inclined causeway was constructed, up which the material traveled to the plateau of the pyramid. All was controlled by the most careful engineering skill, all planned with the most exact calculation. We marvel now to see how each great block fitted upon its neighbor with astonishing perfection, with so narrow a seam sometimes that it can hardly be seen. The whole work is supposed to have taken from twenty to thirty years and to have been done by about a hundred thousand men at a time.

UNIFICATION OF UPPER AND LOWER EGYPT
Project 5—Flooding of the Nile: A Reading, Page 3

TOMBS AND TEMPLES, THE SYMBOLS OF FAITH IN IMMORTALITY

The outer casing was made of smooth and polished blocks, to form an even, shining surface for each face of the four-sided mass; but these are now gone, leaving a series of rough, irregular steps, each so high that to climb them you would have to be pulled and lifted up by native guides.

Standing before the pyramid itself was the pyramid temple, where services were held on feast days; and from this temple a long covered causeway led down to the lower level beside the Nile, where a portico, or secondary temple, stood. Imagine the boats coming along the river and drawing up in front of the lower temple, where priests in their robes and courtly persons in their festive garments, disembarking, would gather for preliminary services before forming a solemn procession through the causeway to the upper temple to perform their rites in memory of the king who had superintended the building of these impressive and massive memorials. And what was the object of all this thought and labor and expense? Simply to honor and glorify the reigning monarch and provide for a safe place for his small but sacred body after death? More than that: it was a symbol of a deep and solemn faith in the immortal life of the soul. The most important thing to do was to plan for the soul's safety and happiness in the after-life, and as this was believed to depend upon the body's being kept whole for the use of the soul, every safeguard must be prepared to protect it from destruction.

There are several groups of pyramids not far from the modern city of Cairo, but none of the others can vie with those of Giza in size or importance. The earliest of them were "step" pyramids, built without the outer layer of facing-stones that came into use afterward.

A pyramid was a tomb for the king or one of his family. Lesser folk than royalty had burial places of different sorts. Near the pyramids were the tombs of officials and nobles connected with the court of the king. They are the kind we know as "mastaba" tombs, so named from the long, flat Egyptian benches, which they resemble. Perneb, Lord

Unification of Upper and Lower Egypt
Project 5—Flooding of the Nile: A Reading, Page 4

Chamberlain, Keeper of the Crowns, and "Companion" to his king, probably of the kings of the Fifth Dynasty, built one of these tombs, in a cemetery near old Memphis, perhaps 4500 years ago.

In it, as in the other mastaba tombs, there were several chambers: a chamber for Perneb's statue carved in cedar; an adjoining chamber shut off from it by a thick wall with only a slit of an opening, through which the family and friends could look at the figure; and the main chamber, entered through a vestibule. The walls of the main room were covered with painted scenes telling the story of the man's daily-life pursuits and showing processions of slaves bearing offerings for his use. One end wall contained the false door, before which food and other gifts were to be placed; and beyond it, but walled from sight, was the top of the deep shaft leading down to the burial chamber.

There is good reason for believing that after a few generations Perneb's descendants began to neglect the duty of bringing him offerings that the tomb gradually passed from their thought and attention, and that robbers broke in to carry off all that was of value. In time the desert sands drifted in, nearly filling the chambers. While the walls of neighboring tombs disappeared in the long course of centuries, the stones being carried off to be used for building houses or other tombs, Perneb's escaped this fate because it was made a dumping place for rubbish cast aside by the ravishers. Then in our own century it came to light again under the spade of an excavator. Stone by stone it was taken down and carried across the ocean to New York City, where it was all put together again inside the Metropolitan Museum of Art.

Tombs that Reveal Very Little About the Past

There, standing opposite the entrance door, you may see on each side of it a picture of Perneb, staff in hand, as if he were about to walk off to attend to some court duty. Inside, you may study the many pictures on the walls, noticing how the people dressed and what they liked to eat or to do. You may face the false door, imagining yourself a member of Perneb's family about to place some choice little gift upon the offering table, that it might be at his disposal whenever he should need it.

For the Egyptians believed that, in some mysterious way, in the new life to which he had gone the departed person would need the same sort of things that he had owned in his earthly life. So, into the burial chambers of royal and rich persons were put their valuable ornaments and other possessions, besides furniture, clothes and food for the use of the spirit who departed. Models of human figures were left there, too, to become companions and servants in the new existence. Every one of these figures and objects was believed to have a double, which would be ready for the double of the dead person at any time.

The sight of these personal belongings brings us closely into touch with the Egypt of three or four thousand years ago. In the great museums at Cairo, Berlin, Paris, London, New York, Boston, Chicago and elsewhere we may see both curious and beautiful reminders of Egyptian life. In the British Museum, for instance, there are cases full of treasures, including dolls with clay beads for hair, other toys, little worn shoes and sandals from the feet of children, a fine lady's dressing-cabinet fitted with jars and bowls for ointments and other appointments, her elbow-cushions and dainty slippers. There, too, are the palette and paints of the scribe, musical instruments—in fact, hundreds of things that bring us almost face to face with the men, women and children to whom they belonged centuries ago.

It is the same in the Metropolitan Museum, in New York, where you will find the most interesting models of buildings and boats, of masters and servants. A great man sits upon the deck of a boat, with musicians to entertain him, lotus lilies to furnish beauty, and scribes to give him reports, as well as rowers, steersmen and fishermen. There are other models of slaves at work in granaries, bakeries or stables—busy with the day's work of gathering or preparing food for many mouths.

These little models were made to be placed in tombs, and there they remained, shut away from the light and from the knowledge of men for centuries.

All these preparations, we must remember, are signs of a strongly fixed belief that the soul would live on and on—a belief that was the central motive of all Egyptian religious thought. Upon the walls of the tomb-chambers there are many representations of the gods worshiped in life and to be met in the nether world after death. It is natural that the sun should have been generally adored as a ruler and life-giver in a land where the days were always flooded with sunshine. As the god Re (or Ra) he sailed across the sky in a celestial boat every day, to return in another boat upon another stream through the underworld.

OSIRIS, ISIS, HORUS AND OTHER GODS OF THE EGYPTIANS

From among the many local deities in different parts of the land a few became generally recognized and worshiped. Foremost among them was a family group of three—Osiris, Isis and Horus—around whom the following legend was woven. When the sun god had been raised to the heavens, Osiris took Re's place as king upon the earth, ruling wisely and beneficently until he was deceived and slain by his wicked brother Set. Isis, the wife of Osiris, after great sorrow and trouble found the body of her husband, and with the help of the jackal-god Anubis prepared it for burial; then by the charms she used she brought back life into the body. Osiris, unable to return to his earthly kingdom, became from that time the ruler of the nether world—lord of departed spirits. But Isis did not rest until their son Horus had avenged his father's death by overthrowing Set and taking his place upon the throne that had once belonged to Osiris.

Anubis, the jackal-headed deity, became known as the god of embalmment and the guide of the spirit to the realm of Osiris. Thoth, with the head of an ibis, was looked upon as the patron of letters, the originator of the fine arts, and the one who acted as scribe to the gods. The sky-goddess—sometimes as Hathor with a cow's head, sometimes as Bast with a cat's head, sometimes in other forms—had especial influence over the life of women. Osiris was the good being; Set the god of evil and harm. Horus, whose symbol was a falcon, had been originally connected with the worship of Re.

PREPARING THE MUMMY FOR ENDLESS YEARS OF WAITING UPON THE SOUL

Because the life of the soul could not go on if the body were not preserved, an elaborate process of embalming it was gradually developed. For the rich and important a long and costly process was used, the very same process, it was claimed, that Anubis had used in preparing the body of Osiris. With accompanying prayers and rites the embalmers proceeded to remove perishable organs, to cleanse the spaces with palm wine and to fill them with aromatic material; then they let the body soak for seventy days in a preservative bath, becoming "slowly impregnated with immortality," as someone expressed it. Meanwhile the family waited in a sorrowful atmosphere, living on plain, coarse foods; allowing themselves to go unkempt; and mingling their tears over the thought of their loss.

The next step in caring for the mummy was to place amulets and rings and dried flowers upon the form and wrap it in layers of linen bandaging soaked in gums with bits of preservative substances tucked in. When the mummy was encased in his coffin he looked like a statue of himself for the coffins were modeled to follow the outlines of the swathed form, the head covering being made to reproduce the features of the dead person, with the eyes of enamel as a final touch. A painted wooden casket or a carven stone sarcophagus made a further guaranty against the body's being molested. Less costly methods and materials were employed for those whose purses were not well lined with gold; but everyone hoped for the survival of his soul through the careful preserving of the body.

The Old Kingdom, with its center at Memphis and its pyramid monuments, had slid into past history before the Eleventh Dynasty brought in a new era of activity, centering at Thebes, farther up the Nile. The kings and nobles of the Theban period were buried in splendid rock sepulchers in the Valley of the Kings' tombs, along the limestone cliffs opposite Thebes. Far into the rock they penetrated, making long galleries and halls to approach the burial chamber with its huge sarcophagus of stone.

Unification of Upper and Lower Egypt
Project 5—Flooding of the Nile: A Reading, Page 7

The Splendid Temples and Painted Walls of Ancient Egypt

Near the ruins of Thebes are the still-imposing remains of magnificent temples, for the pharaohs built the gods dwellings far grander than their own palaces. Even today the great halls, imposing gateways and rows of pillars form a most impressive and beautiful sight, whether in brilliant sunshine or deep purple shadow. As we gaze at them we fancy them once more in their first glory, with long processions of chanting priests and priestesses, a gorgeous display of magnificence when the king came to pay his worship, amidst the stately monuments of gold and silver, adorned with ivory and precious stones.

If we look at the walls and columns of the temples, at the solid vaults, at the coffin-cases, at the sculptures and wall paintings, we shall find most of them covered with picture writing. Until a century ago no one could guess what it all meant. Then at Rosetta, near Alexandria, a soldier of Napoleon's army found an engraved stone that served as a sort of key to unlock the mystery. This stone is now in the British Museum.

How Men Solved the Riddle of the Ancient Writings

On the stone, known as the Rosetta Stone, is a certain decree about keeping a king's birthday, and the same decree is given in three different kinds of writing. The lowest is in Greek, which scholars know well; the top is in the Egyptian picture writing used on the monuments, and the middle one is also in the Egyptian language, but in a more running kind of writing used for everyday purposes by the people.

Learned men, who love to find out the puzzles of the past, set to work to translate this decree. They compared it with certain lists of kings' names they had already studied, till at last it was all straightened out and

UNIFICATION OF UPPER AND LOWER EGYPT
Project 5—Flooding of the Nile: A Reading, Page 8

the values of the signs were discovered, so that we can now stand by and listen to those who know hieroglyphics while they translate the old Egyptian writings almost as easily as if they were in a modern language.

This discovery and study have opened up to us the old books and chapters of books, which are continually being found in the tombs. These were in long rolls, or papyri, so called from the material on which they are written, the inner part of the papyrus reed, which grows in such profusion on the banks of the Nile. From the name papyrus comes our word "paper."

Part of the work of the scribes was to make copies of the papyri; and the one most copied is called the Book of the Dead, sections of which are believed to be older than the pyramids themselves. Certain chapters of this book were always laid beside the mummies, to instruct them what to say and how to behave in the underworld. Our interest in the Book of the Dead is caught partly by the illustrations, but we find it fascinating, too, for the teaching it gives about the religious thought of Egypt: how men tried to fit themselves in life for a happy hereafter, how they expected to be judged, and how they believed they would live and work on their way through the underworld. For instance, it gives a very definite picture of the trial of a man's soul before forty-two judges in the hall of Osiris, when Anubis and Thoth would weigh his heart in the balances of justice and he would have to answer many questions. There are in the book, too, hymns to the gods and magical texts. The British Museum has a fine copy of a large number of its chapters. Besides this and other religious books there are many papyri of great age—fairy tales, war poems, medical and astronomical books, and rules for behavior.

A KING WHO REIGNED NEARLY SEVEN THOUSAND YEARS AGO

Different scholars place the beginning of the story at different dates. The first historical king of all Egypt is put by some in the forty-fifth century before Christ. But some think that Menes, who turned the course of the Nile, united the two kingdoms and founded the First Dynasty, lived about 3400 B.C. Before him there are legends of god-kings and heroes, and of kings of small states. Specimens of very old pottery, with pictures upon it of soldiers and boats, like children's drawings, give an idea of the first known life on the Nile long before Menes.

For the sake of convenience, in dealing with the great number of kings that followed Menes we generally group them into thirty dynasties. Twenty-six of the dynasties ruled between the accession of Menes to the throne and the conquest of Egypt by the Persians, nearly three thousand years afterward. Four others were added before Alexander the Great took the land of the Nile into his empire in 332 B.C. The names are gleaned from lists of kings, on tablets and papyrus, made from time to time through the centuries and still preserved.

When looking at inscriptions we can always distinguish a royal name, because it is surrounded by an oval line, supposed to be a cord tied in a knot to preserve the name from contact with common ones. This oval is called a cartouche. Before the king's name will generally be found some Egyptian words composed of a sign like an umbrella and an insect over two half-circles. These signs mean "King of the North and South," for Egypt is such a long, narrow country that it was long divided into two parts; and so we often hear of the double crown, which is made up of the red crown of North Egypt and the white crown of South Egypt.

UNIFICATION OF UPPER AND LOWER EGYPT
Project 5—Flooding of the Nile: A Reading, Page 9

THE KINGS OF EGYPT WHO CALLED THE SUN THEIR FATHER

Each king called himself the son of a god, usually Son of Re, or the Sun, which is shown by a goose and the sun-disk with a dot in the middle. The names of the kings are made up chiefly from about a dozen signs that we meet with continually in every inscription.

Very little is known of the kings of the first three dynasties. It was under the rule of the fourth, as we have already seen, that the three great pyramids near Cairo are believed to have been built by Khufu, Khafra and Menkaura.

If we would see the lifelike features of Khafra, and note how he sat to give audience to the overseers and officers of his great building works, we can find a cast of his remarkable portrait in the British Museum. There he sits on his throne, surrounded by memorials of the officials who superintended the building of the second pyramid.

THE MERCIFUL KING WHOSE BODY WAS LOST AT SEA

The museum possesses part of Menkaura's skeleton and fragments of his coffin, with an inscription saying he was just and merciful. The rest of the coffin and mummy were lost at sea on the way from Egypt. With Menkaura the power of the Fourth Dynasty dropped away. His statue has been described as that of a "bourgeois royalty, doing his best to look as dignified as becomes the wearer of the double crown, and failing absolutely"—a contrast with the fine dignity of Khafra.

Not far from the Pyramids of Giza is an enormous figure hewn out of the living rock, with a human head and the body of an animal—the Sphinx—so large that it could scarcely be got into the largest of our modern build-ings. From time to time, through the centuries the sand, which drifted over it has been cleared away, and the shape brought to light. An inscription between the forepaws refers to Khafra and seems to show his connection in some way with the great mysterious form.

THE GREAT STONE FACE THAT HAS LOOKED UPON THE WORLD FOR AGES

The face looks out to the far horizon with calm dignity and detachment, changeless through thousands of years, except for the wear of time and the wanton mischief done to it when Mohammedan soldiers used it as a target. It has an impressive majesty of its own. Some travelers have been astonished at noticing how like are the thick lips and the cast of face to those of some of the country girls of Egypt today.

Another striking likeness that connects faraway times with the present is found in the wooden statue of a fat little overseer, whose amusing face makes us smile; though we feel that his sharp eyes would soon find out any wrongdoing in the workers he had to oversee, perhaps four thousand years ago. When this statue was raised from the bed of sand and dust where it had lain for centuries, the watching people called out in amazement: "Shekh el-beled!"—"The chief of the village!" And the statue keeps this name now.

HOW ABRAHAM ENTERED INTO THE BUSY LIFE OF THE NILE VALLEY

Many interesting tombs belong to the period of perhaps 2000 B.C. or earlier. One of them has wall paintings representing the arrival in the country of a family such as that of Abraham, the great founder of the Jewish race. The story of his visit to Egypt in search of food, when there was a famine in his own country beyond the Isthmus of Suez, is familiar to us in the pages of the Bible.

We can well imagine that Abraham would tell his son Isaac stories of this visit to Egypt; that he in turn would tell them to his son Jacob, and Jacob to his sons, among them his favorite, Joseph. Let us follow this son after his brothers sold him. His sad journey lay over the "Bridge of Nations," the Isthmus of Suez and the Peninsula of Sinai, to slavery in Egypt.

Baskets made like those in the Egyptian rooms at the Metropolitan Museum might well have been those which the chief baker carried on his head in Joseph's dream; the models of the granaries show how corn was stored, and bring to mind Joseph's great work of building storehouses and gathering in grain to prepare for the famine that lasted so long, because Father Nile brought too much or too little water to the wide fields.

JOSEPH, HIS BRETHREN AND PHARAOH, WHO WOULD NOT LET HIS PEOPLE GO

Fashions changed so little in Egypt for centuries that we might imagine that the little statue of a treasurer was Joseph himself. We might fancy him earnestly discussing affairs of state with the king, to whom he became as a son, or traveling down the Nile on a tour of inspection in a boat like the model in the case near by. You remember how Joseph's brothers, then his old father Jacob, traveled to Egypt and were given land by the king. There the children of Israel settled and increased in numbers.

Very little is known about the history of Egypt at this time, for the kings who ruled then—believed to be a race of foreign invaders—destroyed monuments instead of setting them up. But when these Hyksos, or Shepherd Kings, passed away, the Eighteenth and Nineteenth Dynasty pharaohs, builders and soldiers, whose names are familiar and famous, took their part in Egypt's history. These were the years when Israel lived in the "House of Bondage." Among these rulers was Thutmose III, who inscribed and set up the great obelisks which we call Cleopatra's Needles, though Queen Cleopatra lived centuries later.

One of the tall stone shafts now stands in London, the other in Central Park, New York. Thutmose III was one of the first kings of Egypt to make war across the Isthmus of Suez, both on the nations in the mountains of Syria and in Mesopotamia, the valley of the two great rivers beyond the desert.

His queen, Hatshepsut, who, as sovereign in her own right, had been chosen "king", shared part of his reign. She, often called Queen Elizabeth of Egyptian history, sent most interesting expeditions to discover unknown countries, and had an account of

UNIFICATION OF UPPER AND LOWER EGYPT
Project 5—Flooding of the Nile: A Reading, Page 11

them, with fine illustrations, engraved on the walls of a magnificent temple which she built near Thebes. There is much that is interesting about this vigorous queen, who for political reasons tried so much to look like a man that she had a beard added to her portraits.

Of this same dynasty—the Eighteenth—was Amenhotep IV, who changed his name to Akhenaten in honor of the god Aten, a universal, or world, god, whose worship he strove to substitute for that of Amen, the deity of Thebes, and other local gods. Amen's name was replaced by that of Aten on statues and monuments. Great temples were built to Aten, and cities were founded in his name. "Truth" was the precious thing that the king most desired. His orders to painters and sculptors were that they should "let the chisel and the brush tell the story of what they actually saw," instead of following the conventions rigidly prescribed by priestly rule.

But the priestly party was strongly set against him, and the inherited faith of centuries was too firmly rooted to be overthrown during the lifetime of one man. Akhenaten's son-in-law, Tukankhaten, was forced to yield to the pressure of the opposition, to restore the worship of Amen and to change his own name to Tutankhamen. The opening of this young king's tomb in 1923 has made him a very real person to us.

Though Akhenaten failed in his effort to revolutionize thought and custom in the old land of the Nile, we find him the most interesting figure in all early history, the first individual in the written story of mankind.

PROUD CONQUERORS AND BUILDERS IN THE NINETEENTH DYNASTY

A little later, when the descendants of Jacob, the children of Israel, had grown to be very numerous, they were harshly treated by the kings of the period, who had built up the empire again. Rameses II, a soldier-king and a mighty builder, is believed to have been the great oppressor of the Israelites, and we can see his face in the huge stone monuments he set up. Of more personal interest still is his mummy, which has been found with that of his father, Seti I, and those of others of his race. They have been placed in the museum in Cairo. Thus, the features into which so many looked with awe, perhaps even the little Moses, are known again to the world more than three thousand years after the great king's death. Of Seti I and Rameses II there are numberless stone portraits in statues and reliefs, giving us interesting impressions of them as men and as rulers. In the Metropolitan Museum there may be seen an earthenware bowl, covered with blue glaze and inscribed with the name of Rameses II, which may have belonged to the great king himself. There, too, is a door lintel taken from one of the temples that he built. As we look at it we wonder how many times his hand may have touched it as he passed in and out thirty centuries ago.

Magnificent were the temples and monuments set up by this dynasty of kings, the Nineteenth. Among them we find the massive ruins at Karnak and Luxor, near Thebes. Bricks such as the Israelites made for use in building store cities for their hard taskmasters; necklaces and jewelry such as they may have taken when they "spoiled the Egyptians," are here in the museum before our eyes. In the great museum at Cairo and in the museums of many European cities we may find endless objects such as the king's daughter may have provided for Moses, whom she rescued and brought up in the palace itself—things which helped to frame his life from childhood onward. The toys and games, especially the animals, must have pleased him, and a garden with trees and a pond, like one that is pictured on a wall, would be delightful for a child to play in. The little Moses may well have heard music from instruments such as the pipes and harps preserved here, and he must have enjoyed sailing and rowing on the Nile in boats like the models on our museum shelves.

The wall paintings from the tombs show in their bright colors how the Egyptians amused themselves in the time of Moses, as well as before and after. There are the gay parties with music and dancing; a father hunting waterbirds with a sort of boomerang, the child holding on to his leg for fear of falling out of the boat; the mother gathering lotus flowers; the family cat retrieving the birds three at a time. When the time came for lessons, reed pens and red and black paints were the sorts with which the boy must have learned to write. We can fancy how he must have enjoyed possessing one of those boxes of pens and paint, and can almost see him poring over the papyrus rolls, which held so much of the learning of the Egyptians.

THE INFLUENCE OF EGYPTIAN LIFE UPON THE HEBREWS

The Ten Commandments, brought down from Mount Sinai by Moses after he had led his people out of Egypt, are foreshadowed in the forty-two commandments in the Book of the Dead. The making and worship of the Golden Calf which so angered the great leader, was suggested by the ancient worship of Egypt, brought home to us in endless forms by paintings and images of every description, as well as by the mummified forms of sacred bulls and other animals held in reverence.

For about a thousand years after the brilliant line of the Rameses dynasty, the history of Egypt, on the whole, was one of gradual decline and gathering trouble. It was during this time that the priests of the splendid temples became richer and richer, more and more powerful, till at last they made themselves king. When examining the mummies and their cases we notice how many are those of priests and priestesses, doorkeepers, incense-bearers, and other officers of the great religious colleges.

Dynasties of foreigners followed the priest-kings, and the country was breaking up into little states and everything was going downhill, when the kings of Assyria—the land of the two rivers—seeing their opportunity for conquest, began to attack Egypt on her own frontier, and then pushed their way over the Bridge of Nations. They overran the whole of the country, spoiling the harvest so that the people starved, and the fine temples and monuments began to fall into decay. We find the account of all this misery in the story of Assyria in the descriptions given by the conquerors with swelling pride of their successes in Egypt.

Egypt revived after this for a little while under kings of the Twenty-sixth Dynasty, with their capital at Sais, not far from old Memphis. In their armies fought soldiers from Greece. But the Nile country was again devastated from end to end by the Assyrians till they, too, fell under a new great power that arose in Asia—that of the Persians.

The Egyptians took every opportunity to revolt against the Persians. Between the second and third revolts, in the fifth century before Christ, a traveler from Greece came to Egypt. He was an author anxious to collect material for his *History of the Persian Wars.* This was Herodotus, the "Father of History," who set down in a pleasant chatty way his impressions of the wonderful country, of the Nile in flood, of the pyramids and other great buildings. Much of his interesting book we can read today, though Herodotus laid down his pen more than two thousand years ago.

The Persians in their turn were driven out by the world-conqueror Alexander the Great, of Greece. His stay was short in Egypt, but his brilliant passage has left marks for all time. He flashed across the desert to worship at the shrine of the god Jupiter Ammon, whom he claimed as an ancestor, and he planned and founded the great city of Alexandria, called after him, which under his successors became one of the most important cities in the world.

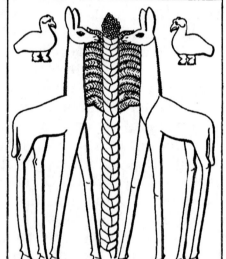

Three centuries before Alexander, as we have noted, an Egyptian king had employed Greek soldiers and had allowed Greek traders to settle in the Delta. Before this Egypt had been closed to foreigners; but after the Greeks found their way into the country, little by little their cleverness in trade, their surpassing skill in art and their learning, spread Greek influence even farther along the Nile. Naucrates became a famous Greek city during this time, and today explorers find Greek treasure of all kinds buried in various parts of the Nile Delta.

THE WORK OF THE PTOLEMIES, GREEK KINGS IN EGYPT

The kings who succeeded Alexander were called the Ptolemies, the first of the name being one of Alexander's generals. They were great builders and restorers. To them we owe the Temple of Edfu and the temples on the Island of Philae, near the great dam at Aswan. The Ptolemies favored the city named Alexandria after the founder of their fortunes, and started in it the famous library which, unfortunately, afterward burned. There, too, they founded a university to which came some of the most famous Greek scholars. Another Ptolemy built the tall lighthouse, which, like the Pyramids, was one of the wonders of the ancient world. The flare from its top guided the shipping of Alexandria safely into its double harbor for long years; but not a trace of it now remains.

The same Ptolemy had the Old Testament, which was originally written in the Hebrew language and was understood by comparatively few people, translated at Alexandria into Greek. This beautiful language was soon to be carried over the known world and to become the language of scholars everywhere. Another good work of this same king was to have a history of Egypt and its religion written by an Egyptian scribe named Manetho, who knew Greek well. Though his actual records have been lost, other writers have made copies from Manetho, and thus the lists of kings and other particulars, which carefully compiled, have been of great use.

UNIFICATION OF UPPER AND LOWER EGYPT
Project 5—Flooding of the Nile: A Reading, Page 14

The Rosetta Stone was set up in the reign of Ptolemy V. We see now how it was that a Greek translation came to be below in Egyptian writing. Both languages were then used in Egypt. And all the time that Egypt was becoming more and more Greek, "a shadow ever lengthening towards the East," was slowly creeping onward from Rome. It passed over Greece itself in the middle of the second century before Christ, and reached Egypt about a hundred years later.

It is a sad and absorbing story, how the end of the independent kingdom came, and how it passed into a Roman province. Upon this foundation Shakespeare constructed his play of Antony and Cleopatra. The beautiful Cleopatra was the last great ruler in the line of Ptolemies. Rather than fall into the hands of the invading Romans, she is said to have allowed a deadly serpent to bite her. So, when they came to her palace they found her in all her regal splendor— dead. In Tennyson's words, Cleopatra says: "I died a Queen. The Roman soldier found Me lying dead, my crown about my brows, A name forever!"

From Menes to Cleopatra, what a perspective of years! As we look back again, much of the old life will seem so vivid and real to us that we can almost hear the dancing feet of children at play in little worn shoes, the sad wailing of mourners carrying the mummy to its hidden tomb, and the hum and clatter of workers building structures of such size and solidity that never on earth have they been outdone. And in and out, among the other sounds, ever the creak and drone of the shadoof, or water-sweep, winds, as the water is lifted from the river to terrace after terrace.

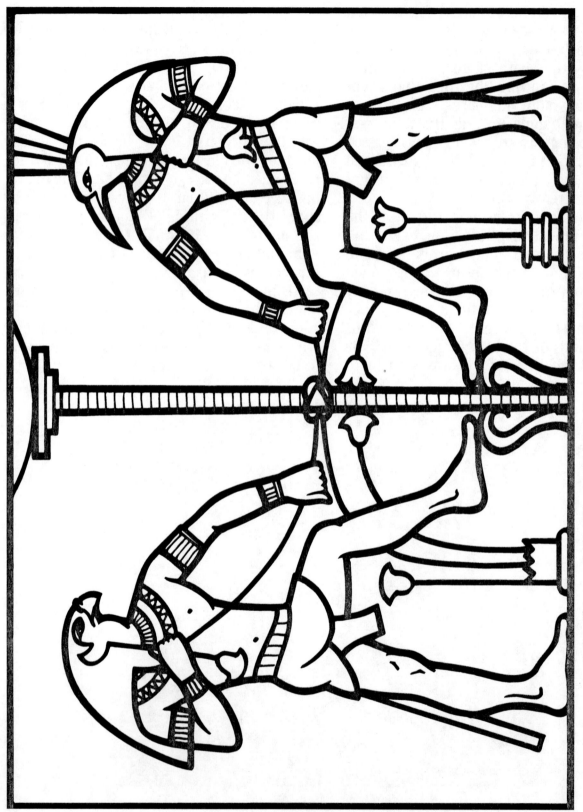

Color this symbolic illustration of the union of Upper and Lower Egypt.

UNIFICATION OF UPPER AND LOWER EGYPT

Test

1. Who was the first known Egyptian pharaoh?

_____

_____

2. At what age did he become pharaoh?

_____

_____

3. What important feat did this pharaoh accomplish?

_____

_____

_____

4. What crown did this pharaoh wear? Why did he wear it?

_____

_____

_____

_____

Review

1. What had God forbidden of Adam and Eve?

_____

_____

2. How did man fall out of fellowship with God?

_____

_____

UNIFICATION OF UPPER AND LOWER EGYPT
Test, Page 2

3. Who was the first baby ever born?

   _____

   _____

4. After the Flood God made a covenant with Noah. What was that covenant?

   _____

   _____

   _____

5. List all events covered in chronological order with biblical references where applicable.

   _____

   _____

   _____

   _____

   _____

   _____

THE OLD KINGDOM IN EGYPT
Worksheet

1. What is the age when pyramids were built known as?

   _____

   _____

2. Why were so many pyramids able to be built during this time period?

   _____

   _____

   _____

3. Name the largest pyramid built? For whom was it built?

   _____

   _____

   _____

   _____

THE OLD KINGDOM IN EGYPT
Worksheet, Page 2

4. How many men labored in a crew to build the largest pyramid?

_____

_____

_____

5. How long did it take to complete the pyramid?

_____

_____

_____

6. Why were the pharaohs so concerned with building pyramids?

_____

_____

_____

7. Does the Egyptian building of pyramids and storage of great wealth follow Jesus' teaching in His Sermon on the Mount *(Do not lay up for yourselves treasures on earth, where moth and rust destroy and where thieves break in and steal; but lay up for yourselves treasures in heaven, where neither moth nor rust destroys and where thieves do not break in and steal. For where your treasure is, there your heart will be also." Matthew 6:19–25)*?

_____

_____

_____

_____

_____

THE OLD KINGDOM IN EGYPT
Project 1—Book of the Dead Painting

Supplies

plaster of Paris

styrofoam vegetable trays
  (available at most groceries stores)

water color paints

pencil

Directions

Mix plaster of Paris according to directions on package. Pour into foam tray, three quarters filled. Allow to dry. Draw an Egyptian picture as they might have used in the Book of the Dead. Using water colors paint the scene. Many of the resources on the card have excellent images to look at for ideas.

THE OLD KINGDOM IN EGYPT
Project 2—Book of the Dead vs. The Bible

The Egyptians were a sinful people who did not worship the living God of Scripture. The Egyptian Book of the Dead was a collection of over 200 magic spells for their religion. Each spell was a prayer intended to help the person on their journey to the afterlife.

During the Old Kingdom the spells were inscribed on the walls of the pyramids. Later they were painted inside coffins and eventually on papyrus.

Standing before Osiris, the god of rebirth, the soul must prove himself worthy to be sent on by saying these typical words from the Book of the Dead:

O ye lords of truth,
I have not secretly done evil
    against mankind;
I have not told falsehoods;
I have not made the laborer do
    more than his daily task;
I have not been idle;
I have not been drunk;
I have not caused hunger;
I have not murdered;
I have not stolen;
I have not cheated the weight of
    the balance;
I have not slandered anyone.

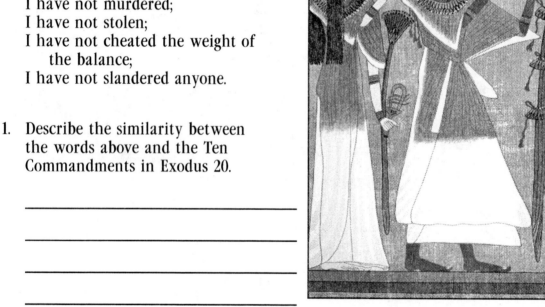

1. Describe the similarity between the words above and the Ten Commandments in Exodus 20.

    _____

    _____

    _____

    _____

2. How do we actually secure life after death?

_____

_____

_____

_____

THE OLD KINGDOM IN EGYPT
Project 3—Hymn to Osiris

Sir E. A. Wallis Budge (1857-1934) was the curator of Egyptian and Assyrian Antiquities at the British Museum, a sometime scholar of Christ's College, a scholar at the University of Cambridge, Tyrwhitt, a Hebrew scholar, a translator, a collector of Coptic, Greek, Arabic, Syriac, Ethiopian, and Egyptian manuscripts, and particpated in many archaeological digs. Yet Budge is best known for his work translating the Papyrus of Ani—the largest and best preserved of The Egyptian Book of The Dead *still in existence.*

The Book of the Dead *are scrolls meant to help the dead along their journey into the afterlife. The Egyptians called these collections of scrolls (up to two hundred, depending on how many a person could afford), "The Chapters of Coming Forth By Day."* Book of the Dead *is the name given to the miscellaneous collection of unconnected spells, hymns, incantations, litanies, words of power and prayers by early nineteeth-century egyptologists. The pious Egyptian held onto these chapters as all-powerful guides into the realms of life and light. Very old even in the reign of Semti, a king of the First Dynasty, these words were copied over and over for over 5000 years and were trusted to be the key to being born again when they met Osiris.*

BOOK OF THE DEAD 1: *Hymn to Osiris*

"Homage to thee, Osiris, Lord of eternity, King of the Gods, whose names are manifold, whose forms are holy, thou being of hidden form in the temples, whose Ka is holy. Thou art the governor of Tattu (Busiris), and also the mighty one in Sekhem (Letopolis). Thou art the Lord to whom praises are ascribed in the nome of Ati, thou art the Prince of divine food in Anu. Thou art the Lord who is commemorated in Maati, the Hidden Soul, the Lord of Qerrt (Elephantine), the Ruler supreme in White Wall (Memphis). Thou art the Soul of Ra, his own body, and hast thy place of rest in Henensu (Herakleopolis). Thou art the beneficent one, and art praised in Nart. Thou makest thy soul to be raised up. Thou art the Lord of the Great House in Khemenu (Hermopolis). Thou art the mighty one of victories in Shas-hetep, the Lord of eternity, the Governor of Abydos. The path of his throne is in Ta-tcheser (a part of Abydos). Thy name is established in the mouths of men. Thou art the substance of Two Lands (Egypt). Thou art Tem, the feeder of Kau (Doubles), the Governor of the Companies of the gods. Thou art the beneficent Spirit among the spirits. The god of the Celestial Ocean (Nu) draweth from thee his waters. Thou sendest forth the north wind at eventide, and breath from thy nostrils to the satisfaction of thy heart. Thy heart reneweth its youth, thou producest the . . . The stars in the celestial heights are obedient unto thee, and the great doors of the sky open themselves before thee. Thou art he to whom praises are ascribed in the southern heaven, and thanks are given for thee in the northern heaven. The imperishable stars are under thy supervision, and the stars which never set are thy thrones. Offerings appear before thee at the decree of Keb. The Companies of the Gods praise thee, and the gods of the Tuat (Other World) smell the earth in paying homage to thee. The uttermost parts of the earth bow before thee, and the limits of the skies entreat thee with supplications when they see thee. The holy ones are overcome before thee, and all Egypt offereth thanksgiving unto thee when it meeteth Thy Majesty. Thou art a shining Spirit-Body, the governor of Spirit-Bodies; permanent is thy rank, established is thy rule. Thou art the

THE OLD KINGDOM IN EGYPT
Project 3—Hymn to Osiris, Page 2

well-doing Sekhem (Power) of the Company of the Gods, gracious is thy face, and beloved by him that seeth it. Thy fear is set in all the lands by reason of thy perfect love, and they cry out to thy name making it the first of names, and all people make offerings to thee. Thou art the lord who art commemorated in heaven and upon earth. Many are the cries which are made to thee at the Uak festival, and with one heart and voice Egypt raiseth cries of joy to thee. Thou art the Great Chief, the first among thy brethren, the Prince of the Company of the Gods, the stablisher of Right and Truth throughout the World, the Son who was set on the great throne of his father Keb. Thou art the beloved of thy mother Nut, the mighty one of valour, who overthrew the Sebau-fiend. Thou didst stand up and smite thine enemy, and set thy fear in thine adversary. Thou dost bring the boundaries of the mountains. Thy heart is fixed, thy legs are set firm. Thou art the heir of Keb and of the sovereignty of the Two Lands (Egypt). He (Keb) hath seen his splendors, he hath decreed for him the guidance of the world by thy hand as long as times endure. Thou hast made this earth with thy hand, and the waters, and the winds, and the vegetation, and all the cattle, and all the feathered fowl, and all the fish, and all the creeping things, and all the wild animals therof. The desert is the lawful possession of the son of Nut. The Two Lands (Egypt) are content to crown thee upon the throne of thy father, like Ra. "Thou rollest up into the horizon, thou hast set light over the darkness, thou sendest forth air from thy plumes, and thou floodest the Two Lands like the Disk at daybreak. Thy crown penetrateth the height of heaven, thou art the companion of the stars, and the guide of every god. Thou art beneficent in decree and speech, the favoured one of the Great Company of the Gods, and the beloved of the Little Company of the Gods. His sister [Isis] hath protected him, and hath repulsed the fiends, and turned aside calamities (of evil). She uttered the spell with the magical power of her mouth. Her tongue was perfect, and it never halted at a word. Beneficent in command and word was Isis, the woman of magical spells, the advocate of her brother. She sought him untiringly, she wandered round and round about this earth in sorrow, and she alighted not without finding him. She made light with her feathers, she created air with her wings, and she uttered the death wail for her brother. She raised up the inactive members of whose heart was still, she drew from him his essence, she made an heir, she reared the child in loneliness, and the place where he was not known, and he grew in strength and stature, and his hand was mighty in the House of Keb. The Company of the Gods rejoiced, rejoiced, at the coming of Horus, the son of Osiris, whose heart was firm, the triumphant, the son of Isis, the heir of Osiris.

On a separate sheet of paper, write a short essay that explains how the Egyptian culture was in violation of God's law as illustrated by this hymn.

THE OLD KINGDOM IN EGYPT
Project 4—Pyramids

Read the books The Great Wonder *by Annabelle Howard and* Pyramid *by David Macaulay. Make a copy of the pyramid book on this and the following pages and answer the comprehension questions. When this is done color the cover and cut out the pyramid shapes and staple them into a triangular book.*

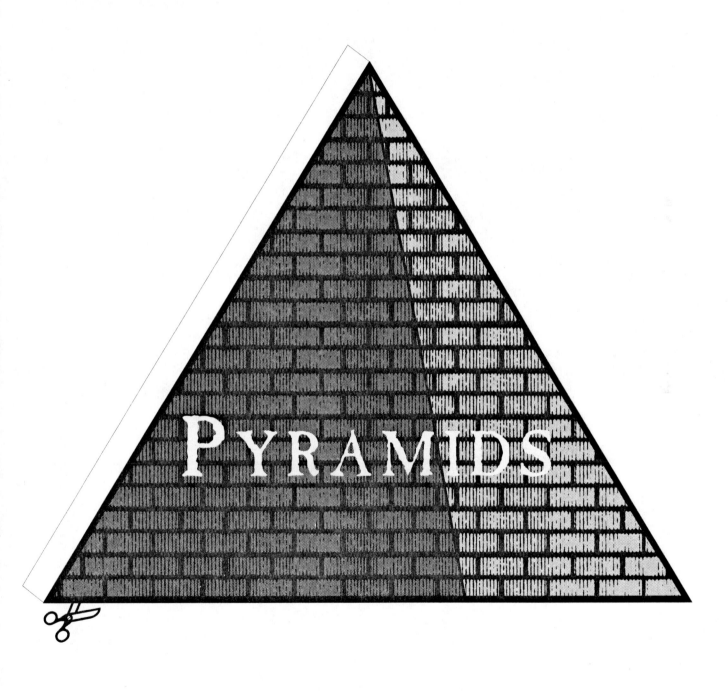

THE OLD KINGDOM IN EGYPT
Project 4, Page 2

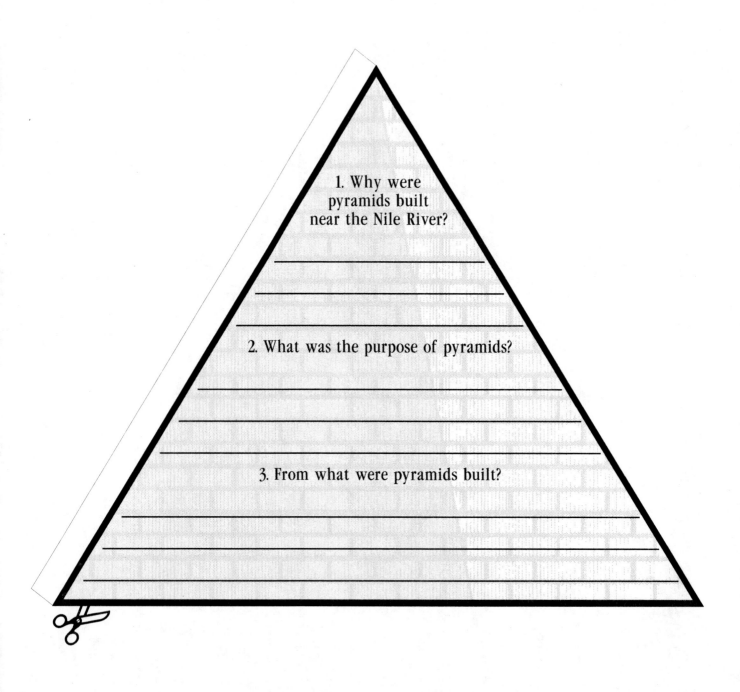

1. Why were
pyramids built
near the Nile River?

_____

_____

_____

2. What was the purpose of pyramids?

_____

_____

_____

3. From what were pyramids built?

_____

_____

_____

THE OLD KINGDOM IN EGYPT
Project 4, Page 3

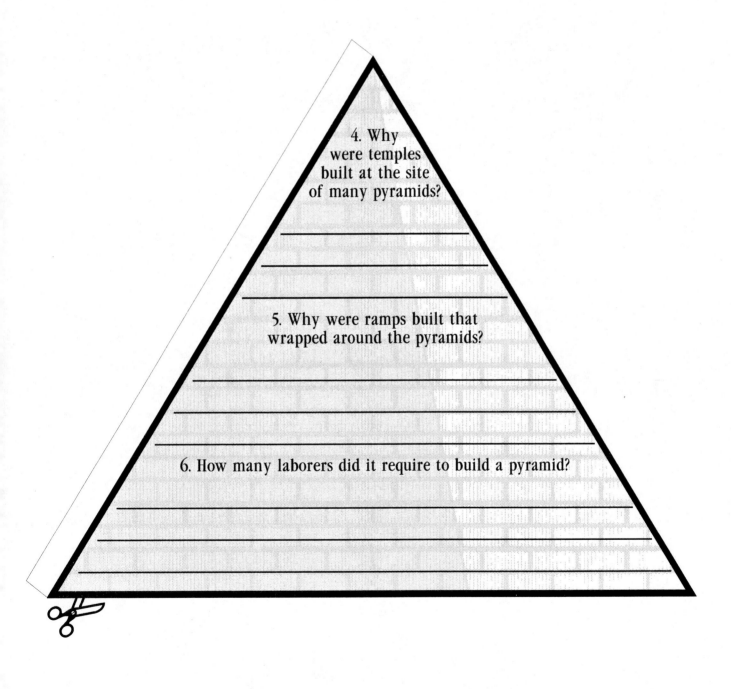

4. Why were temples built at the site of many pyramids?

_____

_____

5. Why were ramps built that wrapped around the pyramids?

_____

_____

_____

6. How many laborers did it require to build a pyramid?

_____

_____

_____

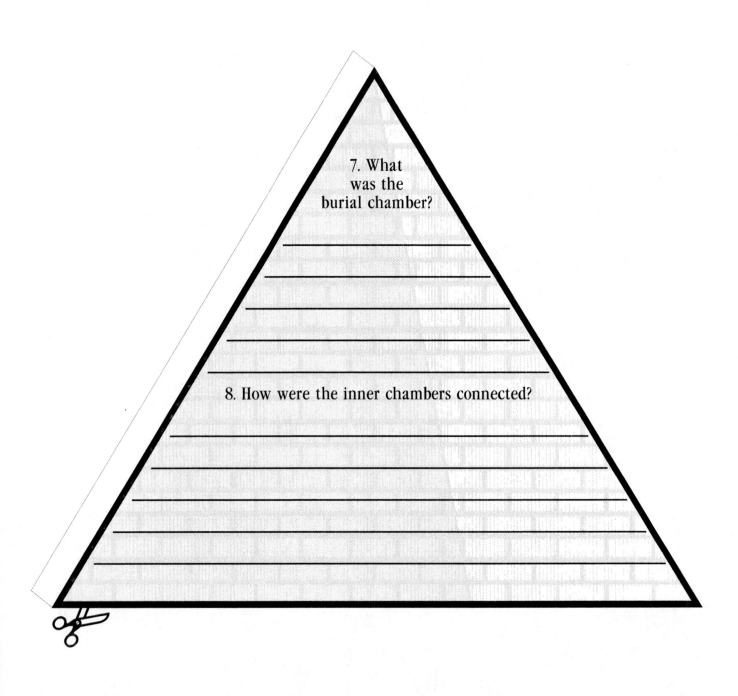

7. What was the burial chamber?

_____

_____

_____

_____

_____

8. How were the inner chambers connected?

_____

_____

_____

_____

_____

THE OLD KINGDOM IN EGYPT
Project 4, Page 5

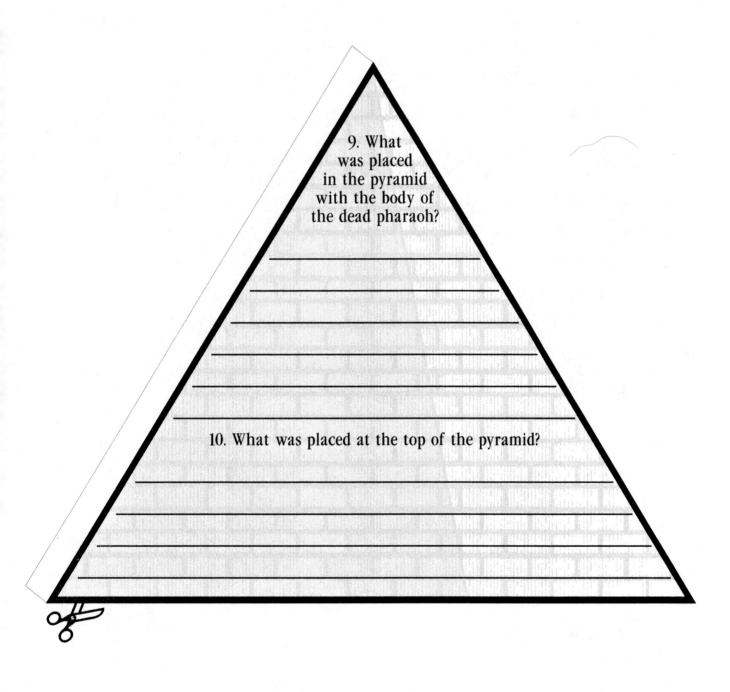

9. What
was placed
in the pyramid
with the body of
the dead pharaoh?

_____

_____

_____

_____

10. What was placed at the top of the pyramid?

_____

_____

_____

_____

THE OLD KINGDOM IN EGYPT
Project 5—Build a Pyramid

Supplies

scissors

crayons

tape or glue

Directions

Color each panel then cut around outside edges. Fold each tab back and then fold each triangle toward the center along the dotted line. Tape or glue each tab behind the panel next to it.

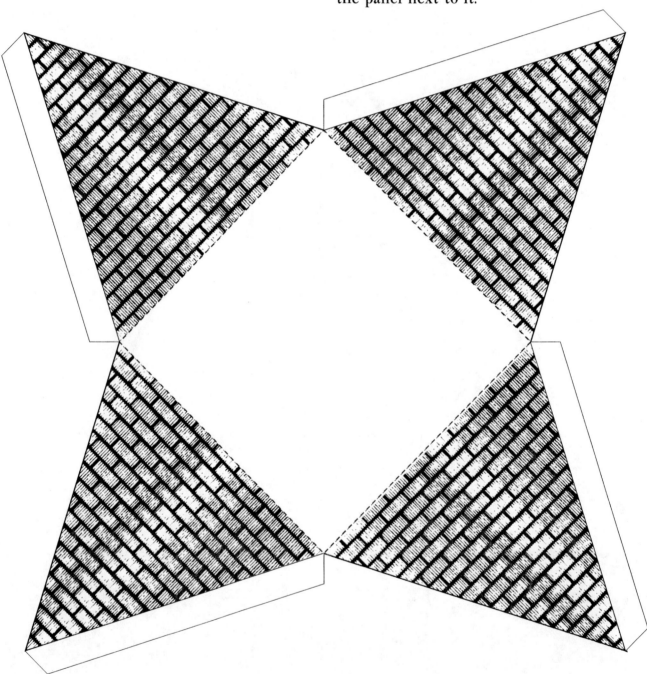

THE OLD KINGDOM IN EGYPT
Project 5—The Great Sphinx Coloring Page

There are so many sphinxes in Egypt that they have come up with names for each kind: *hierocosphinx* (lion body with hawk head), *crisosphinx* (lion body with ram head), and *androsphinx* (lion body with human head). Sphinxes are often found at temple entrances serving as protectors or guardians. And new statues are still being found to this day. The Great Sphinx (an *androsphinx*) was discovered when Napoleon's soldiers came across it in 1798. It is about six miles from Cairo in the necropolis of ancient Memphis near three large pyramids. The Great Sphinx was excavated and carved from natural limestone and measures 241 feet long and 65 feet high. It was probably built at the same time as the nearby Pyramid of Khafre in about 2540 B.C.

Color the Great Sphinx on this page.

THE OLD KINGDOM IN EGYPT
Test

1. For what is the Old Kingdom in Egypt best known?

   _____

   _____

   _____

2. What were the conditions in Egypt during this period?

   _____

   _____

   _____

3. What was the largest of all pyramids? For whom was it built?

   _____

   _____

   _____

   _____

Review

1. What did God create on the second day of Creation?

   _____

   _____

   _____

2. Where in Scripture is the Fall found?

   _____

   _____

   _____

THE OLD KINGDOM IN EGYPT
Test, Page 2

3. Who was the first baby born?

   _____

   _____

4. Why did God flood the earth?

   _____

   _____

   _____

5. Where is the Tower of Babel found in Scripture?

   _____

   _____

6. What is another name for Pharaoh Menes?

   _____

   _____

7. Write the events studied thus far in order. Include biblical references where applicable.

   _____

   _____

   _____

   _____

   _____

   _____

   _____

FIRST INTERMEDIATE PERIOD
Worksheet

1. What are the approximate dates of the First Intermediate Period in Egypt?

   _____

   _____

2. With which dynasties does this period coincide?

   _____

   _____

   _____

3. What activity predominated during this period?

   _____

   _____

   _____

4. What happened to Egypt during this time?

   _____

   _____

   _____

   _____

   _____

   _____

An Egyptian Noble Hunting Wtih A Boomerang

FIRST INTERMEDIATE PERIOD
Project 1—Mythological Mural

During the First Intermediate Period Osiris, an Egyptian god, was designated as ruler of the dead. The Egyptians believed that an underworld existed. They called it Duatt. Parts of Duatt were full of lakes of fire, executioners and snakes. In order to reach the "land of perfect peace" they must journey before the hall of Osiris. Osiris sits on a throne of gold amid 42 solemn judges. Isis, his wife, sits by his side and Anubis, the jackal-headed god, uses scales to weigh men's hearts. Standing before Osiris the soul must prove himself worthy to be sent on to Aalu.

Remind children that this is not biblical truth, but Egyptian mythology.

Read the chapter on Isis and Osiris in Tales of Ancient Egypt *by Roger Lancelyn Green or another reference and make a classroom mural showing the myth of Isis and Osiris. Hang white bulletin board paper on a wall and assign children different parts of the story:*

1. The birth of Osiris.

2. The marriage of Isis and Osiris.
   (Point out the fact that this shows pharaohs marrying their own sisters.)

3. Ra's encounter with the cobra.

4. Isis, Ra, and the secret name.

5. Death of Ra.

6. Osiris, Pharaoh of Egypt.

7. Set's deception.

8. Isis in search of Osiris' body.

9. Temple of Baalat Gebal.

10. Burial of Osiris.

FIRST INTERMEDIATE PERIOD
Project 1—Mythological Mural, Page 2

Egyptian painters followed a grid system to make their artwork. The figures are idealized because that reflected how the people would look like in the afterlife. Objects do not overlap so no details are ever hidden from view. This affected their representation of humans in a way that different viewpoints are often combined, an effect that Picasso and other artists in the twentieth century would revisit and rework in the art movement called Cubism.

Have the students use grid paper to plan out their murals utilizing the system below. Draw a matching grid on the paper hanging up on the classroom walls and then the students can transfer their designs to the wall from their preliminary sketches as the ancient Egyptians did.

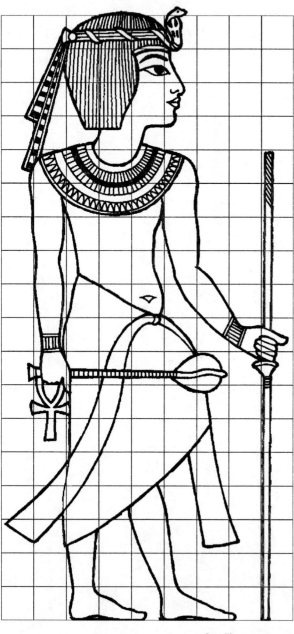

How to Paint the Perfect Egyptian

18 squares	=	the height of the figure
3 squares	=	length of foot
3 squares	=	sole of the foot to midcalf
3 squares	=	midcalf to just above the knee
3 squares	=	just above the knee to the wrist
5 squares	=	shoulders to waist
3 squares	=	shoulders to forehead/wigline
1 square	=	the width of the fist
3 squares	=	wrist to elbow
3 squares	=	elbow to shoulders
2 squares	=	face

First Intermediate Period
Project 2—Mythological Coloring Pages

Color this picture

Tutankhamon in life (left) and as mummified Osiris (right).
Mural from tomb of Tutankhamon.

FIRST INTERMEDIATE PERIOD
Project 2, Page 2

Color this picture

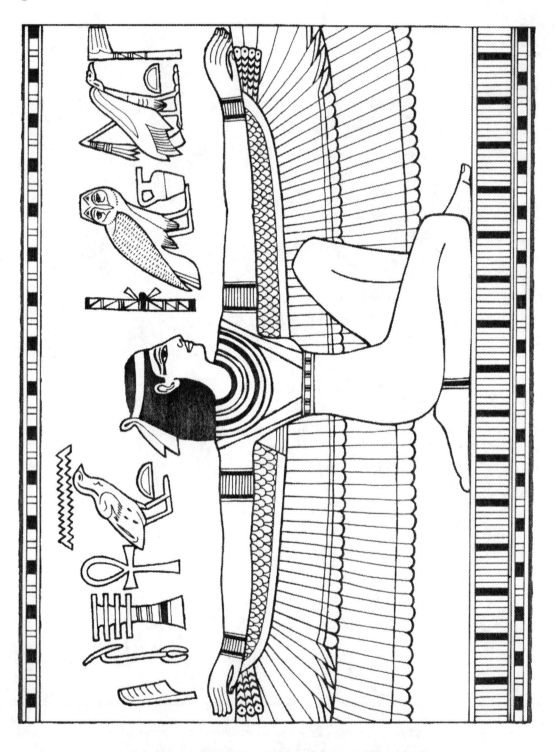

Isis in protective gesture. Mural from tomb of Seti

FIRST INTERMEDIATE PERIOD
Project 3

Using the history card, fill in the missing blanks.

The name of this _____ coincides with dynasties _____ through _____ . During this period _____ _____ predominated in Egypt.

The rich _____ finally grew tired of serving the pharaohs. The nobles grew _____ , and the country was _____ into two sections: north and south. Often _____ kings ruled; one ruled in the _____ , and one ruled in the _____ .

In addition to the nobles, the _____ and temples gained much power. More and more _____ was controlled by the _____ and powerful, and less went to things that helped everyone, like _____ _____ and irrigation. _____ and drought often made things _____ for the common people.

FIRST INTERMEDIATE PERIOD
Test

1. What were the approximate dates for the First Intermediate Period?

    _____

    _____

2. What dynasties coincide with this period?

    _____

    _____

    _____

3. Why did a civil war occur during this period?

    _____

    _____

    _____

Review

1. What happened on the seventh day of Creation?

    _____

    _____

2. What was the result of the Fall in man's relationship with God?

    _____

    _____

    _____

3. What was Cain's occupation? What was Abel's occupation?

    _____

    _____

    _____

FIRST INTERMEDIATE PERIOD
Test, Page 2

4. Who was the one person who remained faithful to God immediately prior to the Flood?

_____

_____

_____

_____

5. At what point did people begin speaking more than one language?

_____

_____

_____

6. Write the events studied thus far in order. Include biblical references where applicable.

_____

_____

_____

_____

_____

_____

_____

_____

THE CALL OF ABRAM
Worksheet

1. What did God tell Abram to do when he was 75 years old?

   _____

   _____

   _____

2. What did God promise (covenant with) Abram?

   _____

   _____

   _____

   _____

   _____

   _____

3. Who accompanied Abram on his journey?

   _____

   _____

   _____

   _____

   _____

4. Where did Abram and his family settle?

   _____

   _____

   _____

   _____

   _____

THE CALL OF ABRAM
Worksheet, Page 2

5. What did God say He would do with the land where Abram settled?

_____

_____

_____

_____

6. What is the approximate date of the Call of Abram?

_____

_____

7. What is the scripture reference for the Call of Abram?

_____

_____

THE CALL OF ABRAM
Project 1—Abram's Times Booklet

On the following pages you will find pictures to turn into a little book for each student. The book will tell about the kind of life Abram, Sarai, and their family lived. Once the booklet is complete, spend time discussing the times of Abram and Sarai.

Supplies

scissors

glue

construction paper

stapler

Directions

Cut construction paper in half as shown below. Fold the halves in two and staple together to form a book. Photocopy the following two pages for each student, then cut the pictures apart and glue onto the construction paper.

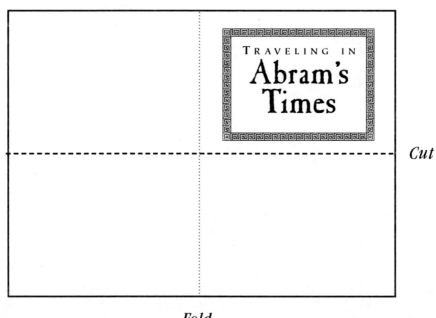

Fold

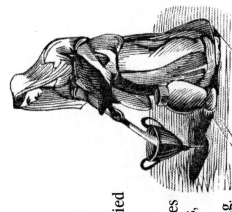

Abram and his family traveled from Ur to Canaan. They rode on camels or walked carrying all their worldly goods with them. They lived a nomadic life and would rise at daybreak, set forth with the sun and travel until mid-afternoon.

Water needed to be carried on the journey. Water would be drawn from wells and put into bottles made from animal skins, which were sewn up leaving only one opening.

TRAVELING IN Abram's Times

They dwelt in tents. The larger tents were divided into three apartments, the inner of which was given to the women and the outer to the servants with the young of the herds. Tents were originally built out of skins stretched upon poles. Linen was substituted later.

THE CALL OF ABRAM

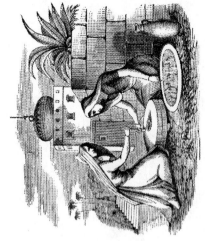

6

Few and simple were the household utensils. A hand-mill consisted of two stones; an upright handle turned the upper upon the lower, while the grain was put in through a central hole. Only women ground the grain.

8

Unleavened bread was a staple of their diet. Sarai may have prepared meals of unleavened bread, milk, and veal. Since Moses and the law as found in Leviticus came later, serving milk and meat at the same meal was not yet prohibited.

5

Digging permanent wells was of great benefit to travelers such as Abram and his family. The water was drawn with pitchers and ropes. The wells were kept covered to keep the sand out. At noon and sunset the stones were rolled away so flocks and herds might be watered and women could draw their household supply.

7

Butter and curdled milk were favorite dishes of the Israelites. The churning was done by putting curdled milk in a goatskin bag which, being tied to a tent pole, was constantly moved back and forth until butter formed.

THE CALL OF ABRAM
Project 2—A Reading About Ur

Read the following background material on Abram's hometown to gain a better understanding of that culture. Then on another sheet of paper draw the four main gods as you imagine them, in the realms they ruled. In the relief below, Enki is the figure second from the right.

The area between the Tigris and Euphrates Rivers, often called the "cradle of civilization," was known in ancient times as Mesopotamia. Sumerians were the first civilization of people found in Mesopotamia. In the Bible, Abram leaves a city in Mesopotamia called Ur. Its ruins are found 140 miles south of Babylon, near the modern city of Baghdad in Iraq, and is now called Tall al Muqayyar.

The ruins of Ur were first found by J.E. Taylor and excavations began there in 1919. Eventually the ziggurat, the temple area, parts of the residential and commercial quarters, and the Royal Cemetary (containing many art treasures) were excavated.

Each city in Mesopotamia had at least one god to worship. The priests who served these gods, or *dingir* as they called them, spoke for the deities. They were very powerful and the high priest often was the king of that city as well.

When the various cities united under one ruler, they developed elaborate mythologies to explain how the gods were related. There was room for every city's gods in the mythology, and new gods were added until the pantheon had no less than 3,000 gods.

Their gods were overexaggerated people, possessing the best and worst of human nature. Though very powerful, the gods acted like humans in their greed, happiness, jealousy and goodness. The universe was divided up into four parts and each of the primary gods ruled these realms. The air was the domain of An, the water was ruled by Enki, the earth was the charge of Ninhursag (sort of like Mother Nature), and Enhil was banished to oversee the underworld because he had broken the laws of the universe. Other deities included Utu the god of the sun (he rode in a chariot across the sky with rays of light issuing from his shoulders) and Ur's god, Nanna the god of the moon (traveling

THE CALL OF ABRAM
Project 2, Page 2

across the night sky in a boat). According to myth, humans were only created to be servants of the gods—one story even said that humanity was made from the blood of an evil god, and thus a man could not help his behavior—an interesting twist on the concept of original sin! In contrast to the afterlife Egyptians professed, in Ur people believed that everyone went to a dreary world like Hell. The only good news was that those who lived good lives on earth did not suffer quite as much as everyone else. When a king or queen died in Ur, dozens of servants followed the royal person into the grave and drank poison so they could serve in the next life as well.

Abram left during Ur's Third Dynasty. His father Terah, was said to be an idol-worshipper (*Then Joshua gathered all the tribes of Israel to Shechem and called for the elders of Israel, for their heads, for their judges, and for their officers; and they presented themselves before God. And Joshua said to all the people, "Thus says the LORD God of Israel: "Your fathers, including Terah, the father of Abraham and the father of Nahor, dwelt on the other side of the River in old times; and they served other gods. —Joshua 24:1-2*), which probably means that he was a priest— and in the Sumerian theocracy that made him a member of the upper class. Abram's wife and half sister was named Sarai, meaning "princess," and the daughter of his brother Haran was named Milcah, which means "queenly"—both suggesting that they may have come from a royal line. When Abram visited Egypt, the Egyptians did not treat him as a common shepherd or backwoods Asiatic trader, but gave him an audience with the pharaoh. Also, as Abram wandered throughout Canaan, he made treaties with the people living there and in the Battle of the Kings, he refused to take any share of the spoils for himself, except to feed the troops that came with him—not the behavior of a lowborn renegade shepherd.

Some have claimed that a cuneiform tablet even mentions Abraham by name. A record of events from the reign of Amar-Sin, the Sumerian king after Shulgi, states that Amar-Sin's seventh year (ca. 2041 B.C.) was the "Year in which the shepherding place of IB.RU.UM was attacked." It is suggested that "IB.RU.UM" is the Sumerian name for Abram.

Josephus wrote in the first century A.D. that "Abraham reigned at Damascus, where he was a foreigner, having come up with an army out of the land above Babylon . . . after a long time, the Lord got him up and removed [him] from that country together with his men and he went to the land then called the land of Canaan but now the land of Judaea." If this is true, then Abram was not a meager shepherd but a Sumerian military commander.

THE CALL OF ABRAM
Test

1. Where in Scripture is the Call of Abram recorded?

   _____

   _____

2. How old was Abram when God promised to make a great nation from his descendants?
   How many children did he have at the time?

   _____

   _____

   _____

   _____

3. Where did God have Abram settle?

   _____

   _____

4. Who went with Abram on his journey to the new land?

   _____

   _____

   _____

5. What did God promise to do with this land?

   _____

   _____

   _____

   _____

6. What is the approximate date of the call of Abram?

   _____

   _____

THE CALL OF ABRAM
Test, Page 2

Review

1. What did God create on the third day of Creation?

    _____

    _____

2. What happened to man as a result of the Fall?

    _____

    _____

    _____

3. What is the biblical reference for Cain and Abel?

    _____

    _____

4. Who was the one person who, with his family, was saved from drowning during the
    Flood?

    _____

    _____

5. Why did God cause the people to speak new languages at the Tower of Babel?

    _____

    _____

    _____

    _____

THE CALL OF ABRAM
Test, Page 3

6. What happened during the Old Kingdom in Egypt?

_____

_____

_____

_____

7. List the events studied to date in chronological order.

_____

_____

_____

_____

_____

_____

_____

_____

_____

GOD'S COVENANT WITH ABRAHAM
Worksheet

1. What was God's promise to Abraham?

   _____

   _____

   _____

2. When God made this covenant with Abraham,

   he and Sarah were too old to have what?

   _____

   _____

3. What did God tell Abraham about the covenant?

   _____

   _____

   _____

4. In what form did God move between the dead animals?

   _____

   _____

5. What sign of the covenant did God later give to Abraham?

   _____

   _____

   _____

6. What is the approximate date of God's covenant with Abraham?

   _____

   _____

7. Where in Scripture do we find the story of God's Covenant with Abraham?

   _____

   _____

GOD'S COVENANT WITH ABRAHAM
Project 1—Genesis 18 Summary

Read Genesis 18. Using complete sentences, write a paragraph describing what is happening in the picture below.

_____

_____

_____

_____

_____

_____

_____

_____

_____

_____

_____

GOD'S COVENANT WITH ABRAHAM
Project 2—Ripped Animals

Supplies

scissors

crayons

glue

Directions

Color each item on the next page. Cut out the elements and tear as needed, then paste onto a sheet of construction paper in a way that shows what happened when Abraham waited on God in the wilderness.

GOD'S COVENANT WITH ABRAHAM
Project 3—Fill in the Blank

Using the history card, fill in the missing blanks.

The Lord _____ Abraham that he would make him a great _____ . When God made this promise Abraham was an _____ man, and he was _____ . His wife, Sarah, was also too old to have children. God, however, made his promise and even told Abraham that his descendants would outnumber the _____ of the sky. Later, God also promised Abraham that his descendants would _____ over a huge area of land, although Abraham _____ no land at the time.

God performed a special _____ to confirm his promise. Abraham cut a heifer, a _____ , a ram, a pigeon, and a turtle dove each into two pieces. Abraham then fell into a deep _____ , and the Lord came down in the form of a smoking _____ and a burning _____ which moved between the pieces of the _____ animals. This type of ceremony was not uncommon in _____ times. When someone made a _____ and then walked between pieces of dead animals they were saying, "Let what happened to the animals happen to _____ if I break this promise." Later, God gave the sign of _____ to Abraham.

Abraham had to wait a _____ time for God's promise to come true.

God's Covenant with Abraham

Test

1. Where in Scripture do we find the story of God's Covenant with Abraham?

    _____

    _____

2. What was the approximate date of God's Covenant with Abraham?

    _____

    _____

3. What was God's promise to Abraham?

    _____

    _____

4. Whom did God say would outnumber the stars in the sky?

    _____

    _____

    _____

5. What sign did God later give to Abraham?

    _____

    _____

    _____

6. Did God's promise to Abraham immediately come true?

    _____

    _____

    _____

God's Covenant with Abraham

Test, Page 2

Review

1. Fill in the days of Creation.

   Day 1: _____

   Day 2: _____

   Day 3: _____

   Day 4: _____

   Day 5: _____

   Day 6: _____

   Day 7: _____

2. With what did God tell Noah to fill the ark?

   _____

   _____

   _____

   _____

3. What happened during the First Intermediate Period in Egypt?

   _____

   _____

   _____

   _____

4. List the events studied to date in chronological order.

   _____

   _____

   _____

   _____

God's Covenant with Abraham
Test, Page 3

4. (continued)

_____

_____

_____

_____

_____

_____

HAGAR AND ISHMAEL
Worksheet

1. What is the approximate date of the departure of Hagar and Ishmael?

   _____

   _____

2. What is the scripture reference for the story of Hagar and Ishmael?

   _____

   _____

3. Why did Sarai ask Abram to take Hagar as his wife?

   _____

   _____

4. What was the name of the son born to Hagar and Abram?

   _____

   _____

5. What was the name of the son born to Abraham and Sarah?

   _____

   _____

6. Why did Sarah ask Abraham to cast Hagar and her son out into the wilderness?

   _____

   _____

7. What did God promise Hagar?

   _____

   _____

   _____

   _____

HAGAR AND ISHMAEL
Project 1—Genesis 16 & 21 Summary

Read Genesis 16 & 21. Using complete sentences, write a paragraph describing what is happening in the picture below.

_____

_____

_____

_____

_____

_____

_____

_____

_____

_____

_____

_____

Hagar and Ishmael
Project 2—Water Bottle

Genesis 21:14–19

So Abraham rose early in the morning, and took bread and a skin of water; and putting it on her shoulder, he gave it and the boy to Hagar, and sent her away. Then she departed and wandered in the Wilderness of Beersheba. And the water in the skin was used up, and she placed the boy under one of the shrubs. Then she went and sat down across from him at a distance of about a bowshot; for she said to herself, "Let me not see the death of the boy." So she sat opposite him, and lifted her voice and wept.

And God heard the voice of the lad. Then the angel of God called to Hagar out of heaven, and said to her, "What ails you, Hagar? Fear not, for God has heard the voice of the lad where he is. Arise, lift up the lad and hold him with your hand, for I will make him a great nation."

Then God opened her eyes, and she saw a well of water. And she went and filled the skin with water, and gave the lad a drink. So God was with the lad; and he grew and dwelt in the wilderness, and became an archer. He dwelt in the Wilderness of Paran; and his mother took a wife for him from the land of Egypt.

After reading the passage above, make this water bottle project to help understand biblical times.

Supplies

two 8.5 x 12 .5 inch pieces of black felt

string or twine

hot glue gun or needle and thread

scissors and chalk

1/2 cup uncooked elbow macaroni or other small pasta

Directions

Cut out the stencil on the following page and trace it on the felt using chalk. Cut out the shape from the felt and wipe off the chalk lines with a damp cloth. Run a line of hot glue along the inside lines, keeping the neck opening free from glue—then glue the two pieces together and allow to cool (or sew the two halves together using small, close stitches). Tie off each of the four leg openings using the string. Fill the bottle with the pasta and tie the neck of the skin closed as you did with the leg openings. Tie three three-foot lengths of twine together at one end of the goatskin. Braid the three pieces of twine and tie off on one of the legs at the other end of the bottle.

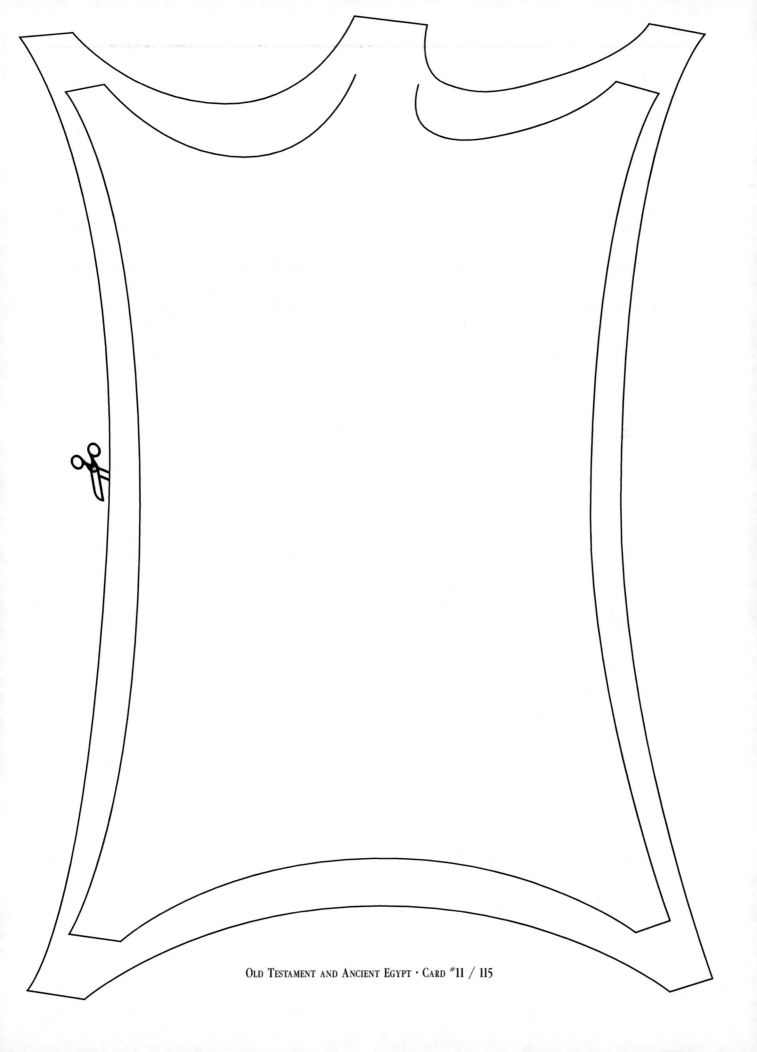

OLD TESTAMENT AND ANCIENT EGYPT · CARD #11 / 115

HAGAR AND ISHMAEL
Test

1. Where in Scripture do we find the story of Hagar and Ishmael?

   _____

   _____

2. Sarai had grown old and had not given birth to a child. What did she tell Abram to do?

   _____

   _____

   _____

3. What was the name of Abram and Hagar's child?

   _____

   _____

4. At the age of ninety Sarah had a child. What was the child's name?

   _____

   _____

5. What did Sarah ask Abraham to do with Hagar?

   _____

   _____

   _____

6. What was God's promise to Hagar?

   _____

   _____

   _____

Hagar and Ishmael
Test, Page 2

Review

1. What is the Scripture reference for the Flood?

   _____

   _____

2. For what purpose were the pyramids built?

   _____

   _____

   _____

   _____

3. What do we mean by the "Call of Abram?"

   _____

   _____

   _____

4. What is the scripture reference for God's Covenant with Abraham?

   _____

   _____

5. Write the events studied to date in chronological order.

   _____

   _____

   _____

   _____

HAGAR AND ISHMAEL
Test, Page 3

5. (continued)

_____

_____

_____

_____

_____

_____

_____

SODOM AND GOMORRAH
Worksheet

1. What is the approximate date of the destruction of Sodom and Gomorrah?

   _____

   _____

2. Where in Scripture can we find the story of the destruction of Sodom and Gomorrah?

   _____

   _____

3. Why did Abraham plead with God not to destroy Sodom and Gomorrah?

   _____

   _____

4. Why did God save Lot?

   _____

   _____

   _____

5. What happened to Lot's wife?

   _____

   _____

   _____

6. Why was this event significant in Abraham's life?

   _____

   _____

   _____

   _____

SODOM AND GOMORRAH
Project 1—News Article

Pretend that you are a reporter for the newspaper Canaan Chronicle *and have just witnessed the destruction of Sodom and Gomorrah. Write an article for the paper reporting what you have seen. Remember to start with a topic sentence. Also make sure that you use complete sentences.*

Sodom & Gomorrah Burn; Woman Turns to Salt

_____

_____

_____

_____

_____

_____

_____

_____

_____   _____

_____   _____

_____   _____

SODOM AND GOMORRAH
Project 2—Lot's Salt Dough Wife

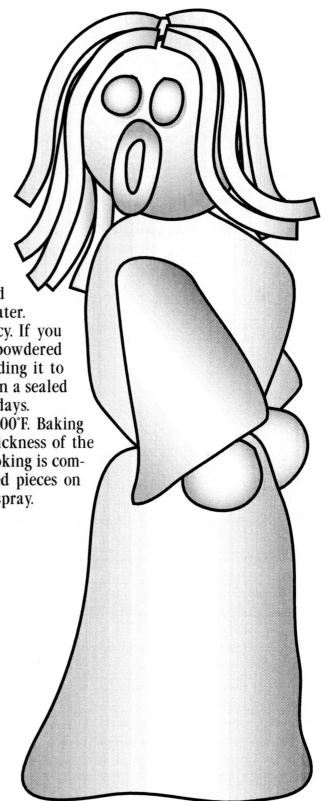

Ingredients

4 cups flour

1 cup salt

1-1/2 cups hot water

clear varnish or polyurethane spray

Directions

Mix the salt and flour together, then gradually add the water until the dough becomes elastic. If the dough is too sticky, add more flour. If it is too crumbly, add more water. Knead the dough until it is a good consistency. If you want colored dough, mix food coloring, powdered drink mix, or paint into the water before adding it to the dry ingredients. Salt dough can be stored in a sealed container in the refrigerator for a couple of days.

Make salt dough sculptures and bake at 200°F. Baking times will vary depending on the size and thickness of the object. If the dough starts to darken before cooking is complete, cover with aluminum foil. Seal finished pieces on all sides with clear varnish or polyurethane spray.

SODOM AND GOMORRAH
Project 3—The Dead Sea

No one knows for sure where the two cities once stood, though many believe the ancient ruins of Sodom lie under the southern part of the Dead Sea. In Lot's day the Dead Sea was much smaller. Using resources in your library or online, write a short report on the Dead Sea as it is today.

_____

_____

_____

_____

_____

_____

_____

_____

_____

_____

_____

_____

_____

_____

_____

SODOM AND GOMORRAH

Test

1. What is the approximate date of the destruction of Sodom and Gomorrah?

    _____

    _____

2. Where in Scripture can we find the story of Sodom and Gomorrah?

    _____

    _____

3. Who was the one righteous man God found?

    _____

    _____

4. When the cities of Sodom and Gomorrah were destroyed what happened to Lot
    and his family?

    _____

    _____

Review

1. What did the devil tempt Eve to do?

    _____

    _____

2. Why did Cain kill Abel?

    _____

    _____

3. Why did the Lord flood the earth?

    _____

    _____

SODOM AND GOMORRAH
Test, Page 2

4. What is the largest pyramid ever built?

_____

_____

5. Where in Scripture can we find the Call of Abram?

_____

_____

6. What promise did God make to Abram?

_____

_____

7. What was the name of Abraham and Hagar's son?

_____

_____

8. Write the events studied to date in chronological order.

_____

_____

_____

_____

_____

_____

_____

_____

_____

_____

BIRTH AND SACRIFICE OF ISAAC
Worksheet

1. What is the approximate date of the Birth and Sacrifice of Isaac?

   _____

   _____

2. Where in Scripture can we find the story of the Birth and Sacrifice of Isaac?

   _____

   _____

   _____

3. How old were Abraham and Sarah when Isaac was born?

   _____

   _____

4. When Isaac was a young boy what did God ask Abraham to do?

   _____

   _____

   _____

   _____

5. Why did an angel of the Lord appear to Abraham?

   _____

   _____

   _____

BIRTH AND SACRIFICE OF ISAAC
Worksheet, Page 2

6. Why was God pleased with Abraham?

_____

_____

_____

7. What can we learn about Abraham's faithfulness to God?

_____

_____

_____

_____

_____

_____

Birth and Sacrifice of Isaac
Project 1—Sacrifices Booklet

On the following pages you will find pictures to turn into a little book for each student. The book will explain the Old Testament sacrificial system.

Read through the following two pages with the children. Discuss the meaning and purpose of sacrifices with particular emphasis on the fact that Christ was the perfect sacrifice ending the need for future sacrifices.

Supplies

scissors

glue

construction paper

colored markers or crayons

Directions

Photocopy the following two pages for each student, then cut the pictures apart and glue onto the construction paper. Cut construction paper in half as shown below. Fold the halves in two and staple together to form a book. Have the children illustrate the different types of sacrifices.

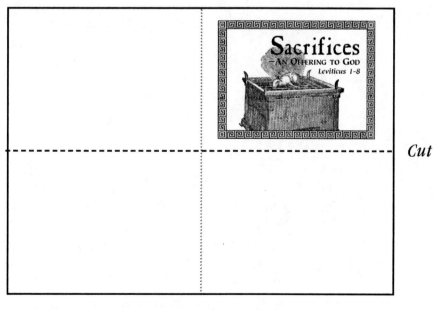

Cut

Fold

BIRTH AND SACRIFICE OF ISAAC

Sacrifices
—AN OFFERING TO GOD
Leviticus 1-8

A sacrifice was the method used in the Old Testament to ask forgiveness for sin or to give thanks and praise to God. Scripture teaches that God is holy and cannot overlook sin, but that sin must be punished. Before Christ, sacrifices of animals and grain were offered to God to atone for sin. However, these sacrifices were imperfect and pointed toward the perfect sacrifice of Christ on the cross.

Altars were made of unhewn stones and later from hewn stones and metal. An altar was not only a place to offer a sacrifice. The word altar means "to approach." Consequently, stepping up to the altar was symbolic of communion with God and an act of remembering His covenant.

Only "clean" animals were allowed as sacrifices. These generally included sheep, goats, cattle, or doves. A grain offering (usually offered with an animal sacrifice) consisted of wheat flour mixed with olive oil, incense, and salt. It was mixed, then baked, fried, or cooked. It symbolized the person's dedication to God.

The "first fruits" were offerings of grain from the first harvest of the year. These offerings differed from other grain offerings in that they were full green heads of grain roasted on the fire. The first fruits were offered to God to give thanks for what He had provided.

On the following pages illustrate the offering described at the top of each page.

Burnt Offering

The whole animal less the skin was burned, symbolizing the total giving of one's self to God.

Peace Offering

The fatty parts of the animal were burned as a sign of fellowship with God. It was unusual in that the priest and the family ate much of the remaining meat.

Trespass Offering

Similar to the sin offering, this offering was for sins of omission, inadvertence or rashness. The fatty parts of the animal were burned and the priests kept the remaining meat. The poor were permitted to offer flour.

Grain Offering

Wheat flour mixed in olive oil, incense and salt. The mixture was then cooked and symbolized the worshipper's dedication to God by giving God of his goods.

Sin Offering

An animal was killed. Its blood was sprinkled on the altar as an atonement for one's sin.

BIRTH AND SACRIFICE OF ISAAC
Project 2—Fill in the Blank

Using the history card, fill in the missing blanks.

Isaac was _____ born to Abraham and Sarah in their _____ age. Abraham was _____ years old, and Sarah was 91. Now they could understand how God would make their _____ a great nation as He _____ .

When Isaac was a boy, God told Abraham to offer Isaac, his only _____ son, as a sacrifice to Him. Abraham's _____ was great, and he _____ God taking Isaac up onto Mount _____ . There he _____ Isaac and placed him on the _____ they had built. But an _____ of the Lord stopped Abraham from _____ Isaac, and they sacrificed a _____ that was caught in the nearby _____ .

God was _____ with the _____ and obedience of Abraham.

BIRTH AND SACRIFICE OF ISAAC

Test

1. What is the approximate date of the Birth and Sacrifice of Isaac?

_____

_____

2. Where in Scripture can we find the story of the Birth and Sacrifice of Isaac?

_____

_____

3. How was God's promise of a great nation finally fulfilled through Abraham?

_____

_____

_____

4. How did God test Abraham's faith?

_____

_____

_____

5. Why did an angel of the Lord appear to Abraham?

_____

_____

_____

Review

1. What did God do at the Tower of Babel?

_____

_____

_____

BIRTH AND SACRIFICE OF ISAAC
Test, Page 2

2. Who unified Upper and Lower Egypt?

_____

_____

3. What happened during the First Intermediate Period?

_____

_____

_____

_____

4. What was the covenant God made with Abraham?

_____

_____

_____

5. What happened to Hagar and Ishmael once they were cast into the wilderness?

_____

_____

_____

_____

6. Why did God destroy Sodom and Gomorrah?

_____

_____

_____

_____

BIRTH AND SACRIFICE OF ISAAC
Test, Page 3

7. List the chronology that you have studied to date. Provide scripture references for biblically recorded events.

_____

_____

_____

_____

_____

_____

_____

_____

_____

_____

_____

THE MIDDLE KINGDOM IN EGYPT
Worksheet

1. What is the approximate date of the Middle Kingdom in Egypt?

   _____

   _____

2. What was the name of the Theban who seized control of Egypt during the 12th dynasty?

   _____

   _____

3. What cultural advances were made during the Middle Kingdom?

   _____

   _____

   _____

   _____

4. What biblical event overlaps with the Middle Kingdom?

   _____

   _____

   _____

5. Who was the most important king/pharaoh of the 12th dynasty and why?

THE MIDDLE KINGDOM IN EGYPT
Project 1—Hieroglyphics

We owe most of our knowledge of ancient Egypt to the inscriptions and manuscripts written in characters called hieroglyphics. This curious style of writing consisted of pictures or symbols representing words or letters. Thus, a circle stood for the sun, a crescent for the moon, an oval figure for the mouth, etc. As different pictures or signs were often used to represent the same word or sound, it is not strange that many centuries passed before scholars were able to decipher the hieroglyphic text. It was not until after 1799 that any clue to their meaning was discovered. In that year the finding of the Rosetta Stone gave the first key to the reading of hieroglyphics. On this stone the same inscription was given in three different sets of characters; the hieroglyphics, the demotic text (a briefer and more running form of hieroglyphics, commonly used in the papyri or manuscripts), and the Greek. By comparing the letters in certain Greek proper names with the letters of the same words in the Egyptian texts, the sounds for which the Egyptian characters stood were discovered.

Eventually, as hieroglyphic writing developed, most of the signs took on phonetic values. They could be used to stand for sounds and used with other hieroglyphs to spell out words.

Make several copies of the next page for each student. Have the students cut them apart and use the hieroglyphics to write a sentence by pasting the letters on construction paper as words. Have the students exchange them to translate another student's work.

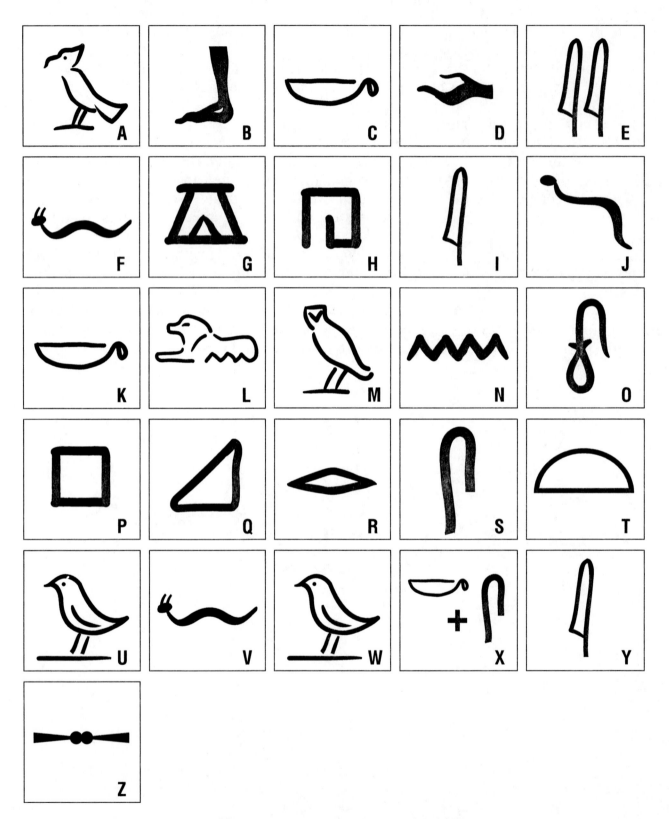

THE MIDDLE KINGDOM IN EGYPT
Project 2—Gateway of Karnak

Supplies

paper

scissors

glue or tape

colored pencils/markers

Directions

Photocopy each page onto white card stock. Color and then cut out along the solid exterior lines. The two small panels on this page are attached to the inside of the gates, and that piece is placed between the two large walls found on the following pages.

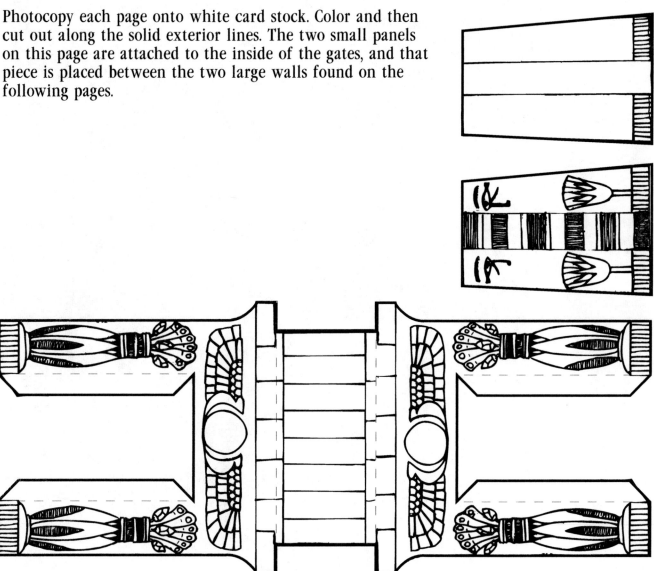

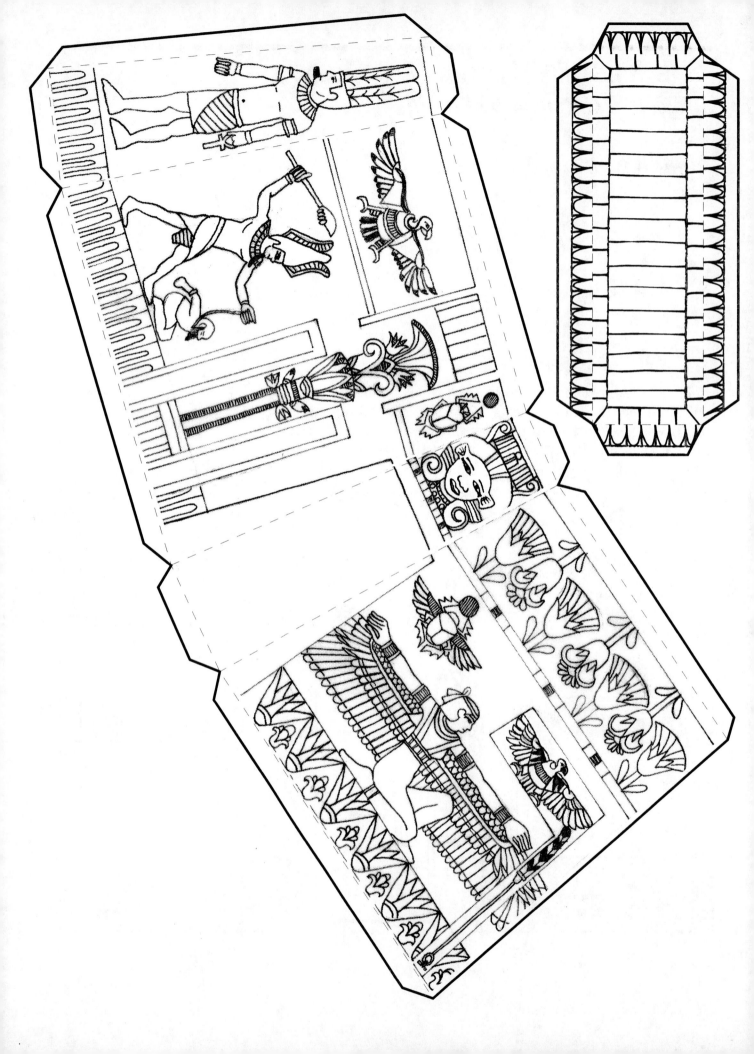

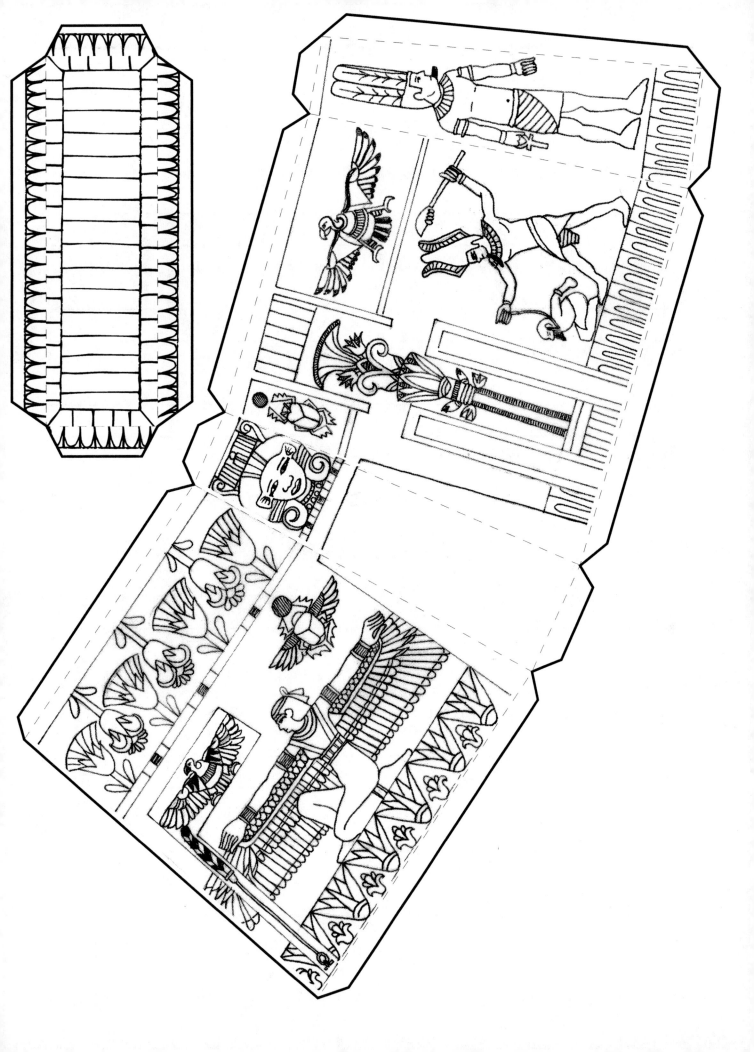

THE MIDDLE KINGDOM IN EGYPT
Test

1. What is the approximate date of the Middle Kingdom in Egypt?

   _____

   _____

2. After Amenemhet seized the throne, what did Egypt enjoy once again?

   _____

   _____

3. What cultural advances were made during the Middle Kingdom?

   _____

   _____

4. Who was sold into slavery during this period?

   _____

   _____

5. Who was the most important king of the 12th dynasty and why?

   _____

   _____

Review

1. What happened on the seventh day of Creation?

   _____

   _____

2. Why did God curse Cain?

   _____

   _____

   _____

THE MIDDLE KINGDOM IN EGYPT
Test, Page 2

3. What was built during the Old Kingdom in Egypt?

_____

_____

4. What did God call Abram to do?

_____

_____

5. What covenant did God make with Abraham?

_____

_____

6. Write the events studied to date in chronological order.

_____

_____

_____

_____

_____

_____

_____

_____

_____

_____

_____

_____

JOSEPH AS A SLAVE
Worksheet

1. What is the scripture reference for Joseph as a Slave?

   _____

   _____

2. What is the approximate date of Joseph's slavery?

   _____

   _____

3. Why did Joseph's brothers envy him?

   _____

   _____

4. What did Joseph's brothers do to him?

   _____

   _____

   _____

5. What did Potiphar do to Joseph?

   _____

   _____

6. Why was Joseph put in prison?

   _____

   _____

7. What responsibility was Joseph given while in prison?

   _____

   _____

8. What remarkable feat did he accomplish while in prison?

   _____

Joseph As a Slave
Project 1

In the "thought clouds" illustrate
Joseph's two dreams from Genesis 37.

JOSEPH AS A SLAVE
Project 2—Genesis 37 Summary

Read Genesis 37. Using complete sentences, write a paragraph describing what is happening in the picture below.

_____

_____

_____

_____

_____

_____

_____

_____

_____

_____

JOSEPH AS A SLAVE
Project 3—Joseph's Grocery Bag of Many Colors

Supplies

paper grocery bag

wallpaper samples

glue

scissors

Directions

Cut circles in the bottom
and sides of the grocery bag
for the neck and arms of the
"coat." Then cut a slit in the
front up to the neck hole.
Cut wallpaper samples into
long narrow strips and glue
to the bag. If an old wallpaper
sample book is unavailable,
paint the bag using tempera
paints and illustrate some of
Joseph's dreams.

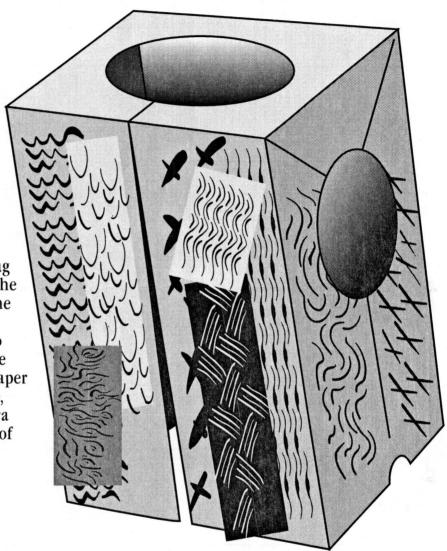

JOSEPH AS A SLAVE
Test

1. What did Joseph dream at the age of seventeen?

   _____

   _____

2. Why did Joseph's brothers envy him?

   _____

   _____

3. What did Joseph's brothers do to him?

   _____

   _____

4. Who was Potiphar?

   _____

   _____

5. Why was Joseph put in prison?

   _____

   _____

6. Whose dreams did Joseph interpret in prison?

   _____

   _____

7. What is the scripture reference for Joseph as a Slave?

   _____

8. What is the approximate date for Joseph as a Slave?

   _____

   _____

   _____

JOSEPH AS A SLAVE
Test, Page 2

Review

1. List what God created on each of the seven days.

   Day 1: _____

   Day 2: _____

   Day 3: _____

   Day 4: _____

   Day 5: _____

   Day 6: _____

   Day 7: _____

2. After Cain killed Abel what was God's judgment on him?

   _____

   _____

   _____

3. What did God command Noah to do?

   _____

   _____

   _____

4. What was the purpose of the pyramids?

   _____

   _____

   _____

5. What is the scripture reference for God's Covenant with Abraham?

   _____

JOSEPH AS A SLAVE
Test, Page 3

6. List all events covered to date in chronological order.

_____

_____

_____

_____

_____

_____

_____

_____

_____

_____

_____

_____

_____

_____

FAMINE IN EGYPT
Worksheet

1. Why did Pharaoh summon Joseph from prison?

   _____

   _____

2. What were Joseph's interpretations of Pharaoh's dreams?

   _____

   _____

3. What job did Pharaoh give to Joseph?

   _____

   _____

4. What did Joseph do to ensure that there would be food during times of famine?

   _____

   _____

5. Who came to visit Joseph during the famine?

   _____

   _____

6. What eventually happened to Joseph and his family?

   _____

   _____

   _____

FAMINE IN EGYPT
Project 1—Genesis 41 Summary

Read Genesis 41. Using complete sentences, write a paragraph describing what is happening in the picture below.

_____

_____

_____

_____

_____

_____

_____

_____

_____

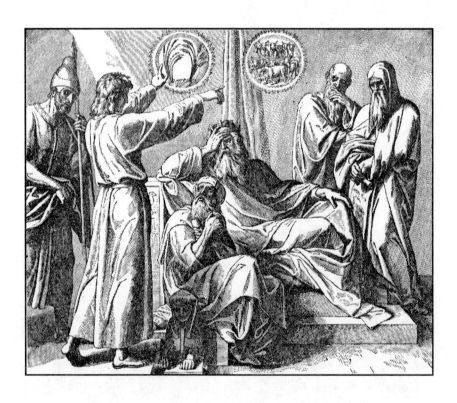

FAMINE IN EGYPT
Project 2—Signet Rings

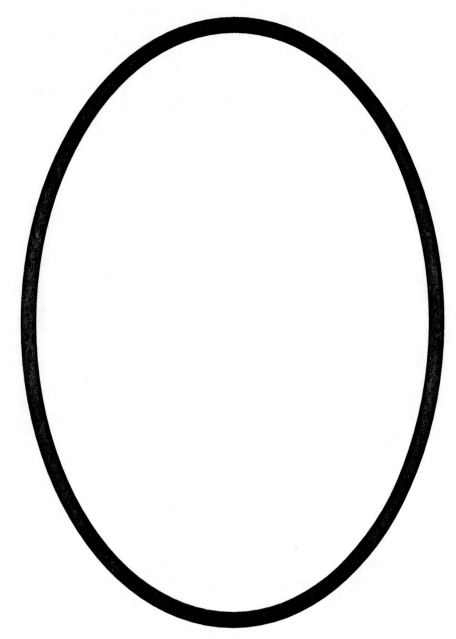

When Pharaoh made Joseph second-in-command he took his signet ring off his hand and put it on Joseph's. He clothed him in garments of fine linen and put a gold chain around his neck. Giving Joseph the signet ring was very symbolic as it transferred power to him. A signet ring was used to sign documents. It would have been pressed into wax or clay as we sign our name to documents today. *Using only pictures, draw a design in the ring below that would symbolize you.*

FAMINE IN EGYPT
Project 3—Grain Crops

Read the following information on the harvesting process and have each child examine a stalk of wheat. Have each child take one stalk apart to see how difficult it was to separate the grain from the chaff. Then make the decorative item below.

Egyptian farmers relied on the Nile River flooding its banks on a yearly basis. If this did not happen the soil would be too dry and infertile for any crops to grow and a famine would occur. Once the flood had subsided the first thing a farmer did was plow his fields with a wooden plow pulled by an ox. The farmer would then walk up and down the fields throwing seeds into the soil. Next the field was either plowed again or animals walked over the soil trampling the seeds into the ground. Once the grain had grown it had to be harvested. The crops were cut and tied into bundles (sheaves). They were then taken to the threshing floor where oxen or donkeys trampled them to separate the grain from the stalks. Now they were ready for a process called winnowing. The trodden grain was sifted and then thrown into the air, using a winnowing fork while a breeze was blowing. The useful grain fell to the ground, but the lighter chaff blew away in the wind. The grain would be sifted through a sieve and placed into sacks in which to be stored.

Survival required much hard work in Egypt at that time. Joseph knew that he must store the grain at the granary if they were not to starve when the drought came and crops could not be grown.

Supplies

one small (3") terra-cotta pot per student

dry foam

paper twist ribbon

12 stalks of wheat per student

hot glue gun

Directions

Cut, fit and hot glue the foam into pot. Insert the wheat into foam. Tie a ribbon around the wheat.

FAMINE IN EGYPT
Project 4—Winnowing Fork

After harvesting wheat, barley and corn, oxen separated the grain from the stalks. Then the grained was sifted using a sieve. Wooden forks called winnowing forks were then used to throw the chaff and grain into the air, and the wind would carry off the chaff.

Follow the directions below to make a small winnowing fork.

Supplies

four craft sticks

hot glue gun

I cup popcorn kernels

4 cups shredded newspaper

1 electric fan

Directions

Glue the craft sticks together as shown in the diagram to the right. Combine the popcorn kernels and shredded paper in a pile on a table. Set the fan so that it will blow over, but not into, the mixture.

Pretend to winnow through the mixture, allowing the lighter "chaff" to be blown away as the grain falls back onto the table.

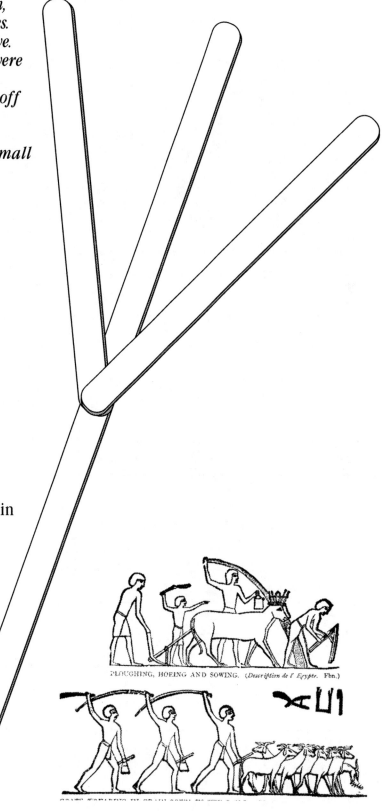

PLOUGHING, HOEING AND SOWING. *(Description de l' Egypte. Fbn.)*

FAMINE IN EGYPT
Test

1. Why did Pharaoh summon Joseph from prison?

_____

_____

_____

2. What was the meaning of Pharaoh's dreams?

_____

_____

_____

3. What job did Joseph do for Pharaoh?

_____

_____

_____

4. Who came to see Joseph during the famine? Did they know who he was?

_____

_____

_____

5. What eventually happened to Joseph and his family?

_____

_____

_____

_____

_____

_____

FAMINE IN EGYPT
Test, Page 2

Review

1. What was Hagar's relationship to Sarai?

    _____

    _____

2. What covenant did God make with Abraham?

    _____

    _____

    _____

3. What occurred during the First Intermediate Period in Egypt?

    _____

    _____

    _____

4. Who unified Egypt and was the first known pharaoh?

    _____

    _____

5. List all events covered in chronological order. Where appropriate, list Bible references.

    _____

    _____

    _____

    _____

    _____

5. (continued)

_____

_____

_____

_____

_____

_____

_____

_____

_____

THE TWELVE TRIBES OF ISRAEL
Worksheet

1. What promise had God made to Abraham?

_____

_____

_____

2. To whom did God reveal this plan?

_____

_____

_____

3. Who are the Patriarchs?

_____

_____

_____

_____

4. To what did God change Jacob's name? How many sons did he have?

_____

_____

5. What happened to each of Jacob's sons?

_____

_____

6. What are Jacob's descendants known as?

_____

_____

7. The _____ were God's _____ people.

THE TWELVE TRIBES OF ISRAEL
Project 1—Breastplate of the High Priest

Under the Mosaic law, the people were not allowed to offer sacrifices themselves to God; a priesthood was instituted to mediate between them and Jehovah. Aaron was the first High Priest, and the office was passed down from father to son and assumed for a lifetime. The robes of glory in which Aaron was arrayed at his consecration, and in which he blessed Israel, are full of symbolic meaning. One of the articles of clothing the High Priest wore was the radiant breastplate which had twelve of the most precious stones set in gold, and fixed upon the beautiful embroidery. The names of the tribes were cut on these stones, and the breastplate was bound close to the heart of the High Priest. This represented the infinite compassion and love of Jehovah for His entire people and the willingness to uphold His followers by the power of His might.

EPHOD→
EX.28

BLUE ROBE→

WHITE→

THE TWELVE TRIBES OF ISRAEL
Project 1, Page 2

Fill in the names of the twelve sons of Israel and color the High Priest.

1. _____

2. _____

3. _____

4. _____

5. _____

6. _____

7. _____

8. _____

9. _____

10. _____

11. _____

12. _____

THE TWELVE TRIBES OF ISRAEL
Project 2—Abraham's Family Tree

Fill in the blanks.

THE TWELVE TRIBES OF ISRAEL
Project 3—Fill in the Blank

Using the history card, fill in the missing blanks.

    Having _____ Abraham that he would cause a great _____ to come from his descendants, God increasingly revealed his _____ through Abraham's son, Isaac, and Isaac's son, _____ . The three are known as the _____ .

    Jacob, whose _____ was _____ by God to Israel, had twelve _____ . They each became a tribe and are known as the twelve tribes of _____ . To this day all their descendants are known as the Israelites or _____ . These were God's _____ people. God _____ them tremendously for their _____ and punished them when they were _____ to Him.

THE TWELVE TRIBES OF ISRAEL
Test

1. What are the scripture references for the Twelve Tribes of Israel?

    _____

2. What is the approximate date of the Twelve Tribes of Israel?

    _____

3. What promise did God make to Abraham?

    _____

    _____

4. To whom did God reveal much of the promise?

    _____

    _____

    _____

5. Who are the Patriarchs?

    _____

    _____

6. To what did God change Jacob's name? How many sons did Jacob have?

    _____

    _____

7. Name Jacob's sons.

    _____   _____

    _____   _____

    _____   _____

    _____   _____

    _____   _____

    _____   _____

THE TWELVE TRIBES OF ISRAEL
Test, Page 2

8. The Israelites were God's _____ people.

Review

1. What may the ziggurat at Marduk be?

_____

_____

2. For whom was the great pyramid at Giza built?

_____

_____

_____

3. What is the approximate date of the Call of Abram?

_____

_____

4. What was the name of the son born to Abram and Hagar?

_____

_____

5. Who was the one righteous man God found in Sodom and Gomorrah?

_____

_____

_____

6. What was the name of the son born to Abraham and Sarah?

_____

_____

_____

THE TWELVE TRIBES OF ISRAEL
Test, Page 3

7. List all events covered in chronological order.

_____

_____

_____

_____

_____

_____

_____

_____

_____

_____

_____

_____

_____

_____

_____

SECOND INTERMEDIATE PERIOD IN EGYPT
Worksheet

1. What is the approximate date of the Second Intermediate Period in Egypt?

   _____

   _____

2. Of what dynasties did the Second Intermediate Period in Egypt consist?

   _____

   _____

   _____

3. How were rulers of this period characterized?

   _____

   _____

   _____

   _____

SECOND INTERMEDIATE PERIOD IN EGYPT
Worksheet, Page 2

4. What did local princes control?

_____

_____

_____

_____

5. What land gains did Egypt make during this period?

_____

_____

_____

_____

_____

_____

_____

Second Intermediate Period in Egypt
Project 1—Making an Egyptian Coffin

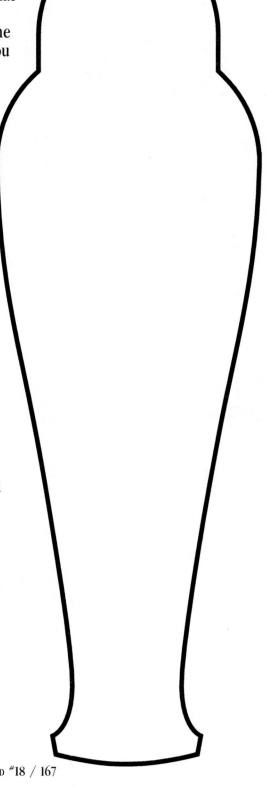

Read the book *Mummies Made in Egypt* by Aliki aloud to your class. This book provides detailed information on how the Egyptians cared for the dead through the entire burial process.

After reading the book have the students define the words on the following page. With younger students you may need to have them copy answers off the board.

After you have done this the children may each make an Egyptian coffin.

Supplies

white bulletin board paper

tempera paint and brushes

newspaper

stapler

pencils

Directions

Have each child lie on his back on the bulletin board paper. Then have another child trace a coffin around him with a pencil. Cut out two of these shapes. Now draw designs on the coffin (refer to the book mentioned above for pictures). Staple the edges of the sarcophagus and fill with crumpled newspaper for stuffing.

SECOND INTERMEDIATE PERIOD IN EGYPT
Project 1, Page 2

Using the book, define the following terms.

ba:

_____

_____

mummified:

_____

_____

_____

fossil:

_____

_____

decay:

_____

_____

pharaoh:

_____

_____

embalm:

_____

_____

natron:

_____

_____

_____

SECOND INTERMEDIATE PERIOD IN EGYPT
Project 1, Page 3

canopic jar:

_____

_____

shroud:

_____

_____

coffin:

_____

_____

sarcophagus:

_____

_____

funeral:

_____

_____

mastaba:

_____

_____

pyramid:

_____

_____

SECOND INTERMEDIATE PERIOD IN EGYPT

Project 2—Cat Mummy

The Egyptians embalmed more than just people. The also made dog, crocodile and baboon mummies. The most common animal mummies were cats because they were thought to be the embodiment of the goddess Bastet. From about 332 B.C. to 30 B.C., animals began to be raised to be turned into mummies. The mummies were sold to people on their way to worship a god and left at the temple as offerings. So many cat mummies were made that one company bought 38,000 pounds of cat mummies in the 1800s to grind up and sell as fertilizer in England.

Supplies

oatmeal container

newspaper

tape

cardboard

colored construction paper

white glue

paint

    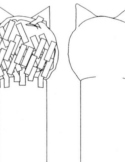   

Directions

Turn the oatmeal canister upside down and tape on it a tight ball of newspaper. Cut out two triangles from construction paper and tape to the top of the ball of newspaper. Dip small strips of newspaper into a mixture of glue and water, then lay over the entire mummy. Allow the piece to dry then paint it gold and add a face. When the paint is dry, cover the canister with the glue and water mixture and overlap two long strips of colored construction paper in a weaving fashion. Brush the glue and water over the woven strips.

SECOND INTERMEDIATE PERIOD IN EGYPT
Project 3—The Artists of the Old Empires: A Reading

Egyptian art differs very greatly in quality from the art of any other early nation, because it was inspired by a definite system of religious thought. It is the first such art in the history of the world. It is the next big thing, in time, to the art of the reindeer-hunters, which was warm and natural and beautiful, and was the work of men who had thought very little. Egyptian art, however, was more cold and less natural, but beautiful—the work of men who had thought a very great deal.

THE TWO THOUSAND STRANGE GODS OF OLD EGYPT

The Egyptians had worked out for themselves a curious religion, a system embracing over two thousand gods and goddesses divided into certain families, or groups. Some of the chief gods have interesting titles. There was Osiris, the man-god who rose from the dead, and was deified and became king of the other world and judge of the dead. There was Set, the principle of evil, the enemy of Osiris. There was Nu, the god of the watery mass whereof the world was made.

There were the goddesses of wisdom, of literature, of earth, sky, rain; almost every physical and mental force had its divinity in the old mental outlook of the Egyptians. Portraits of them are shown in the sacred books and paintings. Generally speaking, from the shoulders down they are very much alike, but are distinguished one from another by the most wonderful head-decorations.

These divinities imposed upon their subjects a certain way of thinking and behaving which had for a foundation two strong beliefs—that this world is of little account, save for the passing happiness it may afford, and that the wicked are punished and the good rewarded in the world to come. It was on the idea of the future life, of which they were so unwaveringly sure, that the Egyptians based most of their literature and art; and we cannot appreciate their painting, their sculpture or their architecture without first understanding this fact.

THE OLD EGYPTIANS' RESTING ROOMS FOR THE LONG, LONG SILENCE

A Greek historian once said that the Egyptians looked on their houses as mere places of passage, and on their tombs as their permanent dwellings. They made tombs fit to outlast time itself, and in them buried their dead, wonderfully embalmed, so that the bodies would be preserved for thousands of years; and they placed in these houses of long silence very beautiful things. It seems strange to us that a nation should concentrate its art on its sepulchres, but perhaps we shall understand it better when we realize that to these far-off people death was only a suspension of life; sooner or later the spirit would return to the body.

This idea was so real to them that they furnished the house of the dead with as much tender care as if the dearly loved person had been alive. Tables, chairs, stools, beautifully decorated bowls for oils and spices, painted and inlaid boxes containing mirrors, hairpins and scents, were among the furniture of the tomb. In a child's tomb they placed its toys, in that of a warrior his spears, in that of a hunter his bows and arrows, in that of a state dignitary his staff of office.

THE LOVELY BOOK LEFT WITH THE DEAD FOR THEM TO READ

In all tombs of any importance they put a remarkable set of writings called the *Book of the Dead,* which was supposed to have been written in the first case by Thoth, the scribe of the gods. It contained religious teaching, stories of the life of the gods, and so on. Each copy was separately written and painted by scribes and artists in bright colors and hieroglyphics—picture-words. And these men put into a work, which would be seen by the spiritual dead all the skill generally put into pictures meant to win worldwide fame.

We can see the kind of illustrations that were painted in the *Book of the Dead* from the magnificent specimens shown in the Egyptian galleries of the British Museum. This collection of papyri is the finest in the world; and it brings back to us a race and a religion and an art that will have a definite place in history as long as history endures.

THE ROYAL TOMBS THAT MADE KINGS SEEM MORE KINGLY

The tombs on which so much time and art were spent were of various kinds: the mastabas of the earlier dynasties—heavy, rectangular constructions; the pyramids of the later centuries; and the rock-hewn tombs of the mountainous parts of the country. Of these last the most famous are the tombs of the kings at Biban-el-Muluk, near Luxor, on the banks of the Nile. The splendors within them make us feel that death had left royalty thrice royal.

Each tomb contained several chambers and passages, and, in some kinds, a shaft led to a remote chamber where the sealed sarcophagus was laid. There was generally placed in or near the tomb a statue of the dead, to which offerings were made. These tombs were built and endowed by the wealthy "for ever." In some there was a chamber where "the sad and solemn priests" made daily offerings for the dead. A temple built near the later tombs took the place of this room. The walls of the chambers, and in some cases the ceilings, were covered with interesting decorations showing men and animals, gods and goddesses.

Second Intermediate Period in Egypt
Project 3—The Artists of the Old Empires: A Reading, Page 3

Figures were often outlined or engraved, sculptured in a slightly raised relief, or sunken.

Where the Dead Wait in Hope of the Life to Come

Usually the decoration was painted in brilliant coloring, and the colors have lasted so well that they are charming today. Often, above and below the rows or groups of figures are beautiful borders of conventional design, using the lotus, the papyrus and other motifs. Almost every shape used was a symbol, and inscriptions in hieroglyphics added further to the richness of the pattern, as well as to the meaning of the whole.

The Egyptian artist had to follow strict rules which were prescribed by religious authority, and which were never cast aside. Everything is painted flat. No modeling is attempted; no light and shade shown; the backgrounds hold no suggestion of the laws of perspective. The figures are always intentionally "out of drawing," with faces, legs and feet in profile, and shoulders and bodies turned full-front. This distortion is all the more marked because the eye shown in the profile is always the eye as it would appear in a full view of the face. The feet were always shown flat to the ground. Any attempt at a light poise, a resting on the toes, or one foot flying, would have seemed to them a contradiction of their standards of art. After a little thought we see that it could not be otherwise. The whole spirit of Egyptian art is the clamping-down of a human being on the Rock of Eternity.

Keynotes of Egyptian Art

The idea that life would go on forever crept into the work even when the artist had no thought of portraying anything of a religious kind. The keynote of their art, so to speak, is a quietness, a waiting, an immobility. In portraits and statues their kings and queens are often shown seated, knees together, feet together, no twist in neck or shoulders, eyes looking calmly out, the face in complete repose. If the figure is standing, it is pulled out to an abnormal length, and has the same movelessness of spirit. Egyptian art, alone in the world, is intensely still.

Wandering about the Egyptian rooms of the Metropolitan Museum in busy, modern New York, you can more than glimpse the life and art of ancient Egypt. You can stand within a tomb-chamber, with rows upon rows of painted scenes around you, and feel yourself in the presence of Egyptian men and women who came to lay gifts upon the offering-table before those painted false doors, from which the spirit of the departed might come forth at will. You can even see how the artist worked; for on the walls there are unfinished bits, showing where figures had been simply outlined in paint, but not yet cut

SECOND INTERMEDIATE PERIOD IN EGYPT
Project 3—The Artists of the Old Empires: A Reading, Page 4

in relief or colored as they were finally to appear. These wall-paintings, the designs on mummy-cases, furniture and chests, and the exquisite jewelry of kings and queens will be proof enough of the Egyptians' love of color and their artists' skill in using it. And, as for their knowledge of nature, their unsurpassed drawings of birds and their expressive studies of animals cannot fail to make us feel how true and sympathetic their vision must have been.

Nearly four thousand years ago a king built lordly temple halls to the glory of himself and his gods. Or, again, a king was buried in state in his tomb by the banks of the Nile. In our own day that vast columned temple reveals to us the thoughts of the far past; the seals of the tomb are broken and its splendid royal trappings become a central interest for the whole world for a time. Not quite three thousand years ago an Assyrian ruler established a great library at Nineveh; and then a Babylonian monarch built shining palaces on the plains of the Euphrates. In these later years, men have dug into the hills of time and unearthed the stone bas-reliefs of the library's walls and thousands of little clay tablets that were the volumes on its shelves. Other men have gathered and pieced together fragments of broken tiles, until we can see the beautiful colored design that adorned the wall of a palace

in Babylon. So, the works of ancient rulers—Rameses and Tutankhamen, Ashurbanipal and Nebuchadnezzar—are brought close to us after having been lost to history for ages.

Color was used for wall-decoration in Babylonia and Assyria as well as in Egypt. In the palaces of Assyria, which was a hill country with a supply of stone, the brick walls of the buildings were often faced with slabs of limestone or alabaster, carved in relief. Sometimes, however, the bricks were simply coated with plaster and this was covered with paintings. In Babylonia, a land of level plains, where stone was scarce, the characteristic finish for decorated walls was that of glazed tiles, some of which had the design raised like a relief, while some were flat, depending upon color alone to show the pattern. In both countries the colors used were brilliant and gay but were not intended to give the effect of nature. Blue, yellow and white were the colors most commonly used. Of these, blue was usually employed for the background, although green sometimes took its place.

Lions frequently appear on the decorative friezes, almost always nobly and vigorously pictured. Two fine examples illustrate very well the color schemes of the old artists in enamel work. First, a lion from a palace at Khorsabad in Assyria is bright yellow against a ground of intense blue, with the mane and some of the muscles brought out in the same strong blue.

The other, belonging to old Babylon, is white with a yellow mane, and stands out against a background of blue. In each case there is a charming border of white rosettes with yellow centers. The Babylonian lion is one of an interesting procession of the kingly beasts forming a frieze on each side of a magnificent festival road built by Nebuchadnezzar from the temple of Marduk, past his own palace, and so on to the Euphrates. Along this road the god Marduk was carried, once a year, to visit the god Nebo on the other side of the river. This lion frieze is probably the highest accomplishment in the art of brick enameling. Enamel was used in Assyria, too, but was not of as fine a quality as that which has been found in Babylon.

Other creatures besides the lion—bulls, dragons, birds and mythical monsters—decorated the gateways and sidewalls in both countries. The palaces were adorned with spirited scenes of warfare and triumph, or of huntsmen on horseback or in chariots pursuing lions and wild boars—

a record of the glories of the kings, their victories and their prowess. For, as the underlying feeling of Egyptian art is that of duration, so the idea most often and most clearly expressed by the Assyrian is strength—strength in action, brute force in full play.

For borders there was a variety of designs. One favorite showed a spiral twist; others were conventionalized flower patterns. All these occur on colored pottery, much of it black, with the lines of the design cut into the surface when it was soft. Then these cut-in lines were filled with a white paste before the clay was baked. The decorations might be in the shapes of fish, boats, waterfowl or geometrical figures. In other cases, stripes of various colors were painted on the bowl or jar by way of ornament.

The art of the Persians closely followed the same lines as that of the Assyrians and Babylonians, with added richness of form and jewel-like radiance of color for their own contribution, and a certain delicacy, which indicates Greek influence.

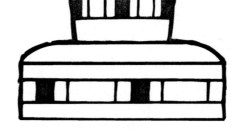

Second Intermediate Period in Egypt
Project 4—Unwrap Your Own Mummy

Photocopy this page onto another sheet of paper then cut out and fold along the dotted lines from right to left. Draw a cover on the final flap that illustrates what will be discovered inside when the mummy is "unwrapped."

Removing the resin-stained strips of cloth finally reveals the shrunken and weathered body of an old man with all of his major organs removed.

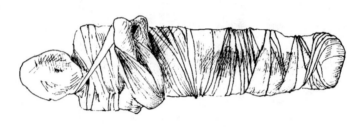

Beneath the resin coating are more bandages and sheets. You can begin to make out an actual human figure.

After the sheets of linen have all been removed, you find that the embalmers had poured a generous layer of resin over the entire mummy that, once dried, had formed a hard, dry preservative.

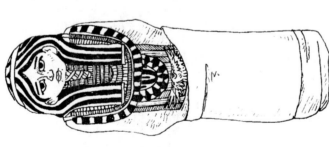

Once the linen is begun to be removed, it is revealed that the face is protected by a gold leaf mask that has a blue and green wig. Red, blue and green beads fill the necklace at the base of the mask.

You have uncovered the ancient tomb of a pharaoh and within the sarcophagus you find a large bundle of cloth. You start unrolling it and find that the mummy is wrapped up in over one thousand square yards of linen.

SECOND INTERMEDIATE PERIOD IN EGYPT
Test

1. What is the approximate date of the Second Intermediate Period in Egypt?

   _____

   _____

2. Of what dynasties did the Second Intermediate Period in Egypt consist?

   _____

   _____

3. What was the character of the rulers during this period?

   _____

   _____

   _____

   _____

4. What areas did the local princes control?

   _____

   _____

   _____

   _____

5. Of what major sites did Egypt gain control?

   _____

   _____

   _____

   _____

   _____

   _____

SECOND INTERMEDIATE PERIOD IN EGYPT
Test, Page 2

Review

1. What is the scripture reference for the Fall in the Garden?

   _____

2. What covenant did God establish with Noah? What sign did he use to signify this?

   _____

   _____

3. Why did God cause man to speak different languages after the building of the Tower of Babel?

   _____

   _____

4. What is the scripture reference for the Call of Abram?

   _____

   _____

5. What did God covenant with Abram?

   _____

   _____

6. Who was the one righteous man God found in Sodom and Gomorrah?

   _____

   _____

   _____

Second Intermediate Period in Egypt

Test, Page 3

7. List all events covered in chronological order.

CODE OF HAMMURABI
Worksheet

1. What is the approximate date of the Code of Hammurabi?

   _____

   _____

2. What land did Hammurabi rule?

   _____

   _____

3. What other landmarks are in this area?

   _____

   _____

   _____

4. Who was the sixth ruler of Babylon?

   _____

   _____

5. What kind of laws did Hammurabi establish?

   _____

   _____

   _____

6. How were these laws recorded?

   _____

   _____

   _____

   _____

CODE OF HAMMURABI
Project 1—Cuneiform

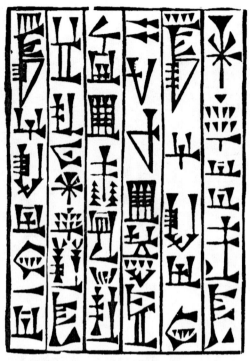

In Ur they used a system of picture writing that included at least 2,500 characters, each representing a different word. That style of writing was eventually replaced by clusters of wedges and symbols. This new system of writing is called "cuneiform" (from the Latin *cuneus,* "wedge-shaped"). Darius I (550–486 B.C.) claimed to have invented cuneiform, but if true, he probably only commissioned his scribes to create the alphabet.

The characters were made by pressing what may have been a chopped off reed into a damp clay tablet. Many of the clay tablets inscribed with cuneiform have been found and contain law codes, war stories, farming advice and stories. One tablet contains one of the oldest recorded customer complaints—Ea-nasir, a copper trader, was told: "You said 'I will give good ingots to Gimil-Sin.' That is what you said, but you have not done so; you offered bad ingots to my messenger, saying, 'Take it or leave it.' Who am I that you should treat me so contemptuously?"

Another story in clay that was discovered on over twenty tablets tells of a student who asked his father to invite the teacher home for dinner because he was tired of being hit by his teacher's cane for breaking rules. When the teacher came for dinner they seated him in a place of honor, the student attended and served the teacher, and the father gave him a new robe and ring to wear. This generosity so overcame him that he forgot the boy's previous conduct. "You have carried out well the school's activities," he told the student. "You have become a man of learning."

Supplies

air-drying clay (such as DAS or Marblex)

clay tools (available at art supply store) or you can use plastic knives

Directions

Give each student a handful of clay. Have them roll it into a ball and then flatten it into an oblong shape. After looking at the image of the clay tablet above have the students use their tools to make a replica of cuneiform writing. Or use the "alphabet" on the next page to try to write out their names (please note, some liberties have been taken with the alphabet to make it match ours). Place the tablets on a tray and allow them to dry.

a   b   c   d   [e]

f   g   h   i   j

k   l   m   n   [o]

p   q   r   s   t

u   [v]   w   y   z

Code of Hammurabi
Project 2—Code of Laws

We have learned that Hammurabi the ruler of Babylon wrote the Code of Hammurabi in order to protect his people. Can you think of something that sounds similar in your life? What about the Ten Commandments or any of the instruction that God has given to His people? Hammurabi lived before the Exodus of the people of Israel. Hammurabi's kingdom was the earliest one established after God spread all the people on the earth at the tower of Babel. The sad thing was these people did not worship God. They were pagans. But people who do not believe in God still need to have laws in order to get along with one another.

Draw a line from the biblical law to the code that matches it most closely.

Laws of Moses

Exodus 22:14 "And if a man borrows anything from his neighbor and it becomes injured or dies, the owner of it being not with it, he shall surely make it good."

Exodus 21:15 "And he who strikes his father or mother shall surely be put to death."

Exodus 21:36 "Or if it was known that the ox tended to thrust in time past, and its owner has not kept it confined, he shall surely pay ox for ox, and the dead animal shall be his own."

Exodus 21:24 ". . . eye for an eye, tooth for tooth, hand for hand, foot for foot . . . "

Exodus 21:16 "He who kidnaps a man and sells him, or if he is found in his hand, shall surely be put to death."

Code of Hammurabi

Hammurabi 251: "If an ox be a goring ox, and it is shown that his is a gorer, and he do not bind his horns, or fasten the ox up, and the ox gore a free-born man and kill him, the owner shall pay one-third of a mina."

Hammurabi 14: "If anyone kidnap the man or son of another, he shall be put to death."

Hammurabi 195: "If a son strike his father, his hand shall be hewn off."

Hammurabi 196: "If a man put out the eye of another man, his eye shall be put out."

Hammurabi 246: "If a man hires an ox, and he breaks its leg or cut the ligament of its neck, he shall compensate the owner with ox for ox."

CODE OF HAMMURABI
Project 3—Fill in the Blank

Using the history card, fill in the missing blanks.

Hammurabi ruled the land of _____ . This land is where the _____ and Euphrates _____ joined. It was in this area that the _____ __ _____ was located.

Hammurabi the Great was the _____ ruler of Babylon. By his efficient, well disciplined rule, his _____ conquered many surrounding lands.

He is known for the _____ he introduced. The laws protected the _____ from the strong and governed all of life including rates of pay and rules of _____ . Anyone breaking the law was severely _____ . These laws are some of the _____ , if not the _____ , to be put into writing. The laws were _____ in _____ in _____ . Cuneiform was the ancient script of the _____ , who lived in Southern _____ , and it was later adapted to the Babylonian language.

CODE OF HAMMURABI
Test

1. Who ruled the land of Babylonia?

_____

_____

_____

2. What other landmarks are in the area of Babylonia?

_____

_____

_____

3. What did the laws contain that Hammurabi established?

_____

_____

_____

_____

4. On what were the laws written?

_____

_____

_____

_____

5. What is the approximate date of the Code of Hammurabi?

_____

_____

_____

CODE OF HAMMURABI
Test, Page 2

Review

1. List all events covered in chronological order. Include all dates and scripture references available.

_____

_____

_____

_____

_____

_____

_____

_____

_____

_____

_____

_____

_____

_____

_____

_____

_____

HYKSOS INVASION OF EGYPT
Worksheet

1. What is the approximate date for the Hyksos Invasion of Egypt?

   _____

   _____

   _____

2. From where did the Hyksos come?

   _____

   _____

   _____

   _____

3. What tools of battle did the Hyksos use that surprised the Egyptians?

   _____

   _____

   _____

   _____

4. After conquering Egypt, where did the Hyksos make their capital?

   _____

   _____

   _____

5. For how many years did the Hyksos rule Egypt?

   _____

   _____

   _____

HYKSOS INVASION OF EGYPT

Project 1–
Coloring Page

Color this.

HYKSOS INVASION OF EGYPT
Project 2—Hyksos Chariot

Supplies

white cardstock

markers, colored pencils, and/or crayons

tape/white glue

Directions

Copy each page with patterns onto white card stock for each student. Color each item and cut out (do not cut along dotted lines, only cut the heavy lines on the chariot wheels). Fold the warrior along the vertical dotted line and glue together. Then fold the tabs at his feet out so he can stand. Fold the horse along the dotted lines below its hooves and glue together, leaving the tabs free from glue and bending those tabs back. Fold the bottom panel of the chariot up and attach to the sides of the chariot, making the floor. Fold the top panel up and glue the tabs to the side of the chariot. Glue the tabs below the feet of the archer to the floor of the chariot and the tabs behind the horse to the front of the chariot.

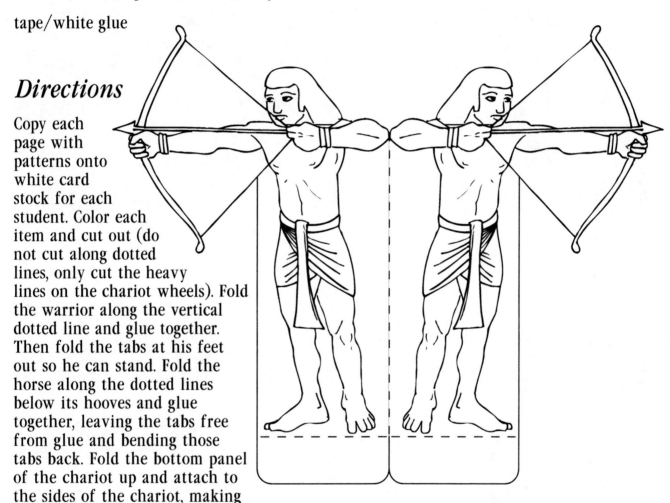

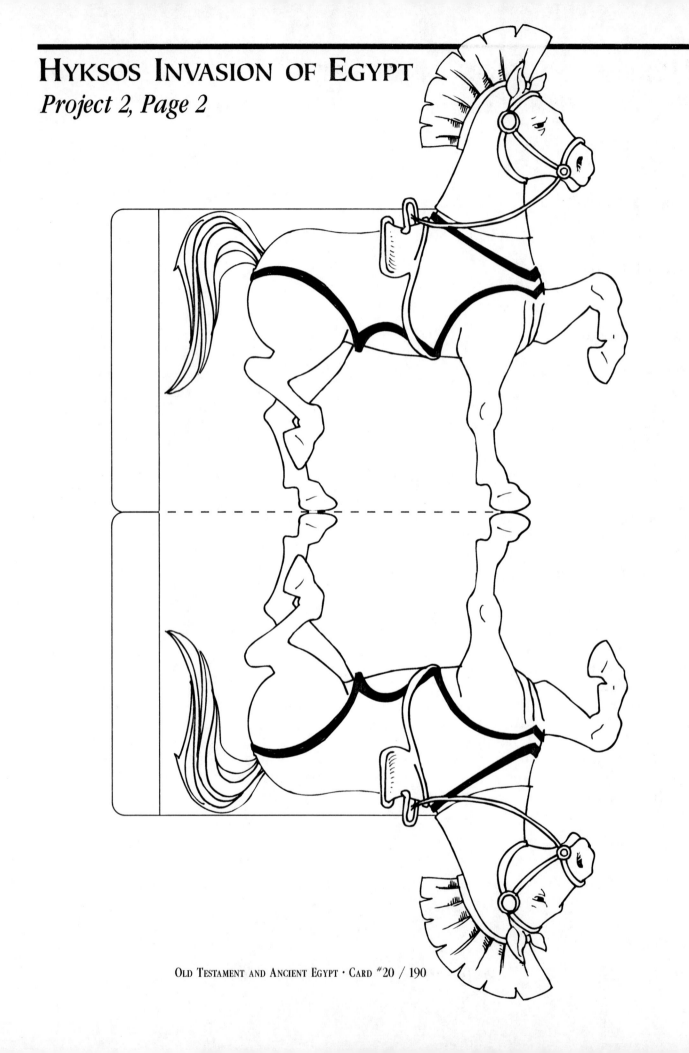

Hyksos Invasion of Egypt
Project 2, Page 3

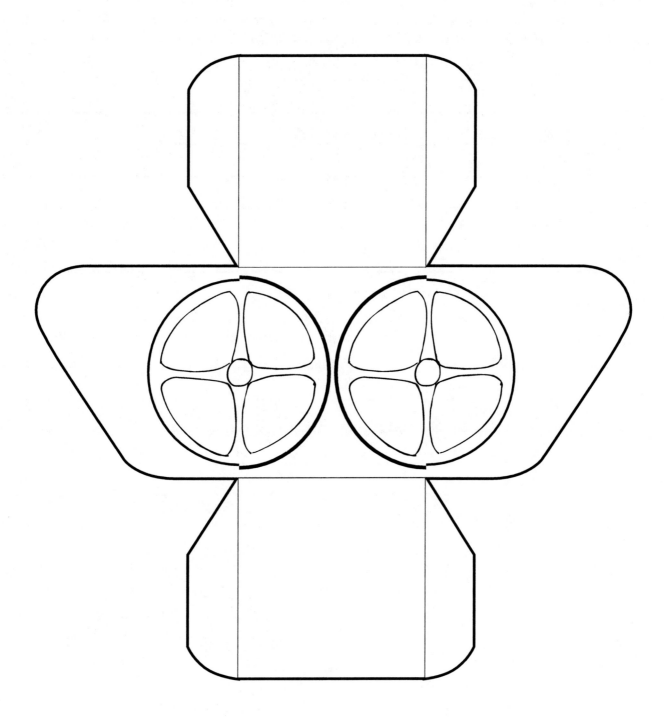

HYKSOS INVASION OF EGYPT
Project 3—Technology Report

The invaders came from Asia, and the Egyptians called them "hyksos" which means kings from foreign lands. The Hyksos changed the way military battles were fought by using horse-drawn chariots and bronze weapons. Using various resources, choose one new technology the Hyksos introduced into Egyptian culture and write about it in the space provided below.

_____

_____

_____

_____

_____

_____

_____

_____

_____

_____

_____

_____

_____

_____

_____

_____

_____

_____

HYKSOS INVASION OF EGYPT
Test

1. What is the approximate date of the Hyksos Invasion of Egypt?

   _____

   _____

   _____

2. What influence did the Hyksos have on the way Egyptians fought future battles?

   _____

   _____

   _____

3. What was the city of Avaris known for during the Hyksos occupation?

   _____

   _____

   _____

   _____

4. For how many years did the Hyksos rule Egypt?

   _____

   _____

   _____

   _____

HYKSOS INVASION OF EGYPT
Test, Page 2

Review

1. What is the scripture reference for the Fall in the Garden?

   _____

   _____

2. Why did God cause the earth to flood?

   _____

   _____

   _____

3. List what God created on the seven days of Creation.

   _____

   _____

   _____

   _____

   _____

   _____

   _____

4. Where did God call Abram to go at the age of 75?

   _____

   _____

   _____

HYKSOS INVASION OF EGYPT
Test, Page 3

5. List all events covered in chronological order.

_____

_____

_____

_____

_____

_____

_____

_____

_____

_____

_____

_____

_____

_____

_____

_____

_____

_____

_____

_____

EARLY NEW KINGDOM IN EGYPT
Worksheet

1. What is the approximate date of the Early New Kingdom in Egypt?

   _____

   _____

2. Of what dynasty did the Early New Kingdom consist?

   _____

   _____

   _____

3. Whom did the Egyptian army defeat in 1570 B.C.? What did the Egyptians learn from these people?

   _____

   _____

   _____

   _____

4. What is the name of the pharaoh that led the Egyptians further north than they had ever been before?

   _____

   _____

   _____

5. What is the name of the Egyptian princess who may have found Moses in the Nile?

   _____

   _____

   _____

   _____

EARLY NEW KINGDOM IN EGYPT
Worksheet

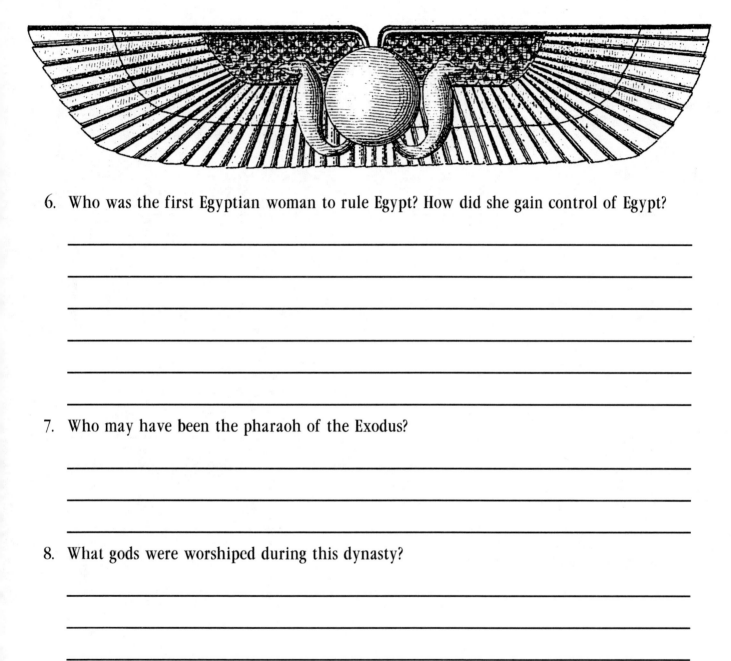

6. Who was the first Egyptian woman to rule Egypt? How did she gain control of Egypt?

_____

_____

_____

_____

_____

_____

7. Who may have been the pharaoh of the Exodus?

_____

_____

_____

8. What gods were worshiped during this dynasty?

_____

_____

_____

_____

EARLY NEW KINGDOM IN EGYPT
Literature Unit—Senefer, a Young Genius in Old Egypt

Either read aloud or have your students read the book titled Senefer, a Young Genius in Old Egypt *by Beatrice Lumpkin. Senefer is an exciting story of a little boy in Ancient Egypt. Although this book has multicultural tendencies, we believe that it is a good book to use when reading about Egypt. On the following page you will find questions about the book Senefer. Following the questions you will find a pattern for an Egyptian paddle doll, and a handout on ancient Egyptian toys.*

1. Who was Senefer?

    _____

    _____

    _____

2. Why did the children in Egypt wear very little clothing?

    _____

    _____

    _____

    _____

3. Where were Senefer and his mother going?

    _____

    _____

    _____

4. What was the black earth?

    _____

    _____

    _____

5. How did some people pay Nefert for her dolls?

    _____

    _____

EARLY NEW KINGDOM IN EGYPT
Literature Unit—Senefer, *Page 2*

6. What do these symbols represent? //////////∩∩

_____

_____

_____

7. Who were the scribes?

_____

_____

_____

8. Why were the scribes impressed with Senefer?

_____

_____

_____

_____

_____

9. What happened to Pepi?

_____

_____

_____

_____

_____

10. Where did they find Pepi?

_____

_____

_____

EARLY NEW KINGDOM IN EGYPT
Literature Unit—Senefer, *Page 3*

11. Where was Senefer invited to attend?

_____

_____

12. What did Nefert paint on the lid of the box for Senefer? What did it represent?

_____

_____

_____

13. What were the boats carrying?

_____

_____

14. Who was Hatshepsut?

_____

15. What was the purpose of the obelisks?

_____

_____

16. What did Senefer grow up to be?

_____

_____

_____

EARLY NEW KINGDOM IN EGYPT
Project 1—Egyptian Paddle Doll

Egyptian children were no different from children today. They liked toys and liked to play. Evidence of balls, rattles, animals on wheels, dolls and games such as senet have been found as archeologists have uncovered the past. One of the favorite toys were paddle dolls. These dolls were made of wood and sometimes had a bead head with hair attached. The dolls were painted with geometric designs. Although we may never know that this was the reason, paddle dolls may have been placed in tombs to act as companions in the afterlife.

Supplies

black yarn

small paint brushes

1/4 inch plywood or foam board

paint

beads

drill

saw

Directions

Copy the outline of the paddle doll onto the plywood or foam board and cut out using appropriate tools. Drill holes in the head for the hair. Allow children to paint the paddle dolls as they like. Then tie yarn on for hair. They may want to tie beads onto the yarn after placing it in the hair.

EARLY NEW KINGDOM IN EGYPT
Project 2—Bird Hat

Make a headress like the one Hatshepsut is wearing on the front of the history card.

Supplies

aluminum foil

posterboard (two 12" strips and one 24")

construction paper (two 12" x 18" light blue)

markers or paint

tape or stapler

Directions

Wrap the 24" strip of board around the head of the student and tape or staple to fit. Crisscross the 12" strips as shown and attach. Cover this form with aluminum foil and tape it. Using markers or paint, create an overall feather pattern on the foil. Photocopy the wings, head and tail on thick paper, color, and cut out. Tape the wings behind the ears. Staple or tape the tail inside the headdress. Tape the head together then attach to the headdress with the extra length wrapping both sides around the front.

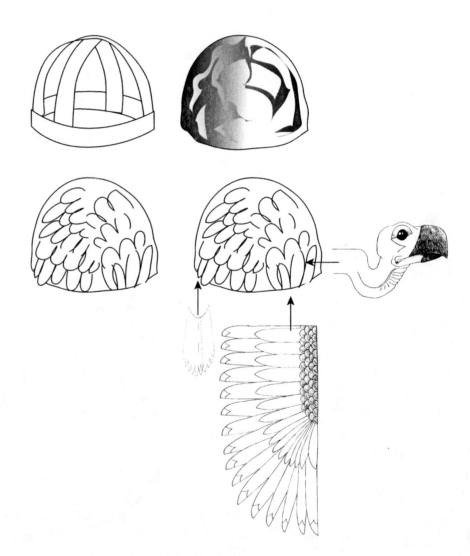

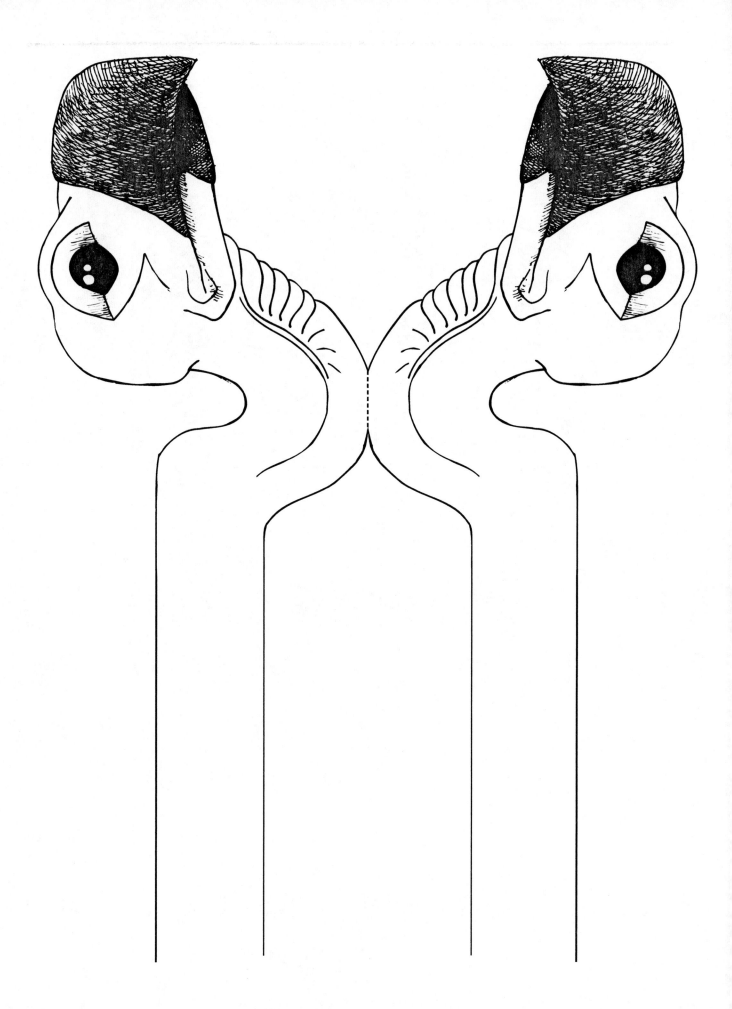

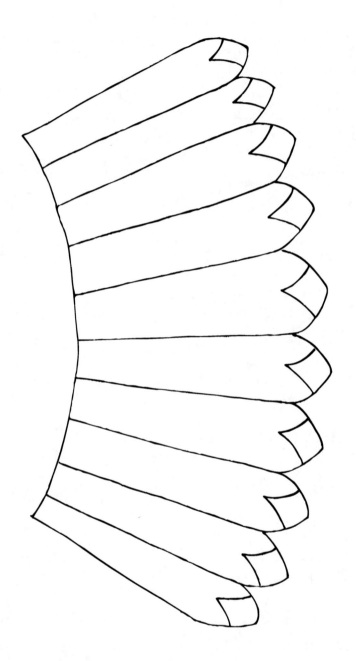

EARLY NEW KINGDOM IN EGYPT
Test

1. What is the approximate date of the Early New Kingdom in Egypt?

_____

_____

2. Of what dynasty did the Early New Kingdom consist?

_____

_____

_____

3. How do Moses and Hatshepsut relate to one another?

_____

_____

_____

4. Who was the first woman pharaoh?

_____

_____

5. Who may have been the pharaoh of the Exodus?

_____

_____

_____

6. Who were Amon and Aton?

_____

_____

_____

_____

Review

1. What did God create on the fifth day of creation?

_____

_____

2. Who tempted Eve to eat of the tree of the knowledge of good and evil?

_____

_____

3. Who were Cain and Abel's parents?

_____

_____

4. Who was the first person to unify Upper and Lower Egypt?

_____

_____

5. What was the largest of all pyramids?

_____

_____

6. What happened during the First Intermediate Period in Egypt?

_____

_____

_____

7. What did God call Abram to do when he was 75 years old?

_____

_____

EARLY NEW KINGDOM IN EGYPT
Test, Page 3

8. What did Sarah ask Abraham to do to Hagar and Ishmael?

_____

_____

9. List all events covered in chronological order.

_____

_____

_____

_____

_____

_____

_____

_____

_____

_____

_____

_____

_____

_____

_____

_____

_____

MOSES' BIRTH
Worksheet

1. Why did the new pharaoh (maybe Thutmose I) fear the Israelites?

    _____

    _____

    _____

2. What order did the new pharaoh give because of his fear?

    _____

    _____

    _____

3. What happened to Moses shortly after his birth?

    _____

    _____

4. Why was Moses now safe?

    _____

    _____

    _____

5. What did the royal family not know about Moses?

    _____

    _____

    _____

    _____

Moses' Birth
Project 1—Exodus 2 Summary

Read Exodus 2. Using complete sentences, write a paragraph describing what is happening in the picture below.

_____

_____

_____

_____

_____

_____

_____

_____

_____

_____

MOSES' BIRTH
Project 2—Basket Weaving

In Biblical times baskets had many purposes. They were made from papyrus, a triangular shaped reed. Papyrus would grow about 13 feet tall along the Nile River. Baskets were woven by craftsmen called weavers or by women at home. Moses' mother may have woven the basket in which he was placed.

You may want to have your students make a basket from reeds. Kits and instructions for doing this may be ordered from: Frank's Cane and Rush Supply, 7252 Heil Avenue, Huntington Beach, CA 92647, tel: 714-847-0707, fax: 714-843-5645, www.franksupply.com. Or follow the instructions below to make a paper basket.

Supplies:

newspaper

scissors

glue stick

tape

craft paints and brushes

Directions:

Make a paper "reed" for weaving out of a 13 1/2 x 22" sheet of newspaper. Starting with a long edge, tightly roll the sheet into a tube. Flatten the tube and use a glue stick to secure the open edge. Assemble seven more reeds.

Lay four of the reeds side by side on a flat surface and weave in the remaining four. Slide the strips together to make the bottom of the basket. Fold the ends of the reeds up to form the side spokes.

Now, cut newspaper sheets into four 11 x 27" rectangles. Using the same method as before, roll four more reeds. Tape the end of a reed to the base of a spoke. Weave the reed in and out of the spokes, around the basket.

Tuck the end behind a spoke. Weave in the other reeds, one above the other. Fold the tops of the spokes into the basket and tuck them behind a reed.

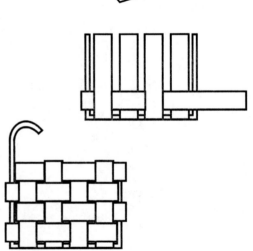

Moses' Birth
Project 3—The Princess and the Nile

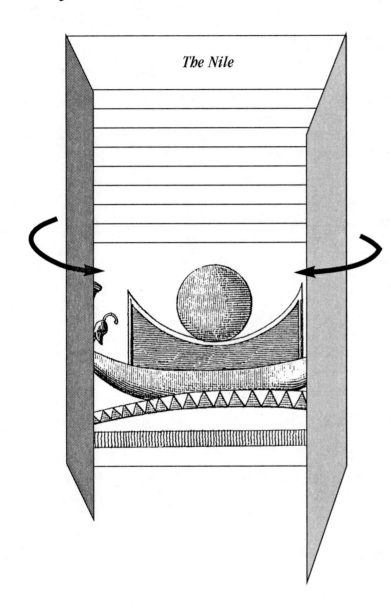

The Nile

Although we do not know the exact pharaoh who reigned during the time of Moses' birth, there are two popular theories. Copy the following two pages so they are back-to-back on one sheet. Using Journey Through the Bible *or another resource, summarize the two theories and write each on the two narrow panels. Then turn the sheet over and write a short report about the Nile River in the lines provided. When you are finished, fold the narrow panels along the dotted lines toward the center as shown in the diagram and trim along the outside solid line.*

Theory One

_____
_____
_____
_____
_____
_____
_____
_____
_____
_____
_____
_____

Theory Two

_____
_____
_____
_____
_____
_____
_____
_____
_____
_____
_____
_____

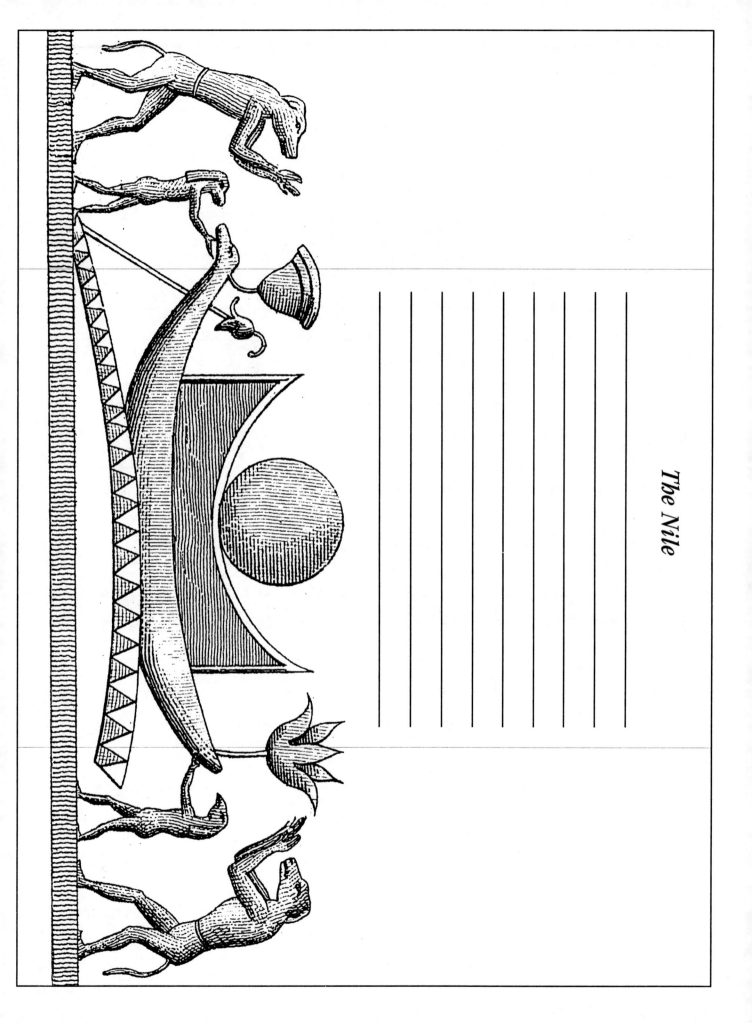

The Nile

Moses' Birth
Test

1. What was the approximate date of Moses' birth?

_____

_____

2. What is the scripture reference for Moses' birth?

_____

_____

3. Why did the new pharaoh fear the Israelites?

_____

_____

_____

4. What did the new pharaoh order the Israelite midwives to do?

_____

_____

_____

5. What did Moses' mother do to save his life?

_____

_____

_____

6. What was Moses safe from because he lived as the son of the princess?

_____

_____

_____

Moses' Birth
Test, page 2

Review

1. What occurred during the First Intermediate Period?

   _____

   _____

2. What promise did God make to Abram?

   _____

   _____

3. Why was Sarah jealous of Hagar?

   _____

   _____

4. What happened to Lot's wife as they fled the burning cities of Sodom and Gomorrah? Why?

   _____

   _____

   _____

   _____

5. What is the scripture reference for the birth and sacrifice of Isaac?

   _____

   _____

   _____

MOSES' BIRTH
Test, page 3

6. List the events studied to date in chronological order.

_____

_____

_____

_____

_____

_____

_____

_____

_____

_____

_____

_____

_____

_____

_____

_____

_____

_____

_____

_____

PLAGUES IN EGYPT
Worksheet

1. What is the approximate date of the Plagues in Egypt?

   _____

   _____

2. What is the scripture reference for the Plagues in Egypt?

   _____

   _____

3. How did God speak to Moses? What did he tell him to do?

   _____

   _____

   _____

4. How many times did Moses return to appeal to Pharaoh to let the Israelites go?

   _____

   _____

   _____

5. What punishment did God send to the Egyptians because Pharaoh would not let the Israelites go?

   _____

   _____

   _____

6. What was the correlation between the plagues and the Egyptian gods?

   _____

   _____

   _____

PLAGUES IN EGYPT
Project 1—Passover Letter

Moses was raised up by God to be the leader of the Hebrews, and their deliverer from "the house of bondage." Pharaoh refused to let the people go, and plagues were sent upon Egypt to bring him into submission. Nine plagues had already visited the land; still Pharaoh's heart was hardened. One plague more, the tenth—terrible, fatal, effectual—was threatened before it came to happen. It was the death of all the first-born in Egypt, from the first-born of "the king upon his throne, to the first-born of the maidservant behind the mill." God, who knew the effect of this terrible stroke, directed that there should be a festival of commemoration of it, and that the Hebrews should stand ready for departure at the appointed time. The festival was called the Passover. The destroying angel would pass over the doors marked with the blood of a lamb which every Hebrew family was directed to slay and eat in the posture of persons ready for a journey. Even now, once every year, Jews celebrate the Feast of the Passover and tell of the wonderful deliverance of the Hebrews. This is an instance from which you see that our blessings should never be forgotten. The record of the Hebrews' remarkable deliverance has come down through the ages.

Pretend that you are a young Hebrew boy or girl and have just survived the plagues and the first Passover. Write a letter on the following page to a friend or grandparent describing what you have just been through.

PLAGUES IN EGYPT
Project 1, Page 2

Plagues in Egypt
Some Egyptian Dieties

1. Athor (corresponded to the goddess Aphrodite of the Greeks)
2. Ptah (pigmy or child)
3. Isis (wife of Osiris, goddess of maternity)
4. Osiris (god of Nile, chief divinity of Egypt)
5. Neith (goddess of wisdom)
6. Bubastis (goddess of fire)
7. Apis (bull, god of nature)
8. Beg (hawk)
9. Ibis (crane)
10. Shau (cat)
11. Scarabaeus (beetle)

PLAGUES IN EGYPT
Teacher's Information

Ask the students what the Bible says about the worship of idols (refer to Exodus 20:1-6).

When the Israelites sojourned in Egypt, they came in contact with more than forty-two deities, fifty local divinities and deified animals. The plagues which God inflicted on Pharaoh and the Egyptians for holding Israel in bondage, were specifically designed to show the utter impotency of their idols and idolatrous worship, and to reveal the might of JEHOVAH. Numbers 33:4 says, "For the Egyptians were burying all their firstborn, whom the Lord had killed among them. Also on their gods the Lord had executed judgments." The Nile and its fish were worshiped: "and all the waters that were in the river were turned to blood; and the fish that was in the water died; and the river stank." The frog was a sacred animal: "and the frogs came up and covered the land of Egypt," and they made everything loathsome. Entire cleanliness of the body was thought to be a religious obligation: "all the dust of the land became lice," so that all were defiled and could not enter their temples. These three plagues came by the delegated hand of Israel's High Priest. Beetles were everywhere sculptures and deified; "the land was corrupted by reason of the swarms of flies," or the great Egyptian beetles. From the cattle of the fields was selected a type of the chief deity: "and all the cattle of Egypt died; but the cattle of the children of Israel died not one." The fourth and fifth plagues came directly from the Lord. Ashes were a means of purification: "and Moses sprinkled it up toward Heaven; and it became a boil breaking forth with blains upon man, and upon beast"—the means of purification became a source of defilement. Nature's fruitfulness was symbolized by a god; each tree was a deity, and the best fruits were votive-offerings to idols: "and the hail smote throughout all the land of Egypt all that was in the field, both man and beast; and the hail smote every herb of the field, and brake every tree of the field." The wind was one of the deities: "and when it was morning the east wind brought the locusts; they covered the face of the whole earth, so the land was darkened; and they did eat every herb of the land, and all the fruit of the trees which the hail had left: and there remained not any green thing in the trees, or in the herbs of the field, through all the land of Egypt." The sun and darkness were each worshiped as gods: "and there was a thick darkness in all the land of Egypt for three days; they saw not one another, neither rose any from his place for three days; but all the children of Israel had light in their dwellings." These four plagues, foreshadowing the ultimate desolation and destruction to befall idolaters, came by the outstretched hand of the Prophet of Israel. The tenth plague was the execution of the final judgement: "and it came to pass, that at midnight the Lord smote all the first-born in the land of Egypt, from the first-born of Pharaoh that sat on his throne unto the first-born of the captive that was in the dungeon; and all the first-born of cattle." Justice was tempered with mercy; all the first-born unto Israel were sanctified: "therefore I sacrifice to the Lord that openeth the matrix, being males; but all the the first-born of my children I redeem." Exodus 7:12, 13:15.

PLAGUES IN EGYPT
Project 2—False Gods Attacked!

Draw an arrow from the plague to the corresponding deity.

Nile changed
to blood

Khnum
controlled the Nile

Frogs overran
the land

Set
god of deserts, storms

Gnats overran
the land

Hathor
depicted with livestock head

Flies infested
Egypt

Heqet
*goddess of birth,
depicted with the
head of a frog*

Cattle found dead

Horus
god of the sun

Boils infected
the Egyptians

Nut
sky goddess

Hail destroyed
the crops

Re
symbolized by the fly

Locusts consumed
the plants

Osiris
god of crops

Darkness covered
the land

Isis
goddess of healing

Egyptian firstborn
children died

Min
god of fertility

PLAGUES IN EGYPT
Project 3—Plague of (Origami) Frogs

Supplies

colored construction paper

Directions

1. Make a fold right through the middle of the corner of a sheet of construction paper, folding the short edge to the long edge. Unfold the paper and lay it flat.
2. Fold the other corner at the short edge as in step one. Unfold the paper to create an X.
3. Fold the paper BACK through the middle of the X and then unfold flat.
4. Push down at "O." Bring up "A" and "B" to meet. Push down and flatten the triangle just formed on the front.
5. Fold the outer corners of the triangle to the corner.
6. Fold the straight sides to the middle.
7. Fold the straight edge to the right.
8. Bring the same edge down to the left.
9. Draw eyes on the frog's "head." Loosen the front and back legs slightly and tap the back to make the frog jump.
10. Repeat steps 1-9 a zillion times more to create the "plague" effect.

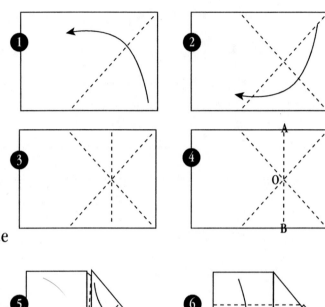

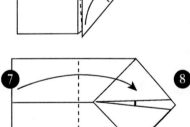

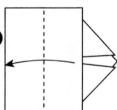

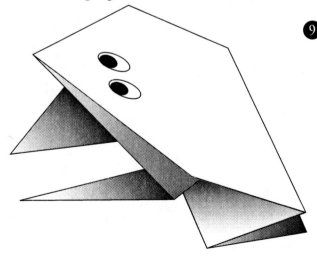

PLAGUES IN EGYPT
Test

1. What is the scripture reference for Plagues in Egypt?

   _____

   _____

2. What is the approximate date of Plagues in Egypt?

   _____

   _____

3. What did God say to Moses through a burning bush?

   _____

   _____

   _____

4. How many times did Moses return to make an appeal to Pharaoh?

   _____

   _____

   _____

5. When Pharaoh refused to listen to what Moses said, how did God punish the Egyptians?

   _____

   _____

   _____

   _____

6. What was the relationship between the plagues and Egyptian gods?

   _____

   _____

   _____

   _____

PLAGES IN EGYPT
Test, Page 2

Review

1. What did God do on the seventh day of Creation?

_____

_____

2. What did Cain and Abel each bring for their sacrifices?

_____

_____

3. What was the name of the son born to Abraham and Sarah?

_____

_____

4. What did Joseph dream about his family at the age of seventeen?

_____

_____

5. To what was Jacob's name changed?

_____

_____

6. Who was the first woman Pharaoh?

_____

_____

PLAGES IN EGYPT
Test, Page 3

7. List all events covered in chronological order.

_____

_____

_____

_____

_____

_____

_____

_____

_____

_____

_____

_____

_____

_____

_____

_____

_____

_____

_____

_____

_____

THE EXODUS
Worksheet

1. What is the approximate date of the Exodus?

   _____

   _____

2. What is the scripture reference for the Exodus?

   _____

   _____

3. What was the tenth plague?

   _____

   _____

   _____

4. How were the Israelites spared from the tenth plague?

   _____

   _____

   _____

5. After this tenth plague, what did Pharaoh tell the Israelites to do?

   _____

   _____

   _____

6. When Pharaoh tried to recapture the Israelites and put them back into slavery, what did God do?

   _____

   _____

   _____

   _____

THE EXODUS
Project 1—Exodus 14 Summary

Read Exodus 14. Using complete sentences, write a paragraph describing what is happening in the picture below.

_____

_____

_____

_____

_____

_____

_____

_____

_____

MOSES

Presented By

_____

THE EXODUS
Project 2, Page 2

Narrator: "The Israelites in Egypt during the captivity became strong and numerous. Pharaoh feared they would take over Egypt and ordered all male Israelite boys to be slaughtered at birth. Moses' mother attempted to hide him by placing him in a reed basket and putting the basket in the Nile river. Pharaoh's daughter found Moses in the Nile and was compassionate towards him. She took him home and raised him as her own. He was raised as an Egyptian, but he never forgot that he was one of the children of Israel. The Pharaoh had no knowledge of Joseph and how helpful the Israelites had been for so long in the past.

Scene One

(Scene opens with an Egyptian taskmaster and slave. Moses watches from the side of stage as the taskmaster strikes the slave.)

Egyptian Taskmaster: (with whip in hand) Work harder! You must make more bricks. We are falling behind and Pharaoh expects us to produce more. (strike the slave)

Moses: Why are you beating the Hebrew slave? He is working as hard as he can.

Egyptian Taskmaster: He is only a slave, Pharaoh's property. He is a Hebrew. They must be treated this way or they may attempt to rebel against us.

Moses: Would you treat me this way? I am a Hebrew. Had I not been raised with Pharaoh you would be treating me this way also.

Egyptian Taskmaster: Work! Work! (striking slave with the whip—he cries out in pain)

Moses: (looks to see if others are watching and picks up a large rock and strikes the Egyptian Taskmaster, killing him) He says angrily while beating him with the rock "You must stop!"

Egyptian Taskmaster: (sighs in pain, falls to the ground dead)

Moses: What have I done? I have killed him. I must bury him quickly. (pulls the body to the side and pretends to dig a hole in the sand. Have some large rocks made out of cardboard or styrofoam to pull him behind.) Pharaoh must not know.

Scene Two

Narrator: Moses thought all night about what he had done. The following day he went back to see the Hebrew slaves. While he was there he encountered two Hebrew slaves fighting with each other. (Open with two Hebrews striking one another.)

Moses: Why are you beating up your brother?

Slave One: Who made you a prince and a judge over us?

Moses: I am only trying to stop you from harming each other. We have enough oppression from the Egyptians without fighting one another.

Salve Two: Do you intend to kill me as you killed the Egyptian?

Moses: (showing fear on his face says to the slave) How did you know about that? (then says to himself) Surely, this thing is known. If Pharaoh hears of this he will have me killed. I must flee.

The Exodus
Project 2, Page 3

Scene Three

Narrator: Moses fled from Egypt and dwelt in the land of Midian. One day he decided to rest and sat down at a well to get a drink.

Moses: I need to rest. I have been walking all day. A drink will cool me down. (Enter Zipporah and her sisters.)

Zipporah: (looks at her sisters) We must draw water from the well to water father's flock.

Sister One: Very soon we will have the troughs filled and we can water the sheep.

Shepherd One: Move away from here. We cannot wait for your sheep to drink, we are in a hurry.

Shepherd Two: Move along, we must water our flock. Away with you!

Zipporah: Please! We have worked hard to fill the troughs. We will be finished and then you may use the well.

Shepherd One: Get out of our way!

Moses: What is the matter? The women were here before you. Don't treat them this way. (Moses picks up a pail of water and helps the women. Shepherds move off to the side.) Let them water their flocks.

Shepherd Two: (looking at Shepherd One) Let's wait, instead of causing trouble. It won't take long. (under his breath he says) We should not have to wait on these women.

Zipporah: (looking at Moses) We can never repay you for what you have done. Please accept our thanks.

Scene Four

(Moses is sitting next to the well and Zipporah enters)

Moses: Why have you come back so soon? Did you leave a watering jug?

Zipporah: We told our father how you helped us today, and he would like you to come home with us for dinner.

Moses: I would like to meet your father.

Zipporah: Follow me. (Moses, Zipporah and sisters walk to one side of the stage.)

Moses: Is that your father I see in the distance?

Jethro: (walk up center aisle from the back) Zipporah, is this the man who helped you today?

Zipporah: Yes, Father, this is Moses.

Jethro: Let us feast. You have shown kindness to my family and I want to break bread.

Moses: That would please me. (Jethro, Moses, Zipporah and sisters sit down to eat)

THE EXODUS
Project 2, Page 4

Scene Five

Narrator: Jethro was so pleased with Moses that eventually he gave Zipporah to him in marriage. Moses tended flocks for his father-in-law and had a son. (Moses in the field tending sheep.)

Moses: Move! (looking at flock.) We must keep moving. We are almost to Horeb. Now you may rest to graze. (Moses sits down to watch the flock. Use party streamers attached to a cardboard rock and blow from underneath with a fan. Flames of fire burst forth from a bush.)

Moses: Gasp!

God from the bush: (Crackle sound . . . use a recording)

Moses: I will now turn aside and see this great sight. Why is the bush not consumed by the fire?

God from the bush: (have someone read from off the stage the parts of the burning bush) Moses, Moses!

Moses: Here I am.

God from the bush: Do not come any closer to this place. Take your sandals off your feet, for the place where you stand is holy ground. I am the God of your Father—the God of Abraham, the God of Isaac, and the God of Jacob.

Moses: (Falls down and hides face.) I must hide my face.

God from the bush: I have surely seen the oppression of My People who are in Egypt, and I have heard their cry because of their taskmasters, for I know their sorrows. So I have come down to deliver them out of the hand of the Egyptians, and to bring them up from that land and to a land flowing with milk and honey, and to a place of the Hittites and Amorites and the Perrizites and the Hivites and the Jebusites. Come now, therefore, and I will send you to Pharaoh that you may bring my people, the children of Israel out of Egypt.

Moses: Who am I that I should go to Pharaoh, and that I should bring the children of Israel out of Egypt?

God from the bush: I will certainly be with you. And this shall be a sign to you: When you have brought the people out of Egypt you shall serve God on this mountain.

Moses: Indeed, when I come to the children of Israel and say the God of your Fathers has sent me to you, and they say to me, "What is his name?" What shall I say to them?

God from the bush: You shall say to the children of Israel I AM WHO I AM has sent me to you. The Lord God of your fathers, the God of Abraham, the God of Isaac, the God of Jacob has sent me to you. This is my name forever, and this is my memorial to all generations. I will bring you out of the afflictions of Egypt. Say to Pharaoh: The Lord God of the Hebrews has met with us. Please let us go three days journey into the wilderness, that we may sacrifice to the Lord our God.

Moses: What if Pharaoh will not let us go?

THE EXODUS
Project 2, Page 5

God from the bush: I am sure that he will not let you go, so I will stretch out my hand and strike Egypt with all my wonders and after that he will let you go.

Moses: What if the people will not believe me?

God from the bush: What is that in your hand?

Moses: A rod.

God from the bush: Cast it onto the ground.

Moses: (throws the rod onto the ground) A serpent! Noooo! (Moses flees)

God from the bush: Reach out and take it by the tail that they may believe that the Lord God of their fathers has appeared to you. (Moses reaches to pick up the snake and it becomes a rod again. Scene ends with lights dimming and Moses saying the following.)

Moses: But Lord, I am slow of speech that they may not believe me.

Narrator: The Lord gave Moses other signs to convince the people of who he was. But Moses was fearful that he could not communicate well. So the Lord agreed to send Aaron, Moses' brother with him. As the Lord foretold, Pharaoh did refuse to let the Israelites go into the wilderness when Moses asked. Moses and Aaron pleaded with Pharaoh, but his heart was hard. God sent plagues to punish the Egyptians. After the tenth and final plague, the death of the first-born, Pharaoh relented and not only allowed them to leave but gave them much to get them to leave quickly. Shortly after they left, Pharaoh changed his mind and took his army after them to bring them back. The Israelites were ushered through the Red Sea on dry land when God parted the water for them and caused the parted water to come crashing down on the Egyptians when they attempted to follow in pursuit. God had faithfully delivered his people from the Egyptian oppression as he had promised.

The End

THE EXODUS
Project 2, Page 6

Moses, a Play (Costume)

1. Use a piece of 45" fabric. A plainer piece of fabric should be used for the Hebrew outfit as they were slaves and dressed more simply. In scenes one and two, Moses should have stipes and jewels as he was part of Pharaoh's household. Measure from the shoulder to just below the knee to determine the amount of fabric needed (approx. 2 yds). Old sheets may be used, too.

2. Fold a two yard length in half as shown on left.

3. Fold on the 45" width then cut out neck hole in the corner with two folds as shown on left. (It's easier to cut a second time than to cut too much the first time.)

4. Cut belt from different colored fabric as shown on left. (Approx. 1.5 yards long) Fringe the edges with scissors. Tie belt around waist.

5. Cut fabric for head piece in one yard squares and cut head band one yard long by one and one half inches wide. Allow children to decorate headbands with markers or paint.

6. Have children wear sandals for shoes.

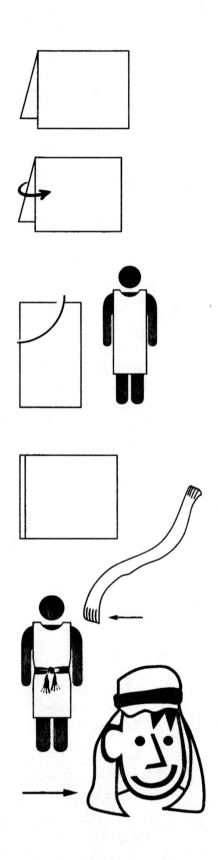

THE EXODUS
Tirzah *Literature Unit*

CHAPTER 1 WHY MUST YOU DIE?
Read Exodus 5–10
1. What are Tirzah and Oren doing at the beginning of the story?
2. What do you learn about Tirzah's brother Oren in the first two pages?
3. Whom do Oren and Tirzah meet while they are working?
4. Briefly describe his appearance.
5. What biblical figure are you introduced to in this chapter?
6. What did their father and other slaves make?
7. How old is Tirzah?
8. What are some of Tirzah's concerns?
9. What is Paser teaching Oren?
10. What do you learn about Tirzah's mother?
11. What happened to Tirzah's father?
12. Who is Caleb?
13. How many times has Pharaoh said he would let them go?
14. What does Aaron say is going to happen in Egypt?

What are the biblical events in this chapter?

CHAPTER 2 DARKNESS OVER EGYPT
Read Exodus 10:21
1. What was the morning like when Tirzah awoke?
2. How old is Tirzah's brother Ram?
3. How does Thotmes describe Egypt?
4. Who is Abihail? What does Tirzah think of her?
5. What was happening in Goshen?
6. What is the prophecy which is repeated over time? (Who said this hundreds of years ago?)
7. Who is Uncle Shobal? What do you learn of him?
8. What kind of home would they have in the desert?
9. How long did the darkness in Egypt last?
10. What was given to Moses and Aaron by an Egyptian as they left the Pharaoh? What do they think of it?
11. What preparations are Moses and Aaron discussing?

What are the biblical events in this chapter?

CHAPTER 3 "GO AND DO NOT RETURN"
Exodus 12
1. How does Oren try to help Pasur?
2. What does Tirzah receive from their neighbor?
3. By evening, what smell filled the room of Tirzah's home? Why?
4. What did old Hanna think she would never see?
5. What does old Hanna say about Tirzah's future?
6. What is the meal they eat?
7. When Tirzah is woken up, what is everyone doing? What time of day is it?
8. As the Israelites are leaving, what is going on around them?
9. What are the men carrying as they leave Egypt?

What are the biblical events in this chapter?

CHAPTER 4 THE TRAP
Read Exodus 13:17–14
1. What discussion goes on between Tirzah's father Jeraheel and Uncle Shobal?
2. What does Jeraheel say to Tirzah to keep her from worrying?
3. What causes Oren's tears and prayers?
4. What is the strange, white, cloud-like mass that hung in front of them? What does this cloud-like mass do?
5. What is the cloud-like mass like at night?
6. What are Ram and her father discussing?
7. What does Jeraheel say to Ram?
8. What does Ram say to Tirzah after her father leaves?
9. What worries Ram and now Tirzah?
10. In the morning, what direction does the

THE EXODUS
Tirzah *Literature Unit*

cloud go? Why does this seem dangerous?
What are the biblical events in this chapter?

CHAPTER 5 THE BOTTOM OF THE SEA
Read Exodus 14
1. What is the donkey's name?
2. What are Jonathan and Ram discussing? Why does this concern Ram?
3. What is Tirzah's mother's reaction to Shobal?
4. What does Moses say to the Israelites in response to those who were rebelling against Moses' leadership?
5. What is the response to Moses?
6. What fearful event seems to loom quickly on the Hebrews?
7. What does Tirzah's family do in response?
8. People cry out in fear to Moses saying Moses brought them out to die. How does Moses respond?
9. What does God do for the Israelites?
What are the biblical events in this chapter?

CHAPTER 6 ESCAPE
Read Exodus 14 and 15
1. Describe the people's reaction to crossing the sea. (Oren, Ram, Abishur and Tirzah)
2. Summarize what happens to the Egyptians.
3. After God gives the victory to the Hebrews, instead of chastising the Israelites for their grumbling hearts, what does Moses teach the Israelites?
4. Write out the words of the song.
5. What does Oren plan to do when he gets to Canaan?
What are the biblical events in this chapter?

CHAPTER 7 FORGIVEN
Read Exodus 3 and 4
1. What causes Ram's anguish?
2. How does his father help him?
3. How does Ram look at his father now?
4. What does Moses say in reply to Ram's asking for forgiveness?
What are the biblical events in this chapter?

CHAPTER 8 MERRIE
Read Exodus 13:19
1. What causes Abihail to worry concerning the journey to the Promised Land?
2. Describe the shoes Benj made for Tirzah and her family. Why were they helpful?
3. What is Jonathan, Tirzah's cousin, discussing with Tirzah concerning the miracle that recently happened?
4. Who is Merrie? Why is she with Hannah?
5. What is Jonathan's response to Merrie?
6. How is Tirzah's response different?
What are the biblical events in this chapter?

CHAPTER 9 MEAT FROM THE SKY
Read Exodus 15:22-15; 16
1. How long have the Hebrews been marching?
2. What was not to be found?
3. How does Moses turn the bitter water to sweet?
4. What great promise did Yahweh give to the Israelites?
5. Why is the whole camp rumbling with unrest? What is the plea?
6. How does Leah help Tirzah know what an omer is?
7. Why does she help her know what an omer is?
8. What does Jerioth say the quail feathers would make?
9. Describe the differences between Abishur and Jonathan.
What are the biblical events in this chapter?

THE EXODUS
Tirzah *Literature Unit*

CHAPTER 10 OLD HANNA'S CHILD
Read Exodus 16

1. List a few of the descriptions of manna as found in the first paragraph.
2. Tirzah collects what she is supposed to. Why does her companion collect more than she needs for one day? How does Tirzah respond to this?
3. What did the manna get baked into? How did it taste?
4. Tirzah asked her mother if there would be manna tomorrow. How does her mother answer?
5. What happened to Ephan's manna that was left over?
6. Describe what happens concerning collecting manna for the Sabbath.
7. How do the Hebrew children treat Merrie when she is drawing water?
8. How does Merrie plan to avoid the problem with children?
9. Give the example of Merrie obeying the Hebrew Sabbath rule.
10. How does Hannah show Merrie that she is special?

What are the biblical events in this chapter?

CHAPTER 11 HIDDEN DANGER
Exodus 17:1-7

1. Copy the words of Moses' song. Think about how encouraging this song would be to people still walking towards the Promised Land.
2. How was Ram encouraged by the words of the song he heard Moses singing?
3. How are Jonathan and the other men stirring up trouble again?
4. What is Ram's response to Jonathan?
5. How do you see Ram's faith in Yahweh strengthened/different after this dialogue?
6. Who is the uncle we are re-introduced to?
7. How does Caleb show he is following Yahweh?

8. What is the miracle Moses performed that Tirzah and Ram are discussing?
9. Reread the dialogue between Ram and Tirzah. Think about how the Israelites are being taught by Yahweh to trust in Him totally as they cross the desert. List examples from the stories that show that God is working for them.

What are the biblical events in this chapter?

CHAPTER 12 WAR
Exodus 17:8-15

1. Who is attacking the Israelites?
2. What is Tirzah's worry? (Is she remembering yet to trust Yahweh? Remember, in the last chapter, Ram said, "When trouble comes, that is the time to show your trust.")
3. What good news does Ram tell Tirzah about the battle?
4. How does Tirzah now show her trust?
5. How are the readers introduced to Joshua?
6. How do different people acknowledge Yahweh's work in the battle?

What are the biblical events in this chapter?

CHAPTER 13 STRANGERS
Read Exodus 18:1-13

1. Who is coming into the Hebrew encampment?
2. Describe the people who came.
3. What was the reaction of Moses to their arrival.
4. Summarize the dispute going on between the men of Dan and Shobal.
5. What is Tirzah's father trying to persuade Shobal not to do.
6. What gossipy, mean-spirited words were being said about Zipporah, Moses' wife?
7. What gift does Tirzah receive and by whom?

What are the biblical events in this chapter?

THE EXODUS
Tirzah *Literature Unit*

CHAPTER 14 THE MOUNTAIN OF GOD
Read Exodus 18:13-27; 19
1. To what job is Tirzah's father, Jeraheel, appointed?
2. Summarize why Merrie cries out, "Yahweh, O Yahweh, help me."
3. Where are the Israelites gathered?
4. Describe what is going on at the mountain to show Yahweh was there.
5. Copy the words that Moses read to the people from the Book of the Covenant.
6. Of what act is Ram a part?
7. What is sprinkled on the people as a sign of the covenant Yahweh had made with them.

What are the biblical events in this chapter?

CHAPTER 15 A GOLDEN IDOL
Read Exodus 32
1. What is Oren keeping track of?
2. Summarize the tension that Oren feels is going through the camp.
3. Summarize what happened to Merrie two days after meeting Manetto at the well and why this happened.
4. What does Merrie cry out to God and how does He answer?
5. Why were the followers of Yahweh hiding in the hills?
6. Summarize what Ram and Abisher hear, as well as know, is going on in the camp.
7. Is Yahweh's presence still above the mountain, despite the activities in the camp?

What are the biblical events in this chapter?

CHAPTER 16 ONE SMALL MIRACLE
Read Exodus 32, 33
1. At the beginning of the chapter, where are the followers of Yahweh going?
2. Why does Tirzah, her mother and her father not go with them?
3. What goes on when they return to their tent?
4. What words of truth does her father give her to give her hope?
5. What tasks does her father give Tirzah to keep her mind off her worries concerning her mother?
6. What is the news when the baby is born?
7. Summarize the story Ram tells about what happened when Moses returned?
8. What happened to Uncle Shobal?
9. What is the good news at the end of the chapter?

What are the biblical events in this chapter?

CHAPTER 17 HANNA
Read Exodus 32:35
1. What did Hanna offer to do?
2. What does Merrie beg of Hanna?
3. What type of sickness has spread through the camp?
4. What do the women do to help the sick?
5. About how many days do they care for the sick together?
6. As they are traveling back to their camp in the hills, what happens to Hanna?
7. What happens to Merrie?
8. Who takes care of Merrie?
9. Where does Jerioth say Hanna is now?

What are the biblical events in this chapter?

THE EXODUS
Tirzah *Literature Unit*

CHAPTER 18 BENJ'S STONE
Read Exodus 35:4-29
1. What is Abishur struggling over?
2. What does Ram say to try to encourage him?
3. What is Benj carrying?
4. What do the coneys look like?
5. Why are peple bringing gifts to Moses?
6. How does Abihail show her interest in Abishur?
7. What does Benj give Tirzah?
8. After Molid finishes the story of Noah, what feelings fill Tirzah's mind?
What are the biblical events in this chapter?

CHAPTER 19 A NEW WAY
Read Exodus 20; 34
1. What is Tirzah learning?
2. What is Tirzah thinking about as she walked home?
3. Why does Abishur say it is a new day?
4. What are Tirzah and her family celebrating, along with the rest of the camp?
5. How does Ephan teach Tirzah the new commandment?
7. How was Merrie? How do some people still treat her?
7. How does Leah, Tirzah's mother, respond to Tirzah's question concerning Merrie and Ram?

CHAPTER 20 HARD LESSONS
Read: Numbers 11, 12
1. Why was the boy stoned to death?
2. What did Ram say to Tirzah concerning this event?
3. At the beginning of the chapter, what mood rolled through the camp? Why?
4. What two things does God send to the Israelites in response to their grumbling?
5. What does Jerioth say to Molid concerning Merrie?
6. What are the rumors concerning Moses which Leah talks about?
7. What happened to Miriam?
8. Why does Jerioth tell Leah that she should make an offering to Aaron and that God was mericful?
9. Why are Oren and Tirzah happy at the end of the chapter?
What are the biblical events in this chapter?

CHAPTER 21 A SONG OF HOPE
1. What did Ephan say scares her?
2. According to Tirzah and Ephan's conversation, who should be coming back soon and from where? How long have they been gone?
3. What was the report concerning what the men saw?
4. How does Joshua encourage the people?
5. How do the people respond to all of this?
6. Contrast Tirzah's reaction to her mother's reaction to the news about the land.
7. After the Israelites had listened to the 10 spies, what were they ready to do?
8. What does Joshua say to them?
9. What does Yahweh do just as Moses and Aaron are about to get stoned?
10. Copy Moses' words to the people after he leaves the Tent of Meeting.
11. Although the ending is sad, what hope is held out to Tirzah's family through their father?
12. How does the Song of Moses conclude the book?
What are the biblical events in this chapter?

THE EXODUS
Tirzah *Literature Unit*

OTHER ACTIVITES

1. Memorize parts of or the whole Song of Moses.
2. Illustrate several favorite sections from the book which correspond to the biblical account, where possible putting characters from the book in your illustrations.
3. First read the story of the Israelites in the wilderness and how God brought them into the Promised Land.
4. Discuss how Tirzah, Jeraheel, Leah, Merrie, and Uncle Shobal showed their trust of God or their fear/lack of trust in different situations. What does their trust or their fear lead them to do?
4. Discuss how the character Ram changes in this book. What is he like and what does he do in the beginning of the book compared to the ending of the book? What events change him?
5. List and discuss who are the faithful followers of Yahweh. How do they live out their trust? Start with discussing Tirzah's father, Jeraheel.
6. Discuss how the author intertwines fiction (the story of Tirzah and her family) with the biblical narrative. Did it help you grasp how the Israelites kept responding to Moses and to Yahweh?

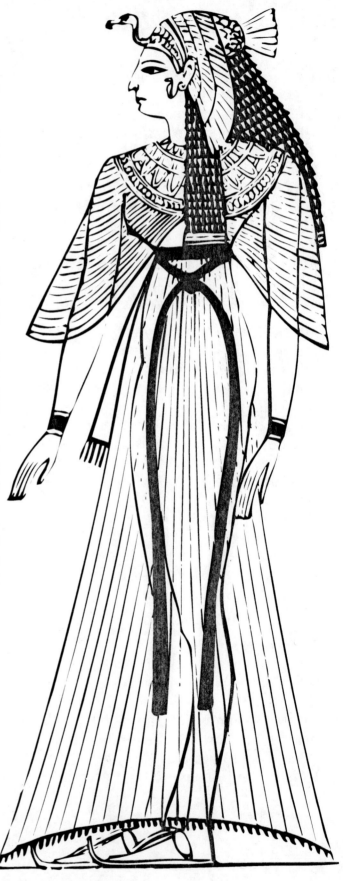

THE EXODUS

Test

1. What is the approximate date of the Exodus?

_____

_____

2. What is the scripture reference for the Exodus?

_____

_____

3. What was the tenth plague?

_____

_____

_____

4. How were the Israelites spared from the tenth plague?

_____

_____

_____

5. How did God keep the Israelites from being taken captive by Pharaoh again?

_____

_____

_____

Review:

1. How did man fall out of fellowship with God?

_____

_____

The Exodus
Test, Page 2

2. What is the scripture reference for the story of Cain and Abel?

_____

_____

3. What did God tell Noah to put into the Ark?

_____

_____

_____

4. What occurred during the First Intermediate Period in Egypt?

_____

_____

_____

5. What was the ancient script of the Sumerians in which the Code of Hammurabi was written?

_____

_____

_____

6. Who was Potiphar?

_____

_____

_____

7. How many sons of Israel were there? Name them.

_____

_____

_____

THE EXODUS
Test, Page 2

8. Why did Moses' mother place him in a basket as an infant and put the basket in the reeds by the Nile River?

_____

_____

_____

9. List all events covered in chronological order.

_____

_____

_____

_____

_____

_____

_____

_____

_____

_____

_____

_____

_____

_____

_____

_____

_____

9. (continued)

_____

_____

_____

_____

_____

_____

TEN COMMANDMENTS
Worksheet

1. What is the scripture reference for the Ten Commandments?

   _____

   _____

2. What is the approximate date of the Ten Commandments?

   _____

3. To whom did God give the Ten Commandments? Where did he do this?

   _____

   _____

4. What purpose do the Ten Commandments serve?

   _____

   _____

   _____

5. Write down each of the Ten Commandments in order.

   _____

   _____

   _____

   _____

   _____

   _____

   _____

   _____

   _____

   _____

Ten Commandments
Project 1—Memory Game

Photocopy the cards below so they back up the next pages and cut out. Shuffle the cards then lay them words down. Take turns lifting two at a time. Replace them face down if they do not match and keep the pair if they do match.

TEN COMMANDMENTS
Project 1, Page 2

THE FIRST COMMANDMENT	THE SECOND COMMANDMENT	THE THIRD COMMANDMENT	THE FOURTH COMMANDMENT
THE FIFTH COMMANDMENT	THE SIXTH COMMANDMENT	THE SEVENTH COMMANDMENT	THE EIGHTH COMMANDMENT
THE NINTH COMMANDMENT	THE TENTH COMMANDMENT	*I. You shall have no other gods before me.*	*II. You shall not make for yourself a carved image.*

TEN COMMANDMENTS
Project 1, Page 3

III. You shall not take the name of the Lord your God in vain.	*IV. Remember the Sabbath day, to keep it holy.*	*V. Honor your father and your mother.*	*VI. You shall not murder.*
VII. You shall not commit adultery.	*VIII. You shall not steal.*	*IX. You shall not bear false witness against your neighbor.*	*X. You shall not covet.*

TEN COMMANDMENTS
Project 2—The Horns of Moses

Michelangelo's magnificent statue of Moses, now in the Church of S. Pietro in Vincoli at Rome, portrays the stammering man of God as a veritable god. The near-perfect man is seated, his head turned, the tablets of the Law held protectively, and—rising from his brow—two small horns! This strikes the modern viewer as odd. Is Michelangelo saying that Moses is a devil?

No, the sculpture was made thus for the same reason the artwork on the flash card shows Moses with what appear to be searchlights shining out of his skull. From the twelfth century, Moses was occasionally depicted with horns due to the Latin Vulgate's mistranslation of Exodus 34:29 and 35 that reads, "And when Moses came down from the mount Sinai, he held the two tablets of the testimony, and he knew not that his face was horned from the conversation of the Lord." "And they saw that the face of Moses when he came out was horned, but he covered his face again, if at any time he spoke to them."

St Jerome had translated the Hebrew verb for "shine" as "horned," since those words were so similar in the language from which he was translating. Following is how the passage reads in the New King James' Version:

Now it was so, when Moses came down from Mount Sinai (and the two tablets of the Testimony were in Moses' hand when he came down from the mountain), that Moses did not know that the skin of his face shone while he talked with Him. So when Aaron and all the children of Israel saw Moses, behold, the skin of his face shone, and they were afraid to come near him. Then Moses called to them, and Aaron and all the rulers of the congregation returned to him; and Moses talked with them. Afterward all the children of Israel came near, and he gave them as commandments all that the LORD had spoken with him on Mount Sinai. And when Moses had finished speaking with them, he put a veil on his face. But whenever Moses went in before the LORD to speak with Him, he would take the veil off until he came out; and he would come out and speak to the children of Israel whatever he had been commanded. And whenever the children of Israel saw the face of Moses, that the skin of Moses' face shone, then Moses would put the veil on his face again, until he went in to speak with Him. —Exodus 34:29–35

TEN COMMANDMENTS
Project 3—Stone Tablets

Write down each of the Ten Commandments next to the appropriate number.

1. _____

    _____

    _____

    _____

2. _____

    _____

    _____

    _____

    _____

3. _____

    _____

    _____

    _____

4. _____

    _____

    _____

5. _____

    _____

    _____

6. _____

    _____

7. _____

    _____

    _____

8. _____

    _____

    _____

9. _____

    _____

10. _____

    _____

    _____

TEN COMMANDMENTS
Test

1. Where did God reveal the Ten Commandments to Moses?

_____

_____

_____

2. Write down each of the Ten Commandments in order.

_____

_____

_____

_____

_____

_____

_____

_____

_____

_____

3. Where can the Ten Commandments be found in Scripture?

_____

_____

Review

1. Write down all the events learned to date in chronological order. Include dates for card numbers 8, 12, and 24 and scripture references where applicable for all events.

_____

_____

TEN COMMANDMENTS
Test, Page 2

1. (continued)

_____

_____

_____

_____

_____

_____

_____

_____

_____

_____

_____

_____

_____

_____

_____

_____

_____

_____

_____

_____

AMENHOTEP IV AND MONOTHEISM
Worksheet

1. What is the approximate date of Amenhotep and Monotheism?

    _____

    _____

2. During what dynasty did Amenhotep IV rule?

    _____

    _____

    _____

    _____

3. What was the name of
    Amenhotep's wife?

    _____

    _____

    _____

    _____

    _____

4. Which god did Amenhotep declare
    as the only god?

    _____

    _____

    _____

    _____

    _____

AMENHOTEP IV AND MONOTHEISM
Worksheet, Page 2

5. What is monotheism?

_____

_____

_____

_____

_____

6. Why did Amenhotep change his name to Akhnaton?

_____

_____

_____

_____

7. Who was Tiy?

_____

_____

_____

_____

AMENHOTEP IV AND MONOTHEISM
Project 1—Coloring Page

Amenhotep and his queen Nefertiti playing "Senet." The most controversial figure in Egyptian history, Amenhotep IV (reigned 1361–1344 B.C.) changed his name to Akhnaton after transferring his worship from the many national gods, headed by Amon-Re, to Aton, the solar disk, in a nearly exclusive cult. The stiff resistance to his intention of converting the whole country led to his creation of a new capital city far from Thebes, in an area of present day Tell el-Amarna. The art that he commissioned was unlike that of any other reign, showing the royal family in many non-ceremonial activities.

Color this picture.

AMENHOTEP IV AND MONOTHEISM
The Golden Goblet *Literature Unit*

CHAPTER 1

1. Put into your own words "molten gold" and "flame-colored liquid." Use a dictionary for help and make sure it agrees with the context of the story.
2. What is this boy's name?
3. What is he doing when we are introduced to him in the beginning of the story?
4. Ranofer does a lot of daydreaming throughout this story. What is he dreaming about when we are introduced to him?
5. What is his reaction to Gebu? Why does he live with Gebu?
6. Describe the month of Hathor.
7. Who is Ibini? What is Ranofer's reaction to him?
8. What does Gebu do with the wine that Ibini gives him? What does Ranofer think of this?
9. What is missing from Rekh the Goldsmith's place?
10. "Why must they make me talk of these things that I wish to forget?" List 3 things he would like to forget.
11. What does Ranofer need proof of?

CHAPTER 2

1. Describe the differences between the different parts of Thebes as presented at the beginning of this chapter.
2. What is the best protection from Egypt's glaring sun?
3. List the craftsmen/artisans mentioned in this chapter. For what were most of their objects fashioned?
4. Put in your own words the two aspects of Gebu's personality (you may need a dictionary).
5. What grows in the marshes?
6. When someone says to a neighbor or companion "May your Ka be joyful" what do they mean?

7. What is Ranofer's worry concerning the wineskins?
8. What is Ranofer's biggest longing as well as his biggest disappointment?
9. What is the name of the street on which Gebu's house is located?
10. Before going to sleep, what does Ranofer decide to do?

CHAPTER 3

1. What is the "Great Lord Ra" which "bursts over the eastern horizon?"
2. What does "this Heqet must be the drollest fellow in Egypt" mean? Find out what droll means. Using this chapter for help, find an example of why Ranofer thinks this of Heqet.
3. What happens during the morning ritual?
4. Define *mollified*.
5. Describe the incident which shows that Ranofer would make a good goldsmith.
6. What does Rekh tell Ranofer to do that brings Ranofer such joy?
7. Does Ranofer fulfill his desire in regards to the wineskin and "the Babylonian?"
8. How does Gebu respond to Ranofer's actions.
9. With what does Gebu threaten Ranofer?

CHAPTER 4

1. What or who does Ranofer think helped him in the middle of the night?
2. Why does Ranofer place some food at his father's statue?
3. What does Heqet say to Ranofer to gain Ranofer's trust?
4. Briefly explain Ranofer's plan and how it includes Heqet.
5. Why does Ranofer receiving the wineskin spoil his plan?
6. What mood is Gebu in when Ranofer arrives with the wineskin?
7. What does Gebu say in an undertone to

Amenhotep IV and Monotheism
The Golden Goblet *Literature Unit*

Wenamon when he receives the wine-skin?

8. How does Gebu reward Ranofer?
9. Describe how Ranofer feels about Wenamon.
10. What does Ranofer do with his coin.

Chapter 5
1. Define *joviality*.
2. Why is Ranofer worried?
3. Why is someone being executed?
4. What do Egyptians believe happens to the pharaoh if his tomb is robbed?
5. What has caused Ranofer to be "buoyant with triumph and overflowing with energy?"
6. What then causes him to be depressed?
7. What happens to Ibini?
8. What does Gebu say to Ranofer in regards to working at the goldsmith's?
9. What does Ranofer beg of Gebu in the middle of the night? How does Gebu respond?

Chapter 6
1. How does the author describe the difference between the stonecutter's shop and the goldsmith's shop?
2. What is made in this shop? Explain what these are.
3. Who is Zahotep and does he help Ranofer?
4. What does the reader learn about Pai's character after Ranofer meets him? List 3 characteristics.
5. How does Ranofer respond to his new work surroundings? What does he think of it? Find a direct quote and copy it.
6. Why does Ranofer need to pay close attention to this work? (Why is this job possibly dangerous for Ranofer and his dreams?)
7. Define *appropriated*. What does Gebu

appropriate from Ranofer?

8. What strange noise does Ranofer hear one night? What is Ranofer's reaction to it?
9. Does Ranofer hear the same noise again? What other noises does he hear?

Chapter 7
1. Paragraph one describes the landscape based on the rhythm of the Nile. Describe what happens in the fall, in the winter and after the winter.
2. Describe what occurs during harvest time.
3. What humor does Heqet use to say that Ranofer has been a stranger?
4. What idea does Heqet present that Ranofer positively accepts?
5. How is Heqet's friendship helpful to Ranofer?
6. What does Heqet plan to teach Ranofer?
7. How does the Ancient One help the two friends?
8. List five characteristics of or facts about Ancient.
9. What unexpected goodness comes to Ranofer?

Chapter 8
1. What happens to the river and the weather in the spring? What do Ranofer and Heqet do in the spring?
2. What wisdom does Ancient give to Ranofer? How did Ancient gain this wisdom?
3. Of what job does Heqet have that he asks Ranofer to come with him?
4. What is Ranofer's daydream?
5. List five details concerning the part of town they walk to reach Zau's place?
6. Who is Zau? How did Ranofer know him before?
7. What does Ranofer ask of Zau?
8. How and why does Zau say he will help Ranofer? Explain Ranofer's responses.

AMENHOTEP IV AND MONOTHEISM
The Golden Goblet *Literature Unit*

9. Copy Zau's response to Ranofer in regards to his being able to teach Ranofer in the future.
10. Why was there no miracle that night?

CHAPTER 9
1. Ranofer realizes there is a change in Gebu's physical appearance. List three examples.
2. Why does Ranofer think Gebu is stealing again?
3. What is their plan to catch Gebu?
4. What else does Heqet propose to do?
5. What kindness does Ancient do to Ranofer which brings tears to his eyes?
6. What does Ancient make Ranofer promise?
7. What does Ranofer do in the time between coming home from the stonecutters and going to bed?
8. Do his activities prove to be successful? Why or why not?

CHAPTER 10
1. What does Wenamon's wife's voice sound like? Do you think this is a nice description of her? Why or why not? What other information does the reader find out about her?
2. Why was Ranofer disappointed with Heqet's story? Did anything important happen when Ancient was watching Setma?
3. How long does nothing happen while the three are spying? What is Heqet's explanation for this?
4. From what or whom does Heqet save Ranofer? Does anything else important happen that night?
5. The author described Ancient's face as "seamed." What does this mean?
6. Why does Ranofer start to lose hope in spying on Gebu and Wenamon?
7. What does Ranofer realize Gebu is after

and what part of the day does he go after it?
8. What does Ranofer find on a drawing on a scroll that puzzles him? When he asks Gebu about it, how does Gebu respond to Ranofer?
9. Why does Ranofer decide to defy Gebu and go up into the upper room?
10. What does Gebu discover in Gebu's room which makes him go "numb all over?" What does Ranofer realize Gebu has done?
11. What trouble does Ranofer realize he is in?

CHAPTER 11
1. Because of the problem he has, what does Ranofer tell himself he must be? What does he do to try to fix his problem? List five things in order.
2. In what state does Gebu come back to the house? How does this help Ranofer?
3. What does Ranofer daydream about?
4. Why are his hopes dashed?
5. What did Ancient see? Who was quarreling and how did it end? What do you think they were quarreling over?
6. What is Gebu carrying into the shop the morning Ranofer is following him? After he goes into the office, does he come out empty-handed? How does Ranofer respond to this?
7. When Ranofer is sent into the storeroom for a scroll, what does he do?

CHAPTER 12
1. What is Ranofer's dilemma in regard to Heqet? What does he decide to do?
2. For what does Heqet think the little room is used. What is the problem with this idea?
3. What event are all looking forward to? What do they expect to receive from the

AMENHOTEP IV AND MONOTHEISM
The Golden Goblet *Literature Unit*

Pharaoh?

4. On the day before the festival, Heqet ends up doing some spying. What does he see and hear?

5. Because of Heqet's story, Ranofer realizes something about Gebu's plans. What is it?

6. Of what does Ranofer ask Ancient concerning the hangings of the tomb robbers? What does he learn?

7. In this chapter, does Ranofer tell his two friends what he knows about Gebu and the golden goblet? Why do you think this?

8. What decision does he make concerning "tomorrow," the Feast Day?

CHAPTER 13

1. "The stars still spangled the sky . . ." What is the author describing?

2. Does Ranofer feel positive about what lays ahead of him on this feast day? Why or Why not? Give two examples from the first, second and third paragraphs of this chapter to support your answer.

3. What are the two reasons why Ranofer is following Gebu to the tombs today, instead of going to the feast.

4. After following Gebu and Wenamon for awhile, he comes upon them "working busily" at something. What are they doing? What does Ranofer find?

5. What answer does Ranofer come up with concerning the "little room" on the tomb drawing (the one Ranofer questions Gebu about, but got hit for instead).

6. Heqet and Ancient spend time waiting for Ranofer. At first, why do they think he is late? How do they realize where Ranofer is? What do they decide to do?

7. What do Ancient and Heqet see at the "boulder strewn sands?" Who was also frightened by it?

CHAPTER 14

1. After following Gebu through the dark passageways, what does Ranofer find Gebu doing?

2. Why do Heqet and Ancient decide that Ranofer could not have gone into the tomb?

3. What is a ushabit? Why are its eyes smashed out?

4. List ten items found in the tomb.

5. What is the title of the tomb?

6. Ranofer sees the seal of who is buried in the tomb. Who is it and why are they important?

7. Why do Gebu and Wenamon realize Ranofer is there? What does Ranofer do to keep them from getting him?

8. Does Ranofer escape them? How?

CHAPTER 15

1. What story about Gebu does Ranofer tell Ancient and Heqet?

2. What does Ancient tell Ranofer he and Heqet will do to help Ranofer?

3. Where does Ranofer head for first in his quest for help? Was there help?

4. Where does he decide to go next? What keeps him going in this direction?

5. After an exciting chase through the stable, kitchen and garden, now what happens to Ranofer?

6. Do people believe him at first?

7. After being held by the soldier, whom does Ranofer meet and to whom does he tell his story?

8. Where is Ranofer going at the end of this chapter?

CHAPTER 16

1. List and briefly describe 5 items in the room he is in when he enters the palace.

2. Who is Ranofer going to see with Qanefer?

AMENHOTEP IV AND MONOTHEISM
The Golden Goblet *Literature Unit*

3. What is the test the queen puts to Ranofer to see if he is lying?
4. What is Ranofer's answer? Does this prove he was telling the truth?
5. What does the queen tell people to do after she hears his answer?
6. After Ranofer is escorted out of the queen's room, who asks Ranofer a question? What is this man's job? What question does he ask Ranofer?
7. Who is sent to look for the goblet? Where are they told to especially look?
8. What were the orders Qa-nefer had concerning Ranofer? List a few nice things that happened to Ranofer before he sees the queen.
9. Were Gebu and Wenamon captured? What happened to the gold and jewels they were trying to capture?
10. Was the golden goblet found? Where does Ranofer see it?
11. Were Ancient and Heqet safe after guarding the two thieves?
12. The queen wants to bestow a reward on Ranofer. What is his request?
13. As Ranofer walks through the City of the Dead, he is carrying or accompanied by several rewards. List four.
14. Now Ranofer can return to Zau and say, "_____."

DISCUSSION QUESTIONS

1. What is Ranofer like at the beginning of the book? How is he very different at the end? What events or people helped to bring about this change?
2. This story shows the importance of true friends. Throughout the entire story, how do Ancient and Heqet prove to be good friends to Ranofer.
3. Think of a few events that show Ranofer has become a brave and strong person by the end of the story.
4. Through most of the story Ranofer is fearful of Gebu. By the end, is this true? Why or why not?
5. Describe the character of Ranofer, Ancient, Heqet and Gebu.
6. Ranofer daydreams quite often. Why do you think he daydreams so much? What are some of his dreams? Which of his dreams do come true?
7. The theme of the book is established by Zau. What does he say to Ranofer? How does Ranofer accomplish this?
8. What does the reader learn about the culture and land of Ancient Egypt by reading this book?
9. What was your favorite event in this book?
10. Discuss with someone who has read *Great Expectations* or *Nicholas Nickleby* by Charles Dickens how this book is similar to these two books. Especially think about Ranofer and Gebu and the involvement of Ranofer's friends.

Amenhotep IV and Monotheism
The Golden Goblet *Project—Make a Golden Goblet*

Supplies

plastic 16.9 fl. oz. bottle

scissors

hot glue gun

gold paint

Directions

Remove label, wash, and rinse bottle. Cut all the way around below where label had been on the bottle (usually there is a slight indent there). Remove any burrs or sharp places on both pieces. Run a thick bead of hot glue around the top (mouth) of the bottle. Turn the bottle over and place the opening with the hot glue on it centered on the inside of the base in the middle. You may need to run another line of glue around the point where the two pieces meet. Let cool then paint.

AMENHOTEP IV AND MONOTHEISM
Project 3—Senet

This game is very old and was very popular. It was found in many tombs from all levels of society. The oldest known reference to Senet is in a wall painting in the tomb of the Third Dynasty Pharaoh Hesy c. 2650 B.C.

Supplies

scissors

markers or colored pencils

tape

one die

Directions

Copy the following two pages. Color the pieces and the game board as desired, then cut them out. Tape the game board together (panels overlap).

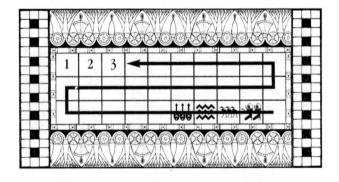

No one knows what the real rules for this game were in antiquity. This version of the rules is based on those proposed by R.C. Bell, The Boardgame Book, *1979, Marshall Cavendish Ltd, London.*

Rules

Each player has 10 game pieces. At the beginning of the game the board is empty.

Each player in turn rolls the die, and puts his game pieces on the board on the squares with the symbols (roll a 1 = the blank square in the lower right corner, roll 3 = birds, etc.).

When a game piece arrives on a square already occupied by an opponent game piece, the opponent is removed and must restart from the beginning. This rule does not apply for the squares with pictures, which are shelters.

A player may either move one game piece or add a new game piece to the board, if possible, with each roll.

The first game piece to snake its way along a backwards "S" path to square number 1 (upper left corner) determines the goal of the game: that player's other game pieces have to reach odd squares whereas the opponent must reach the even squares. The game ends when the game pieces of the two players are alternately placed on the first and second rows.

When a game piece has reached its last square, it cannot be attacked.

The first player to have put all his game pieces on his own squares wins the game.

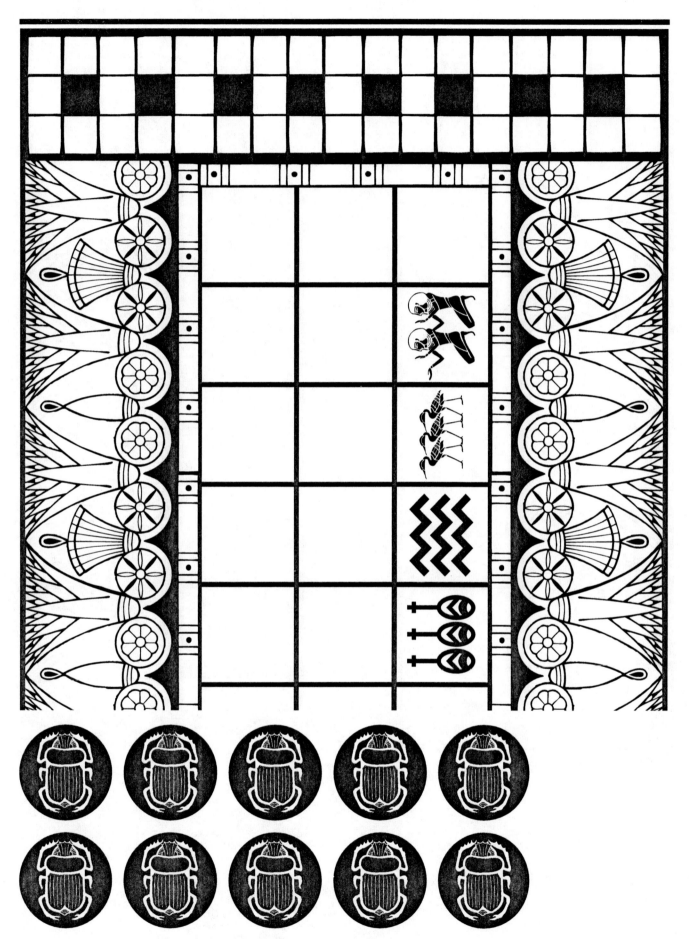

AMENHOTEP IV AND MONOTHEISM
Project 4—Fill in the Blank

Using the history card, fill in the missing blanks.

Amenhotep IV ruled during the _____ dynasty. His father was Amenhotep III. He married _____ . In the second or third year of his reign he began to build a new city, _____, named after the god _____ . He believed Thebes, the old capital, was dominated by a god named _____ .

Then he changed his _____ . He no longer wanted to be called _____ relating him to Amon, but _____ after a god named _____ . He decreed _____ to be the only god, establishing _____ , and closed the temples of all other gods. Many believed he did this because he wanted to _____ the power of the priesthood of _____ .

Amenhotep III died and his wife _____ came to see her son Akhnaton and his wife _____ . What happened next is a _____ . It appears that Tiy argued with her son about monotheism. He became very ill. _____ was sent away from the palace with her servants and _____ (who was, perhaps, Akhnaton's half-brother).

Smenkhkare married Akhnaton's oldest daughter and was named co-ruler of Egypt. Three years later Smenkhkare, his wife, and Pharaoh Akhnaton were dead. Tutankhaton, whose _____ was changed by the priest of _____ to Tutankhamon would be Pharaoh.

Amenhotep IV and Monotheism
Test

1. What is the approximate date of Amenhotep IV?

   _____

   _____

2. Who was the wife of Amenhotep IV?

   _____

   _____

   _____

3. Why did Amenhotep decree Aton to be the only god?

   _____

   _____

   _____

4. To what did Amenhotep change his name?

   _____

   _____

Review

1. What did God create on the fifth day of Creation?

   _____

   _____

2. What is the scripture reference for the Fall in the Garden?

   _____

   _____

AMENHOTEP IV AND MONOTHEISM
Test, Page 2

3. What is the scripture reference for the Tower of Babel?

_____

_____

4. Who was the first person to unify Upper and Lower Egypt?

_____

_____

5. What was the name of Abraham's wife?

_____

_____

6. What was the name of the one righteous man that God found living in Sodom and Gomorrah?

_____

_____

7. List all the events learned to date in chronological order.

_____

_____

_____

_____

_____

_____

_____

_____

_____

7. (continued)

_____

_____

_____

_____

_____

_____

_____

_____

_____

_____

_____

_____

_____

_____

_____

REIGN OF TUTANKHAMON
Worksheet

1. What is the approximate date of the Reign of Tutankhamon?

_____

_____

2. What was one of the largest archeological finds in history, made on November 4, 1922? Who made this discovery?

_____

_____

_____

_____

_____

_____

_____

3. How old was Tutankhamon when he ascended the throne?

_____

_____

_____

4. How long did he reign?

_____

_____

_____

REIGN OF TUTANKHAMON
Worksheet, Page 2

5. How old was Tutankhamon when he died?

_____

_____

_____

6. Why was Tutankhamon's name changed during his life?

_____

_____

_____

_____

7. Why was the discovery of Tutankhamon's tomb so important?

REIGN OF TUTANKHAMON
Tut's Mummy Lost . . . and Found *Literature Unit*

CHAPTER ONE: THE KING IS DEAD

1. How old was Tutankhamon when he died?

_____

_____

2. What is the Land of the Dead? Describe it.

_____

_____

_____

3. What did the Egyptians believe they needed to take with them to the Land of the Dead?

_____

_____

_____

4. What was the purpose of mummies?

_____

_____

_____

5. How many days did it take to make a mummy?

_____

_____

6. Where was Tutankhamon buried?

_____

_____

REIGN OF TUTANKHAMON
Tut's Mummy Lost . . . and Found *Literature Unit*

7. Draw a picture of Tutankhamon's funeral parade.

8. The priest would touch the mouth, eyes, and ears on the mummy. Why did they do this?

    _____

    _____

    _____

9. Contrast the Egyptians' view of death with Jesus' teachings about death. (Mathew 6:19-21 and John 14:1-6)

    _____

    _____

    _____

    _____

REIGN OF TUTANKHAMON
Tut's Mummy Lost . . . and Found *Literature Unit*

CHAPTER 2: THE LOST KING

1. What is an archeologist?

   _____

   _____

   _____

2. What did archeologists find in Egypt in the 1800's?

   _____

   _____

3. What was the Valley of the Kings? What were they hoping to find in the Valley of the Kings?

   _____

   _____

   _____

   _____

4. Who was the one archeologist who never gave up looking for lost tombs?

   _____

   _____

   _____

REIGN OF TUTANKHAMON
Tut's Mummy Lost . . . and Found *Literature Unit*

CHAPTER THREE: THE SEARCH

1. Howard Carter believed he would find Tutankhamon's tomb. Who did he get to finance his expedition?

    _____

    _____

    _____

2. What were the conditions in which Carter and his men worked?

    _____

    _____

    _____

3. After five years and no significant finds Lord Carnarvon was ready to give up. What was Carter's response?

    _____

    _____

    _____

    _____

4. In November, 1922, Carter and his men began digging again. What happened on the third day of the dig?

    _____

    _____

    _____

5. For whom did Carter send?

    _____

    _____

REIGN OF TUTANKHAMON
Tut's Mummy Lost . . . and Found *Literature Unit*

CHAPTER FOUR: THE DISCOVERY

1. What did Carter see as he looked in the hole in the door of the tomb?

_____

_____

_____

2. What did the air smell like that escaped from the tomb?

_____

_____

_____

3. Why was Howard Carter so excited? What did he see all around him?

_____

_____

_____

REIGN OF TUTANKHAMON
Tut's Mummy Lost . . . and Found *Literature Unit*

CHAPTER FIVE: THE KING IS DEAD

1. Why did the discovery of Tutankhamon's tomb make headlines all over the world?

   _____

   _____

   _____

2. What name did newspapers give to Pharaoh Tutankhamon?

   _____

   _____

3. After months of clearing away hundreds of treasures Howard Carter was finally ready to open the sealed door. What did he find?

   _____

   _____

   _____

4. What happened to Lord Carnarvon? What did the newspapers say about him? Why?

   _____

   _____

   _____

   _____

REIGN OF TUTANKHAMON
Project 2—King Tut Mask

Supplies

paper

foil

glue

paint

scissors

clear spray acrylic

Directions

1. Copy the patterns onto card stock and cut out the pieces.
2. Attach tin foil to both pieces of mask—spray glue works best.
3. Spray paint them gold.
4. Have students score the lines on the foil with pencil by using various pictures in books. (One of the best is *Tut's Mummy Lost . . . and Found,* page 44.)
5. Paint the face mask with acrylic paint.
6. Spray the pieces with clear spray acrylic to seal it.
7. Glue the piece below to the forehead of the mask. You may want to glue the completed mask to foamboard or cut holes in the eyes so the student may "wear" the mask.

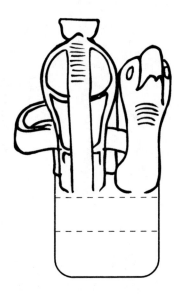

REIGN OF TUTANKHAMON
Project 3—King Tut, Tomb of Treasure

View King Tut, Tomb of Treasure, *produced by Public Media Home Video. Experience the wonder and mystery of King Tutankhamon's tomb. Visit the actual tomb, the Cairo Museum, and the New Orleans Museum of Art for a glimpse at the magnificent artifacts that were buried with Tut.*

Jim Packer
presents
Narrated by
Allen Ludden

King Tut
Tomb of Treasure

REIGN OF TUTANKHAMON
Test

1. What was the approximate date of the Reign of Tutankhamon?

   _____

   _____

2. What discovery did Howard Carter make?

   _____

   _____

3. How old was Tutankhamon when he ascended the throne?

   _____

   _____

4. How long did Tutankhamon reign?

   _____

   _____

5. Why did Tutankhamon change his name?

   _____

   _____

6. Why was the finding of Tutankhamon's tomb such an important archeological discovery?

   _____

   _____

   _____

REIGN OF TUTANKHAMON
Test, Page 2

Review

1. What covenant did God establish with Noah?

   _____

   _____

2. What occurred during the Old Kingdom in Egypt?

   _____

   _____

   _____

3. What is the scripture reference for God's covenant with Abraham?

   _____

   _____

4. How did God test Abraham's faith?

   _____

   _____

   _____

   _____

5. Name the twelve sons of Israel.

   _____   _____

   _____   _____

   _____   _____

   _____   _____

   _____   _____

   _____   _____

REIGN OF TUTANKHAMON
Test, Page 3

6. Who was Hammurabi?

_____

_____

_____

7. How did the Hyksos take Egypt by surprise?

_____

_____

_____

8. Where was Moses raised?

_____

_____

_____

9. List the events covered to date in chronological order.

_____

_____

_____

_____

_____

_____

_____

_____

_____

9. (continued)

_____

_____

_____

_____

_____

_____

_____

_____

_____

_____

_____

_____

_____

_____

_____

LATER NEW KINGDOM
Worksheet

1. What is the approximate date of the Later New Kingdom?

   _____

   _____

2. What gains were made during the Later New Kingdom?

   _____

   _____

   _____

   _____

3. Who was the first pharaoh of the 19th Dynasty?

   _____

   _____

   _____

4. Place the following names in order of father, son, and grandson: Seti, Ramses II, Ramses I

   _____

   _____

5. What is the most depicted event in Egyptian history?

   _____

   _____

   _____

6. What is Ramses II known for building?

   _____

   _____

   _____

   _____

LATER NEW KINGDOM
Project 1—Visit to the Temple

Read the section entitled "Visit to a temple" in the Time Traveler Book of Pharaohs and Pyramids. *Using complete sentences, compare the Egyptian view of worship to the Hebrew/ biblical view of worship.*

_____

_____

_____

_____

_____

_____

_____

_____

_____

_____

_____

_____

_____

_____

_____

_____

_____

_____

LATER NEW KINGDOM
Project 2—Egypt: Quest for Eternity

View with your students the 60 minute video
Egypt: Quest for Eternity *produced by National
Geographic Video Classics. This exceptional video
will help in understanding Egyptian culture.*

Join egyptologists as they unravel and interpret the riddles of Egypt's intriguing past.

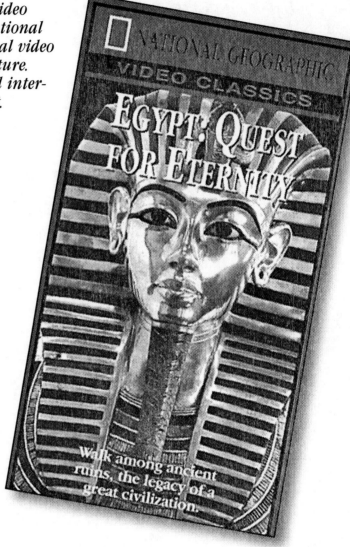

LATER NEW KINGDOM
Project 3—Travel Brochure

*On the following two pages is a shell for a three-panel brochure. After copying back-to-back,
fold along the dotted lines and fill in the spaces provided with pictures and/or information
related to the titles provided.*

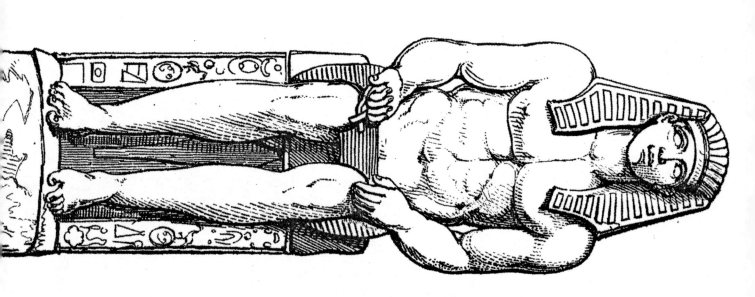

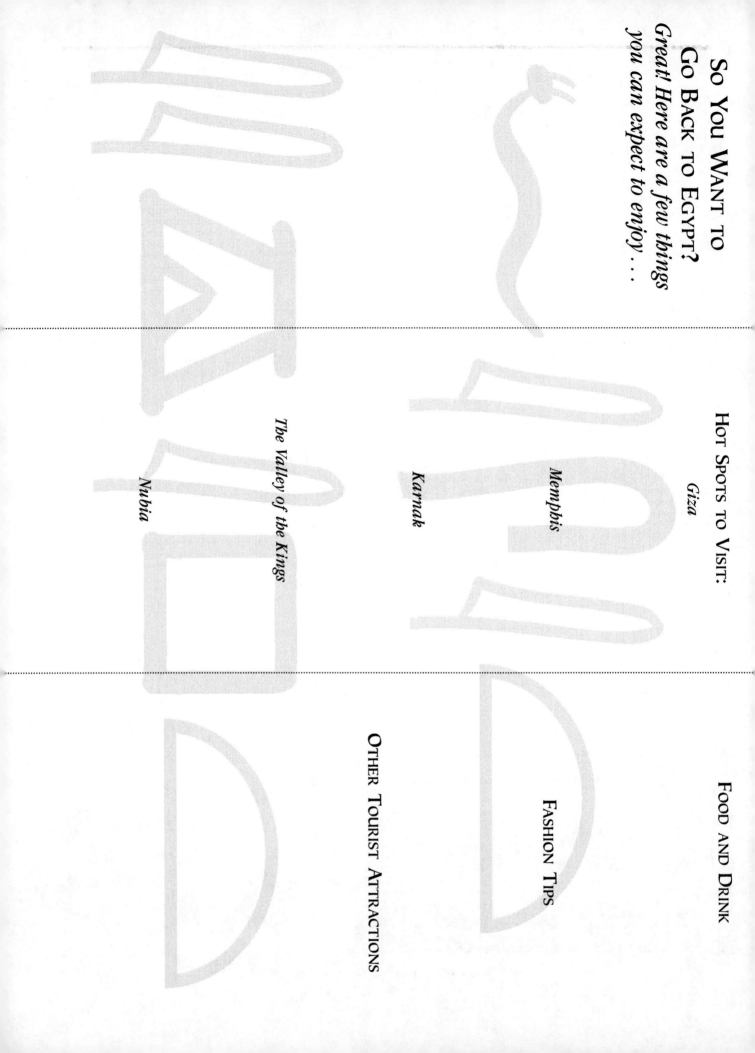

So You Want to Go Back to Egypt?

Great! Here are a few things you can expect to enjoy . . .

Hot Spots to Visit:

Giza

Memphis

Karnak

The Valley of the Kings

Nubia

Food and Drink

Fashion Tips

Other Tourist Attractions

LATER NEW KINGDOM
Test

1. What is the approximate date of the Later New Kingdom in Egypt?

_____

_____

2. What gains did Egypt make during this period?

_____

_____

_____

_____

3. To which dynasty does Ramses I belong?

_____

_____

4. What is the most depicted event in Egyptian history?

_____

_____

5. Who led Egypt in the battle of Kadesh?

_____

_____

LATER NEW KINGDOM
Test, Page 2

Review

1. List the twelve sons of Israel.

   _____   _____

   _____   _____

   _____   _____

   _____   _____

   _____   _____

   _____   _____

2. List the Ten Commandments. Where can the Ten Commandments be found in Scripture?

   _____

   _____

   _____

   _____

   _____

   _____

   _____

   _____

   _____

   _____

   _____

   _____

LATER NEW KINGDOM
Test, Page 2

3. List all the events covered to date in chronological order.

_____

_____

_____

_____

_____

_____

_____

_____

_____

_____

_____

_____

_____

_____

_____

_____

_____

_____

LATER NEW KINGDOM
Test, Page 3

3. (continued)

_____

_____

_____

_____

_____

DAVIDIC KINGDOM
Worksheet

1. What is the scripture reference for the Davidic Kingdom?

   _____

   _____

2. What are the approximate dates of the Davidic Kingdom?

   _____

   _____

3. With God's direction where did the prophet Samuel visit to find the next king of Israel?

   _____

   _____

   _____

4. Who was selected as Israel's next king?

   _____

   _____

5. Whom did David defeat?

   _____

   _____

6. Why did King Saul become jealous of David?

   _____

   _____

   _____

7. What did King Saul attempt to do to David?

   _____

   _____

   _____

DAVIDIC KINGDOM
Worksheet

8. How long was David's reign over Israel?

_____

_____

_____

DAVIDIC KINGDOM
Project 1—Draw David's Life

After reading about David in I & II Samuel and I Chronicles choose four favorite events and illustrate them in the frames below.

DAVIDIC KINGDOM
Project 2—I Samuel 16 Summary

Read I Samuel 16. Using complete sentences, write a paragraph describing what is happening in the picture below.

_____

_____

_____

_____

_____

_____

_____

_____

_____

_____

_____

_____

DAVIDIC KINGDOM
Project 3—Who Were the Philistines?

David gained fame among the Israelites due to his success in battle against the Philistines, especially when he killed their warrior Goliath. But who were these people that beset the chosen people of God? Write a short report describing where they lived, what group of people they were and what trade or arts they were known for?

_____

_____

_____

_____

_____

_____

_____

_____

_____

_____

_____

_____

_____

_____

_____

_____

_____

_____

_____

DAVIDIC KINGDOM
Test

1. Where in Scripture can we find the Davidic Kingdom?

   _____

   _____

2. What are the approximate dates of the Davidic Kingdom?

   _____

   _____

3. At the direction of God whom did Samuel choose to be the next king of Israel?

   _____

   _____

   _____

4. Why did King Saul become jealous of David?

   _____

   _____

   _____

   _____

5. Who was Goliath?

   _____

   _____

   _____

6. Approximately how many years did David reign as king of Israel?

   _____

   _____

   _____

DAVIDIC KINGDOM
Test, Page 2

Review

1. When God decided to flood the earth, who was the one man who found favor in God's sight?

   _____

   _____

   _____

2. What do some archeologists believe may be the ruins of the Tower of Babel?

   _____

   _____

   _____

3. What was the purpose of the pyramids?

   _____

   _____

   _____

4. Where in Scripture can we find the Call of Abram?

   _____

   _____

5. What major advances occurred during the Middle Kingdom in Egypt?

   _____

   _____

   _____

   _____

Davidic Kingdom
Test, Page 3

6. When Pharaoh found out that Joseph's brothers had come to see him, what did he do?

_____

_____

_____

7. Who may have been the princess that pulled Moses from the Nile River?

_____

_____

_____

8. What is the Fifth Commandment?

_____

_____

_____

9. List all the events covered to date in chronological order.

_____

_____

_____

_____

_____

_____

_____

_____

_____

DAVIDIC KINGDOM
Test, Page 4

9. (continued)

_____

_____

_____

_____

_____

_____

_____

_____

_____

_____

_____

_____

_____

_____

_____

SOLOMON'S REIGN
Worksheet

1. What is the scripture reference for the Reign of Solomon?

   _____

   _____

2. What are the approximate dates of the Reign of Solomon?

   _____

   _____

3. After David died who became king?

   _____

   _____

4. In a dream God asked Solomon, "What shall I give you?" For what did Solomon ask?

   _____

   _____

   _____

5. What plan of his father's was Solomon able to carry out?

   _____

   _____

   _____

6. What famous queen came to seek out Solomon's wisdom?

   _____

   _____

   _____

7. What happened to Solomon's relationship with God before he died?

   _____

   _____

   _____

SOLOMON'S REIGN
Project 1–Building the Temple

With the instructions below turn your classroom (or a room at home) into a replica of Solomon's Temple. Talk to the children about how many years went into the planning and building of the Temple. Read I Kings 6–8 and possibly Journey Through the Bible, *pages 132-133.*

After reading this let the students come up with ideas for turning your room into the Temple. It is also a good idea to see if a local pastor or someone with knowledge of the Temple can come in upon completion and discuss the symbolism with the children.

Below are some ideas for implementing this. They are in no way complete. Be creative and have fun. You should allow one Friday afternoon for this project and speaker. It also helps to have a couple extra moms to help (or to work with other homeschool families).

1. Hang brown bulletin board paper on a few of the walls to represent cedarwood. Draw on the paper flowers, cherubim, and palm trees to represent those carved in the wood.
2. At the front of the room make the inner sanctuary. Hang yellow bulletin board paper to represent the gold overlay. (Gold foil is better, but more expensive.)
3. Put a desk in the outer sanctuary to represent the altar and cover it with yellow paper. Cover another desk with yellow paper to use as the table of gold on which the show bread was kept.

4. Make two cherubim by drawing, painting, and cutting them from refrigerator boxes. Put them in the inner sanctuary.
5. Using another refrigerator box, make a door for the inner sanctuary. Use desks or other furniture items to separate the inner sanctuary from the outer.
6. Make lampstands from cardboard (or borrow from a party rental store). Place the lampstands in front of the inner sanctuary.
7. Have students bring in bowls, ladels, etc. and cover them with gold foil for use in the temple.

SOLOMON'S REIGN
Project 1, Page 2

8. Make the Ark of the Covenant from a box and cover it with yellow paper. Attach two dowels/rods to the sides with which to "carry" it. Place the Ten Commandments inside it. (Remember the stone tablets from the card #25 project?) Make two more cherubim and place on the top facing each other. Place the Ark in the inner sanctuary.

This is not intended to be an exact replica. The engravings of worship elements on these two pages are from the Tabernacle. Those found in the Temple would have been more grand and not designed for travel. The more resources you have the more elaborate you may want to be. The ultimate idea is to teach the children about the extraordinary symbolism and work that went in to building a temple by God's design.

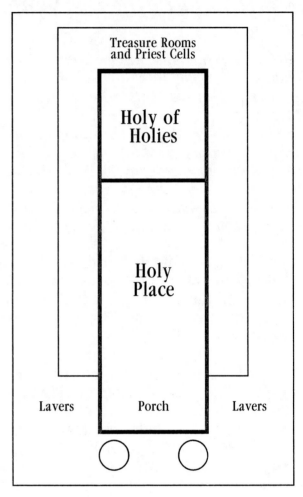

Treasure Rooms and Priest Cells

Holy of Holies

Holy Place

Lavers   Porch   Lavers

Molten Sea

Altar of Sacrifice

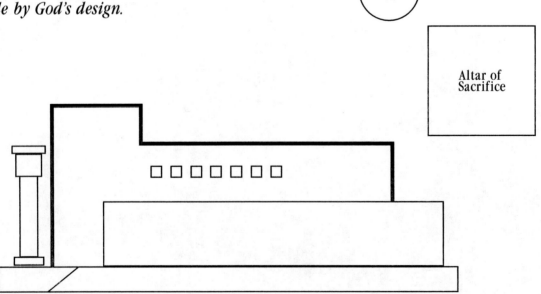

SOLOMON'S REIGN
Project 2—Fill in the Blank

Using the history card, fill in the missing blanks.

After _____ died, Solomon, his son, became the _____ of Israel. In a _____ God asked King Solomon, "What shall I give you?" Solomon requested _____ . Because he asked for _____ from God rather than _____ or long life, God gave him _____ and wealth. He became the _____ and wealthiest man in all the earth.

Now that there was _____ in the land, Solomon was able to carry out his father's _____ to build a _____ to worship God. The temple was elaborately decorated with _____ . It was built by the most talented workers and _____ in the land and was located on Mt. _____ . The innermost sanctuary, the Holy of Holies, was where the Ark of the _____ was kept.

Solomon's _____ and accomplishments were so well known that visitors came from _____ lands to see the _____ and his wealth. The _____ of _____ came to ask him _____ and see his wealth and was very impressed with how God had _____ him.

But Solomon, tempted by foreign _____ , turned from God and became _____ before he died. He reigned over Israel for _____ years, and his son Rehoboam became _____ .

SOLOMON'S REIGN
Project 3—Art of the Temple

Read the following material and make the booklet on the following page, illustrating it with the art of the Temple.

When many people go to church nowadays they expect their ears to experience beauty in hymns and spiritual songs, rich prayers, and in the proclaimation of the Word of God. But they do not expect to *see* anything beautiful.

In the third and fourth chapters of 2 Chronicles we find out that has not always been the case. David gave his son Solomon plans for the Temple, the patterns of which God had told him what they would look like. As we saw in the Tabernacle, God cared deeply about beauty in worship. So much so that the first person He ever filled with his Spirit was an artist.

So what kind of artwork would be found in the Temple? There wasn't just artwork *in* it, the building *itself* was beautiful. Francis Schaeffer points out in *Art and the Bible*, "Notice this carefully: the temple was covered with precious stones *for beauty*. There was no pragmatic purpose. God simply wanted beauty in the temple. God is interested in beauty." Schaeffer is referencing 2 Chronicles 3:6, "And he decorated the house with precious stones for beauty, and the gold was gold from Parvaim," which also mentions gold—the whole Temple was overlaid inside with pure gold! These gold walls were carved with palm trees and chainwork. This kind of art is called BAS-RELIEF (sculpture in which the projection from the surrounding surface is slight and no part of the modeled form is undercut). In the Holy of Holies Solomon had free-standing THREE-DIMENSIONAL SCULPTURES made —two giant carved cherubim (the wings of the cherubim alone were about thirty feet in overall length) and covered them with gold. TEXTILES is the next artwork listed in the text. The famous veil hiding the Holy of Holies was a veil of blue, purple, crimson, and fine linen, woven with representations of cherubim. Following this is a description of what in museums today would be called INSTALLATION ART —Jachin (means "he establishes") and Boaz (means "in him is strength"). The Bible says that Solomon— following plans given to David by God—placed in front of the temple on the left and right, two pillars each over fifty feet high with wreaths of chainwork on top and one hundred pomegranates in the chainwork. Again, Francis Schaeffer points out, "Here are two free-standing columns. *They supported no architectural weight and had no utilitarian engineering significance.* They were there only because God said they should be there as things of beauty. Upon the capitals of those columns were pomegranates

SOLOMON'S REIGN
Project 3, Page 2

fastened upon chains—artwork upon art-work. If we understand what we are reading here, it simply takes our breath away. This is something overwhelmingly beautiful."

That is more than enough art for a "church," right? No, God wants more beauty in His house where His chosen worship. Next we read of a bronze altar and then the Sea of cast bronze—a pool that might have held up to 10,000 gallons of water. This rested on a base of twelve carved oxen—nonreligious representational art in the center of worship. Finally, around the outside walls was more art. In 1 Kings 6:29 it says, "Then he carved all the walls of the temple all around, both the inner and outer sanc-tuaries, with carved fig-ures of cherubim, palm trees, and open flowers." Schaeffer writes that it was like God was saying, "'I'll even have lions in my house, carved lions, oxen and cherubim.' Not for a pragmatic function, just for beauty."

Then add to all that visual art the performing arts:

"Praise the LORD!
Sing to the LORD
    a new song,
And His praise in
    the assembly of saints.
Let Israel rejoice in their Maker;
Let the children of Zion be joyful in
    their King.
Let them praise His name with the dance;
Let them sing praises to Him with the
    timbrel and harp." —*Psalm 149:1-3*

Finally the crafts are represented in car-pentry and JEWELRY: "Thus Solomon had all the furnishings made for the house of God: the altar of gold and the tables on which was the showbread; the lampstands with their lamps of pure gold, to burn in the pre-scribed manner in front of the inner sanctu-ary, with the flowers and the lamps and the wick-trimmers of gold, of purest gold; the trimmers, the bowls, the ladles, and the cen-sors of pure gold. As for the entry of the sanctuary, its inner doors to the Most Holy Place, and the doors of the main hall of the temple, were gold."

Supplies

scissors

pencil

colored pencils

Directions

Copy the next page, then fold in half vertically, then in half horizontally and half again along the dotted lines. Unfold completely, then fold in half horizon-tally and cut halfway across along the solid black line. Unfold then fold ver-tically again. Push both ends toward the cen-ter so the center panels fold outwards mak-ing a booklet with the two illustrated panels being the front and back cover. Illustrate the book with pictures of the art of the Temple indicated on the top of each page.

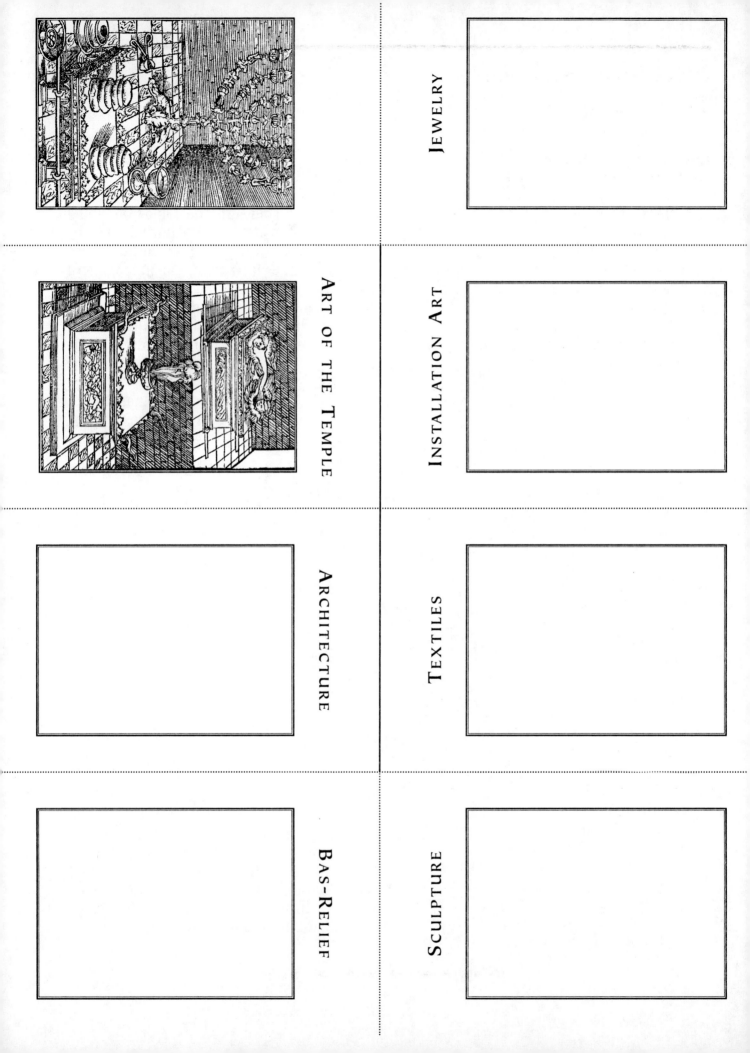

JEWELRY

ART OF THE TEMPLE

INSTALLATION ART

ARCHITECTURE

TEXTILES

BAS-RELIEF

SCULPTURE

SOLOMON'S REIGN
Test

1. What are the approximate dates of Solomon's Reign?

   _____

   _____

2. What is the scripture reference for Solomon's Reign?

   _____

   _____

3. Who succeeded David as king?

   _____

   _____

4. What request did Solomon make of God?

   _____

   _____

   _____

5. In the later years of Solomon's life what happened to his relationship with God?

   _____

   _____

   _____

6. Who succeeded Solomon as king?

   _____

   _____

Solomon's Reign
Test, Page 2

Review

1. List all events covered to date in chronological order. Place scripture references at the appropriate events. List dates for events numbered 9, 14, and 24.

_____

_____

_____

_____

_____

_____

_____

_____

_____

_____

_____

_____

_____

_____

_____

_____

_____

_____

SOLOMON'S REIGN
Test, Page 3

1. (continued)

_____

_____

_____

_____

_____

_____

_____

_____

ALEXANDER THE GREAT CONQUERS EGYPT
Worksheet

1. What is the approximate date of Alexander's conquering Egypt?

   _____

   _____

2. In 525 B.C. which Persian ruler conquered Egypt? What did this ruler not approve of?

   _____

   _____

   _____

   _____

3. Who conquered the entire Persian empire including Egypt?

   _____

   _____

   _____

4. Why was Alexander welcomed by the Egyptians?

   _____

   _____

   _____

   _____

   _____

ALEXANDER THE GREAT CONQUERS EGYPT
Worksheet, Page 2

5. What did Alexander tell his generals about who should succeed him upon his death?

_____

_____

_____

_____

6. Who was Ptolemy I?

_____

_____

_____

_____

Alexander the Great Conquers Egypt
Project 1—Persians

Rameses III ruled as the empire collapsed. Historians believe his reign ended in his untimely murder in 1158 B.C. Thieves began to break into the royal tombs at Thebes and Asian territories were lost. Then a Libyan dynasty was set up in the Nile delta which was followed by civil war, resulting in Nubian kings taking control of Memphis and Thebes. The Assyrians then invaded in 663 B.C., sacking and looting the great treasures of Thebes. Babylonians soon followed, with the Persians on their coat tails, winning a great victory under Cambyses at Pelusium in 525 B.C. Egypt was under the rule of Persia until Alexander the Great conquered Egypt.

Write a report to explain who the Persians were and the extent of their empire from 525–332 B.C.

_____

_____

_____

_____

_____

_____

_____

_____

_____

_____

_____

_____

_____

_____

_____

_____

ALEXANDER THE GREAT CONQUERS EGYPT
Project 2—Alexander the Great Triumphant

Dynasties 28–30 represented a last flickering of a relative independence for Egypt before Persia took over again (Dynasty 31, the last numbered one). When Persia finally lost Egypt, it had almost lost everything: Alexander the Great (lived 356–323 B.C), the world-conquerer from Macedonia, "delivered" Egypt in 332 B.C., only months before his decisive victory over the Persian empire in Mesopotamia. Crowned as pharaoh at Memphis, Alexander founded the city of Alexandria at the western end of the Delta. This was destined to become one of the greatest cities of the world. After Alexander's death, his vast empire was divided among his leading generals, who launched new dynasties. The line founded by his general Ptolemy, who became pharaoh in 305, was to last until 30 B.C.

Color this.

ALEXANDER THE GREAT CONQUERS EGYPT
Project 3—Fill in the Blank

Using the history card, fill in the missing blanks.

In 525 B.C. Cambyses, the _____ ruler, conquered Egypt. Cambyses was brutal and didn't approve of the local Egyptian _____. A series of Egyptian dynasties _____, but none lasted long.

In the late _____ century B.C., Alexander, the _____ of Macedonia, conquered the entire Persian empire including _____. Alexander was welcomed because of the Egyptians' _____ of the Persians. He founded a town near the mouth of the Nile and named it after himself: _____.

Before Alexander died, he told his _____ that the strongest one of them should reign after him. Upon his death, the _____ strongest generals divided up his kingdom. _____ claimed Egypt as his share. He and his descendants ruled Egypt for _____ years. The last of the _____ (and the last of the pharaohs) was _____.

ALEXANDER THE GREAT CONQUERS EGYPT
Project 4—The Pharos Lighthouse

In Plutarch's *Life Of Alexander,* he says that when Alexander took Egypt he decided to found: "a large and populous Greek city which should bear his name, and by the advice of his architects was on the point of measuring off and enclosing a certain site for it. Then, in the night, as he lay asleep, he saw a wonderful vision. A man with very hoary locks and of a venerable aspect appeared to stand by his side and recite these verses:

> *'Now there is an island*
> *in the much-dashing sea,*
> *In front of Egypt;*
> *Pharos is what men call it.'"*

In Book IV of Homer's *The Odyssey* Menelaus tells Telemachus how he was stranded on the shores of Egypt on an island that offered a good harbor. So, according to Plutarch, Alexander set himself before the isle of Pharos and "saw that Homer was not only admirable in other ways, but also a very wise architect, and ordered the plan of the city to be drawn in conformity with this site." Alexander did not stay to see the construction of a city that would become the Seventh Wonder of the World.

The Pharos Lighthouse was likely begun by Ptolemy Soter, one of Alexander's generals, and finished by his son, Ptolemy Philadelphus, around 285 BC. The lighthouse was designed by Sostrates of Knidos, but Ptolemy II insisted that the structure have only his own name carved into the foundation. Sostrates obeyed Ptolemy—sort of. He first chiselled the inscription:

"Sostratos of Cnidus, son of Dexiphanes, to the savior gods, for sailors" then covered it with plaster. Then he had Ptolemy's name cut into the plaster. Over the years the plaster chipped and wore away to reveal the inscription underneath.

It is believed that the lighthouse stood almost 400 feet tall (the equivalent of a 40-story modern building) on the eastern tip of the island and that it was built in three stages: the first square, then octagonal and the last circular. A long ramp led up to the tower and a spiral staircase rose up inside of it. The dedicatory inscription carved into the wall of the lighthouse referenced the "saviour gods" a phrase that usually refered to the twin sons of Zeus, Castor and Pollux. And ancient texts mention a statue standing on the top of the tower. The lighthouse served for seventeen centuries, surviving into the 14th century until earthquakes k it down.

As to the beacon, ancient travelers tell sometimes of a mirror that could be used to focus the sun and set enemy ships on fire, or a huge lens designed to increase the range of the light to 100 miles out to sea. Implausible as these stories sound, there must have been some arrangement to deal with the hot fire burning beneath the copula since the constant heat would certainly crack the masonry. Many scholars believe that the Ptolemies mixed their own culture with that of the Egyptians when constructing the lighthouse, using Egyptian stone covered in white marble.

ALEXANDER THE GREAT CONQUERS EGYPT
Test

1. What is the approximate date of Alexander the Great Conquers Egypt?

   _____

   _____

2. Who was Cambyses?

   _____

   _____

3. When Alexander conquered Egypt why was he so welcomed by the Egyptian people?

   _____

   _____

   _____

   _____

4. Who came to rule over Egypt after Alexander's death?

   _____

   _____

   _____

Review

1. What is the scripture reference for Creation?

   _____

   _____

2. Why did God curse Cain?

   _____

   _____

ALEXANDER THE GREAT CONQUERS EGYPT
Test, Page 2

3. What was another name for Pharaoh Menes?

_____

_____

4. What did God covenant with Abraham?

_____

_____

5. What happened when Lot's wife looked back as they fled from Sodom and Gomorrah?

_____

_____

6. Why did Joseph's brothers sell him into slavery?

_____

_____

7. What did Joseph do to secure food for Egypt during the famine?

_____

_____

8. What was each plague in Egypt a direct attack against?

_____

_____

ALEXANDER THE GREAT CONQUERS EGYPT
Test, Page 3

9. What was the Exodus?

10. List all the events covered to date in chronological order.

ALEXANDER THE GREAT CONQUERS EGYPT
Test, Page 4

10. (continued)

_____

_____

_____

_____

_____

_____

_____

_____

_____

_____

_____

_____

EGYPT FALLS TO ROME
Worksheet

1. What was the approximate date when Egypt fell to Rome?

   _____

   _____

2. What Roman general supported Cleopatra during the Civil War in 48 B.C.?

   _____

   _____

3. Who murdered Julius Caesar?

   _____

   _____

4. Who ruled the Roman Empire after Julius Caesar died?

   _____

   _____

5. Whom did Cleopatra marry?

   _____

6. Why did Anthony and Cleopatra kill themselves?

   _____

   _____

   _____

EGYPT FALLS TO ROME
Worksheet, Page 2

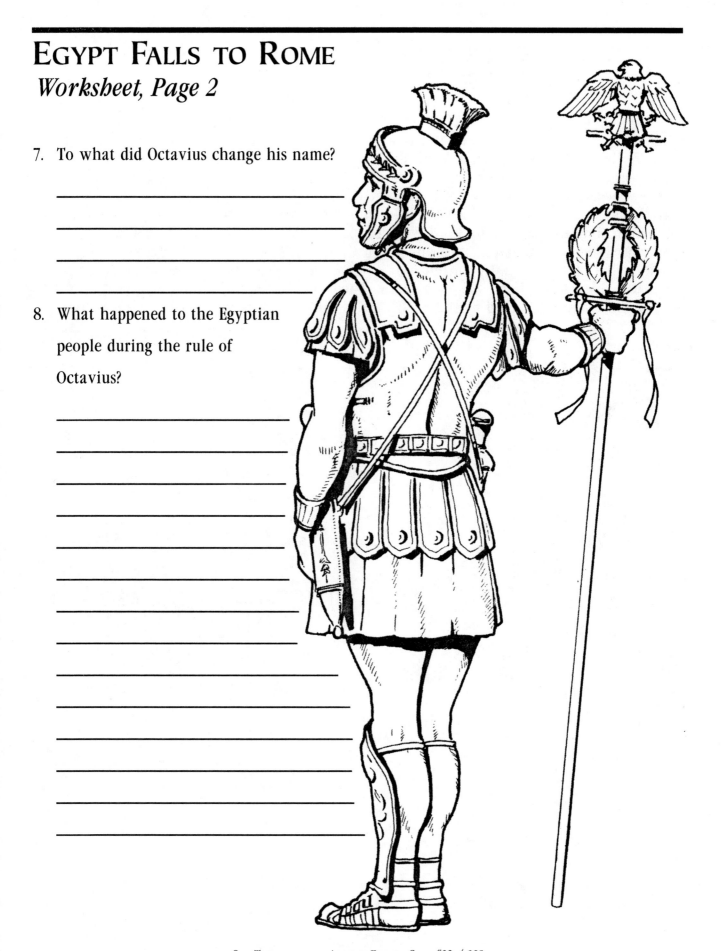

7. To what did Octavius change his name?

_____

_____

_____

_____

8. What happened to the Egyptian people during the rule of Octavius?

_____

_____

_____

_____

_____

_____

_____

_____

_____

_____

_____

_____

_____

EGYPT FALLS TO ROME
Project 1—Caesar and Cleopatra

Julius Caesar, arriving in Egypt in 48 B.C. in pursuit of Pompeii, his rival for supremacy in Rome, fell in love with Cleopatra VII and supported her disputed claim to the throne. After Caesar's assassination in 44 B.C., a new contender for Roman leadership, Mark Antony, became Cleopatra's new champion. They jointly ruled Egypt and large parts of the Near East until defeated by Augustus (Octavius), soon to become the first Roman emperor. Antony and Cleopatra committed suicide in 30 B.C., and Egypt became a province of the Roman Empire, supplying Rome with much of its grain. When the Empire split in two, in A.D. 395, Egypt found itself in the eastern, Byzantine, half. One of the great centers of early Christianity, Egypt was the original home of monasticism. The so-called Coptic art of this period is highly regarded today. Conquered by the Arabs in the 640's, Egypt has been Islamic ever since.

Color this.

EGYPT FALLS TO ROME
Project 2—Cleopatra's History

Cleopatra VII's (69–30 BC) father was Ptolemy XII Neos Dionysos. He was nicknamed Auletes (Greek for *flute-player*), which implied he was a do-nothing weakling. His rule of Egypt began in 80 B.C. but was interrupted when Berenice IV took over the kingdom, forcing Auletes to escape to Rome. Ptolemy XII returned in 55 B.C. and had Berenice IV beheaded, ruling Egypt until his death.

Cleopatra was about 17 years old when her father died. Cleopatra and her 12 year old brother, Ptolemy XIII, ruled jointly. Brother-sister marriages had been established by Ptolemy II, and the siblings were named Queen and King of Egypt in 51 B.C. Ambitious Cleopatra left Ptolemy XIII out of the ruling of Egypt. Then power-hungry advisers manipulated the young Ptolemy and succeeded in kicking Cleopatra out of the palace in 48 B.C. Cleopatra responded to this action by creating her own army.

When Caesar arrived in Alexandria, Cleopatra rolled herself in a carpet to deliver herself across enemy lines to Caesar. The Alexandrian War followed, and Cleopatra's brother died while trying to flee. Cleopatra was installed as the only ruler of Alexandria and was worshiped as a pharaoh. Caesar and Cleopatra's son, Caesarion (Ptolemy Caesar) was born on June 23, 47 BC. Caesar brought Cleopatra back to Rome with him, but when he was murdered, Cleopatra returned to Egypt.

Marc Anthony had control of Egypt for Rome. Cleopatra met Marc Anthony, and they fell in love. Marc Anthony divorced his wife (the Caesar's sister) to be with Cleopatra. The Caesar did not like this, so as an excuse to attack Egypt, he said she was a sorceress and an enemy of Rome. The war began, Cleopatra was captured, and then she committed suicide.

EGYPT FALLS TO ROME
Project 2—Cleopatra's Wig

Supplies

black paint

scissors

tape

black yarn

glue

paper grocery bag

Directions

Cut a paper bag along the dotted lines as shown. Adjust the width to fit the student's head and tape in place. Paint the exterior black and then take black yarn and dip it in glue. Arrange yarn on the wig and let dry.

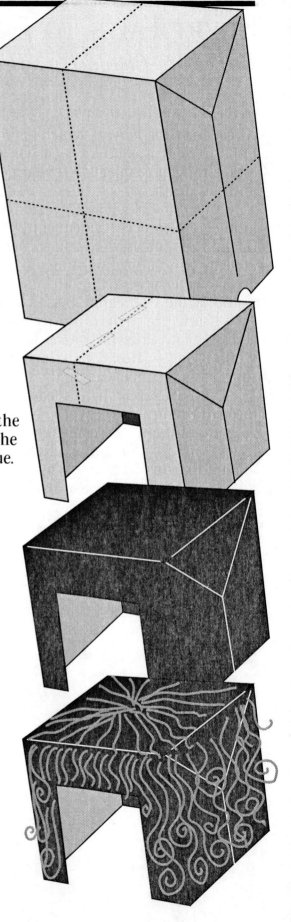

EGYPT FALLS TO ROME
Project 4—Cleopatra's Necklace

Supplies

cardboard

paint

yarn

pasta

Directions

Paint the pasta in red, orange, blue, turquiose, ivory and gold. Cut a 3" circle out of cardboard then cut it in half. Punch four holes in the semi-circles as shown. Tie two pieces of yarn on each hole. String the pasta on the yarn, weaving a piece of yarn through each end of the pasta so they criss-cross. Tie off the yarn on the other semi-circle of cardboard when you have the length necklace desired. Connect the two semi-circles with a piece of yarn long enough to fit over the student's head.

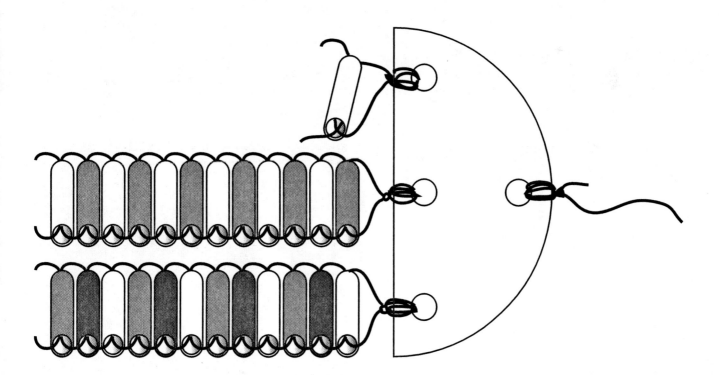

EGYPT FALLS TO ROME
Project 5—Caesar's Breastplate

Supplies

metallic gold paint

six milk lids

scissors

hot glue

black marker

paper grocery bag

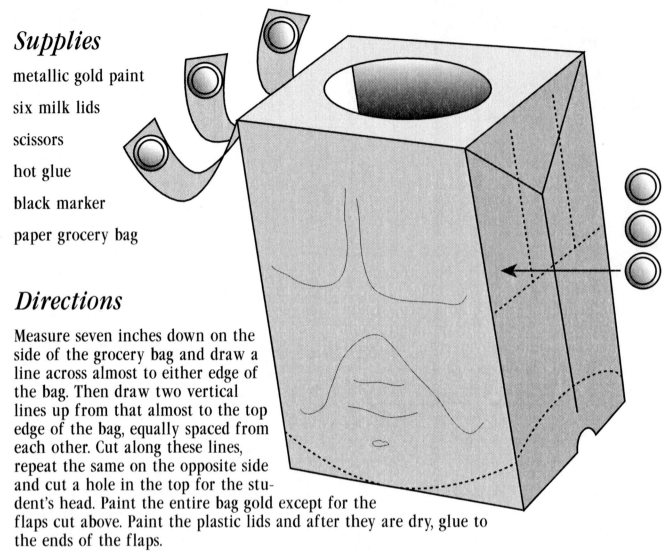

Directions

Measure seven inches down on the side of the grocery bag and draw a line across almost to either edge of the bag. Then draw two vertical lines up from that almost to the top edge of the bag, equally spaced from each other. Cut along these lines, repeat the same on the opposite side and cut a hole in the top for the student's head. Paint the entire bag gold except for the flaps cut above. Paint the plastic lids and after they are dry, glue to the ends of the flaps.

Optional: Cut along the bottom of the bag as shown in the diagram above. Draw designs on the front to look like a human torso.

EGYPT FALLS TO ROME
Test

1. What is the approximate date of Egypt's fall to Rome?

   _____

   _____

2. Who was Julius Caesar?

   _____

   _____

   _____

3. Who murdered Julius Caesar?

   _____

   _____

4. Whom did Octavius go to war against?

   _____

   _____

   _____

   _____

5. Why did Antony and Cleopatra commit suicide?

   _____

   _____

6. To what did Octavius change his name?

   _____

   _____

EGYPT FALLS TO ROME
Test, Page 2

Review

1. Why did God cause people to speak so many new languages at the time of the Tower of Babel?

_____

_____

_____

2. What is the period in Egypt's history when pyramids were built known as?

_____

_____

_____

3. What is the scripture reference for the Call of Abram?

_____

_____

4. What did God ask Abraham to do to Isaac?

_____

_____

_____

5. What did Joseph do for Pharaoh while in prison that resulted in Pharaoh putting Joseph in command of all Egypt?

_____

_____

_____

_____

_____

6. What term is given to describe Abraham, Isaac, and Jacob, collectively?

_____

_____

7. What is Hammurabi best known for?

_____

_____

_____

8. What did the Hyksos introduce to the Egyptians?

_____

_____

_____

9. Who is believed to be the pharaoh of the Exodus?

_____

_____

10. List all the events covered to date in chronological order.

_____

_____

_____

_____

_____

_____

_____

_____

EGYPT FALLS TO ROME
Test, Page 4

10. (continued)

_____

_____

_____

_____

_____

_____

_____

_____

_____

_____

_____

_____

_____

_____

_____

_____

_____

_____

_____

_____

_____

OLD TESTAMENT AND ANCIENT EGYPT
Memory Song Lyrics

First came creation, seven days, listen to what God did: He created everything and this is how it went . . . Day One day and night, Day Two heaven and earth, Day Three seas and land, Day Four sun, moon and stars, Day Five creatures of the sky and of the sea, Day Six creatures of dry land and then came man. Then God saw that it was good, all of His creation, so He took the seventh day and on that day He rested.

Second came the Fall in the Garden of Eden,

Third was Cain and Abel,

Fourth the Earth was flooded,

Fifth came the Tower of Babel,

Sixth the Unification of Upper and Lower Egypt by Pharaoh Menes.

Seven, the Old Kingdom in Egypt,

Eight, the First Intermediate Period,

Nine, The Call of Abram,

Ten, God's Covenant with Abraham.

Eleven, Hagar and Ishmael,

Twelve, was Sodom and Gomorrah,

Thirteen, the Birth and Sacrifice of Abraham's son named Isaac,

Fourteen, the Middle Kingdom,

Fifteen, Joseph as a Slave,

Sixteen, the Famine in Egypt, then came number seventeen. God gave Isaac's son named Jacob twelve sons of his own. They became the patriarchs of all the tribes of Israel. Rueben, Simeon, Levi—Judah, Issachar, Zebulun, Joseph and brother Benjamin, still four more left to name. Dan and brother Naphtali, Gad and Asher, this is why God gave Jacob twelve sons so that He could make a great nation.

Eighteen, came the Second Intermediate Period in Egypt,

Nineteen, came a list of laws, the Code of Hammurabi.

Twenty, the Hyksos invaded Egypt,

Twenty-one, the Early New Kingdom,

Twenty-two, the Birth of Moses,

Twenty-three, the Plagues in Egypt,

Twenty-four, came the Exodus in 1446 B.C.

Twenty-five, the Ten Commandments,

Twenty-six, Pharaoh Amenhotep, worshiped only one god. This was monotheism.

Twenty-seven, came the famous reign of Pharaoh Tutankhamen,

Twenty-eight, came the Later New Kingdom, the Golden Age in Egypt,

Twenty-nine, the Davidic Kingdom, 1011 B.C.,

Thirty, came the Reign of Solomon—builder of the Temple,

Thirty-one, came Alexander, Alexander the Great, he led Greece in conquering Egypt 332 B.C.

Number thirty-two was last but certainly not least: Egypt fell to Roman rule and so came to an end. Egypt fell to Roman rule and so came to an end.

OLD TESTAMENT AND ANCIENT EGYPT
Ten Commandments Song Lyrics

God gave Moses Ten Commandments
After he delivered Israel
Out of Egypt, out of bondage
These were God's own words.

First Commandment, God said "You shall have no other gods before me,"
Second, you shall not make for yourself a carved image.
Third, you shall not take the name of the Lord your God in vain,
Fourth, God said "Remember the Sabbath day, to keep it holy."

Fifth, honor your father and your mother,
Sixth, you shall not murder.
Seven, God said "You shall not commit adultery."

Eighth Commandment, you shall not steal.
Ninth Commandment, you shall not bear
False witness against your neighbor.
Ten, you shall not covet.

God descended in a fire
Down upon the mount of Sinai.
On the mount he spoke to Moses,
These the Ten Commandments.

ANSWERS

CREATION
Worksheet
1. Genesis 1–2
2. Always
3. Day 1: Day and night
   Day 2: Heaven and earth
   Day 3: The seas and the land
   Day 4: The sun, moon and stars
   Day 5: The creatures of the sky and sea
   Day 6: The creatures of the dry land, and man
   Day 7: Nothing; He rested.

Project 1—Creation Mobile
For both younger and older students

Project 2—Creation Myths
For both younger and older students

Test
1. Genesis 1–2
2. God
3. Day 1: Day and night
   Day 2: Heaven and earth
   Day 3: The seas and the land
   Day 4: The sun, moon and stars
   Day 5: The creatures of the sky and sea
   Day 6: The creatures of the dry land, and man
   Day 7: Nothing; He rested.

THE FALL IN THE GARDEN
Worksheet
1. Satan
2. Adam, yes.
3. a beautiful garden
4. cursed the world and punished Adam and Eve
5. We became guilty before God.

Project 1—Briars and Weeds
For both younger and older students

Project 2—The Cunning Serpent
For younger students

Project 3—Paradise P.I.
For both younger and older students
1. True. *Now the serpent was more cunning than any beast of the field which the LORD God had made. And he said to the woman, "Has God indeed said, 'You shall not eat of every tree of the garden'?"*
2. False. Eating of it would make her *like God,*

knowing good and evil.
3. False. *So when the woman saw that the tree was good for food, that it was pleasant to the eyes, and a tree desirable to make one wise, she took of its fruit and ate.*
4. False. *. . . she took of its fruit and ate.*
5. False. *. . . and they sewed fig leaves together and made themselves coverings.*
6. True. *And they heard the sound of the LORD God walking in the garden in the cool of the day . . .*
7. True. *. . . Adam and his wife hid themselves from the presence of the LORD God among the trees of the garden.*
8. False. The serpent tricked only Eve. *. . . The woman said, "The serpent deceived me, and I ate."*
9. True.
10. True. *Then the man said, "The woman whom You gave to be with me, she gave me of the tree, and I ate."*
11. False. There is no place in the text where Adam is said to rule over his wife before they fell. Only after they fell does Adam rule over her. *Your desire shall be for your husband, And he shall rule over you.*
12. False. *Also for Adam and his wife the LORD God made tunics of skin, and clothed them.*

Project 4—Fill in the Blank
For both younger and older students
tree, good, evil, word, die, tree, serpent, Eve, word, fruit, eyes, God, sinned, fruit, gave, Adam, sin, parents, head, cursed, death, Adam's, Adam, Eve, birth, sin, guilty, law, seed, Satan, Jesus

Test
1. The chance to be like God
2. He ate it.
3. Because Adam and Eve had disobeyed him by eating the fruit
4. We became guilty before God.

Review
1. Day 1: Day and night
   Day 2: Heaven and earth
   Day 3: The seas and the land
   Day 4: The sun, moon and stars
   Day 5: The creatures of the sky and sea
   Day 6: The creatures of the dry land, and man
   Day 7: Nothing; He rested.

ANSWERS

CAIN AND ABEL
Worksheet
1. Genesis 4
2. Cain, Adam and Eve
3. Abel
4. A farmer, a shepherd
5. Cain brought fruit. Abel brought the firstborn of his flock.
6. Cain; he was jealous.
7. He was unable to grow crops and had to be a vagabond and wanderer.

Project 1—Genesis 4 Bible Summary
For both younger and older students

Project 2—Matching
For younger students
CAIN: corn, banana, orange, peas, grapes, wheat, pepper
ABEL: lamb, bird, rabbit, antelope

Test
Answers will vary

Review
1. Genesis 1-2
2. Satan, the serpent
3. The Creation, the Fall in the Garden, the story of Cain and Abel

THE FLOOD
Worksheet
1. Genesis 6-9
2. Because man's every intent was wicked and continuously evil
3. Noah, build an ark and fill it with the male and female of every species, and also his own family
4. He sent a flood. It rained for 40 days and 40 nights
5. a promise between two persons
6. It was a sign of God's promise to never flood the earth again.

Project 1—The Ark's Size
For younger students
600 years old/keep trying to do what God tells us, no matter how long it takes
Project 2—Ark Model
For both younger and older students

Project 3—Dove Pop-Up Card
For both younger and older students

Project 4—You Expect Me to Believe That?
For older students

Test
1. Genesis 6-9
2. because man's every intent was wicked and continously evil
3. Noah
4. build an ark and fill it with the male and female of every species, and also his own family
5. A rainbow, it was a reminder of God's promise to never again flood the whole earth.

Review
1. because Adam and Even disobeyed Him by eating the fruit of the tree of knowledge of good and evil
2. God was pleased with Abel's sacrifice but not with Cain's.
3. because he murdered his brother Abel
4. See the master list on page 362.

THE TOWER OF BABEL
Worksheet
1. Genesis 11
2. One
3. He caused the people to speak many different languages and to scatter all over the earth.
4. the ziggurat of Marduk at Babylon

Project 1—Ziggurat Model
For both younger and older students

Project 2—Ziggurat Drawing
For both younger and older students

Project 3—Fill in the Blank
earth, language, tower, heavens, proud, God, many, scatter, over, ziggurat, Marduk, 300

Test
1. Genesis 11
2. God made all the people speak many different languages to scatter them all over the earth.
3. The ziggurat of Marduk at Babylon

ANSWERS

Review
1. Day 1: Day and night
   Day 2: Heaven and earth
   Day 3: The seas and the land
   Day 4: The sun, moon and stars
   Day 5: The creatures of the sky and sea
   Day 6: The creatures of the dry land, and man
   Day 7: Nothing; God rested.
2. when Adam and Eve disobeyed God in the Garden
3. Cain
4. that he would never again destroy the whole earth with a flood
5. See the master list on page 362.

UNIFICATION OF UPPER AND LOWER EGYPT
Worksheet
1. Menes (also known as Narmer), 15
2. He conquered Lower Egypt, built a new city, and ruled two kingdoms.
3. A double crown of red and white; it represented that he ruled both Upper Egypt and Lower Egypt (the Delta region).

Project 1—Hunting Expedition
For both younger and older students

Project 2—The Nile Flood Project
For both younger and older students

Project 3—Salt Relief
For both younger and older students

Project 4—Crown of Upper and Lower Egypt
For younger students

Project 5—Flooding of the Nile Reading
For older students

Project 6—Coloring Page
For younger students

Test
1. Menes (also known as Narmer)
2. 15
3. He conquered Lower Egypt, built a new city, and ruled two kingdoms.
4. A double crown of red and white; it represented that he ruled both Upper Egypt and Lower Egypt (the Delta region).

Review
1. To eat the fruit of the tree of knowledge of good and evil
2. He disobeyed and ate the fruit.
3. Cain
4. He promised that He would never again destroy the earth with a flood, and He gave the rainbow as a reminder of the covenant.
5. See the master list on page 362.

THE OLD KINGDOM IN EGYPT
Worksheet
1. The Old Kingdom
2. Egypt was at peace.
3. the Great Pyramid at Giza; Pharoah Cheops (also called Khufu)
4. one hundred thousand men at a time
5. twenty years
6. They thought their pyramids would prepare and help them on their journey into the afterlife.
7. no

Project 1—Book of the Dead Painting
For both younger and older students

Project 2—Book of the Dead vs. the Bible
For both younger and older students
1. both speak against false witnessing, murder, and stealing
2. Life is found by grace through faith in the person and work of Jesus Christ.

Project 3—Hymn to Osirus
For older students

Project 4—Pyramids Booklet
For younger students

Project 5—The Great Sphinx Coloring Page
For younger students

Test
1. The pyramids were built
2. Egypt was at peace. The pharaohs were secure. Peasants farmed the land and built the pyramids.
3. the Great Pyramid at Giza; Pharaoh Cheops (also called Khufu)

ANSWERS

Review
1. Heaven and the earth
2. Genesis 3
3. Cain
4. Man was wicked.
5. Genesis 11
6. Narmer
7. See the master list on page 362.

FIRST INTERMEDIATE PERIOD IN EGYPT
Worksheet
1. c. 2200–2050 B.C.
2. Dynasties seven through eleven
3. Civil war
4. Rich nobles grew powerful and the country was split between north and south. Rival kings ruled, one in the north and one in the south. Priests and temples grew more powerful and poor people got poorer.

Project 1—Mythological Mural
For both younger and older students

Project 2—Mythological Coloring Pages
For younger students

Project 3—Fill in the Blank
For younger students
period, seven, eleven, civil war, nobles, powerful, split, rival, north, south, priesthood, wealth, rich, public works, Famine, worse

Test
1. c. 2200–2050 B.C.
2. Dynasties seven through eleven
3. The rich nobles got tired of serving the pharoahs and wanted to rule themselves.

Review
1. God rested.
2. He became a sinner and guilty before God.
3. A farmer, a shepherd
4. Noah
4. when God judged the people building the Tower of Babel

THE CALL OF ABRAM
Worksheet
1. Leave his home in Ur, Mesopotamia
2. To bless him and make him a great nation
3. Sarai (his wife) and Lot (his nephew)
4. Canaan
5. Give it to Abram's descendants
6. c. 2091 B.C.
7. Genesis 12–13

Project 1—Abram's Times Booklet
For younger students

Project 2—A Reading About Ur
For older students

Test
1. Genesis 12–13
2. 75, none
3. Canaan
4. Sarai (his wife) and Lot (his nephew)
5. Give it to Abram's descendants
6. c. 2091 B.C.

Review
1. the seas and the land
2. He became a sinner, guilty before God.
3. Genesis 4
4. Noah
5. because they were sinfully proud and God wanted to stop them from building the tower
6. The pyramids were built.
7. See the master list on page 362.

GOD'S COVENANT WITH ABRAHAM
Worksheet
1. to bless him and make him a great nation
2. children
3. that his descendants would outnumber the stars in the sky and they would rule over a huge area of land
4. a smoking oven and a burning torch
5. circumcision
6. c. 2082 B.C.
7. Genesis 15–17

Project 1—Bible Summary
For both younger and older students

ANSWERS

Project 2—Ripped Animals
For younger students

Project 3—Fill in the Blank
For younger students
promised, nation, old, childless, stars, rule, owned, ceremony, goat, sleep, oven, torch, dead, ancient, promise, me, circumcision, long

Test
1. Genesis 15-17
2. c. 2082 B.C.
3. to make him a great nation
4. Abraham's descendants
5. circumcision
6. no

Review
1. Day 1: Day and night
   Day 2: Heaven and earth
   Day 3: The seas and the land
   Day 4: The sun, moon and stars
   Day 5: The creatures of the sky and sea
   Day 6: The creatures of the dry land, and man
   Day 7: God rested.
2. A male and female of all species, and Noah's family
3. Civil war, rich nobles grew powerful and the country was split between north and south.
4. See the master list on page 362.

HAGAR AND ISHMAEL
Worksheet
1. c. 2068 B.C.
2. Genesis 16 and 21
3. Sarah was old and hadn't borne Abram any children.
4. Ishmael
5. Isaac
6. Ishmael was scoffing at Isaac.
7. to take care of Hagar and Ishmael and to make a great nation from Ishmael

Project 1—Genesis 16 & 21 Summary
For both younger and older students
Answers will vary

Project 2—Water Bottle
For younger students

Test
1. Genesis 16, 21
2. take her maidservant, Hagar, for his wife so that Hagar could have a child for them
3. Ishmael
4. Isaac
5. sent her and Ishmael away
6. to protect her and to make a great nation from Ishmael

Review
1. Genesis 6-9
2. They were tombs for the pharoahs, meant to help them enter the afterlife.
3. God called Abram to leave his home and follow God's leading to Canaan.
4. Genesis 15-17
5. See the master list on page 362.

SODOM AND GOMORRAH
Worksheet
1. c. 2080 B.C.
2. Genesis 18-19
3. because his nephew Lot lived there, and because there might be other righteous people living there
4. because he was righteous
5. She was turned into a pillar of salt.
6. It taught him to keep the way of the Lord and to do righteousness and justice.

Project 1—News Article
For both younger and older students
Answers will vary

Project 2—Lot's Salt Dough Wife
For both younger and older students

Project 3—The Dead Sea
For older students

Test
1. c. 2080 B.C.
2. Genesis 18-19
3. Lot
4. They escaped, but Lot's wife looked back at the cities and God turned her into a pillar of salt.

Review
1. eat of the fruit from the tree of knowledge of good and evil
2. He was jealous of Abel because God was pleased

ANSWERS

with Abel's sacrifice but not with Cain's.
3. because everybody was wicked and continually evil
4. the Great Pyramid at Giza
5. Genesis 12–13
6. to make him a great nation
7. Ishmael
8. See the master list on page 362.

BIRTH AND SACRIFICE OF ISAAC
Worksheet
1. c. 2066 B.C.
2. Genesis 21–22
3. Abraham was 100, Sarah was 91.
4. offer Isaac as a sacrifice to God
5. to stop Abraham from sacrificing Isaac
6. because he had faith in God and was obedient
7. Answers may vary.

Project 1—Booklet
For younger students

Project 2—Fill in the Blank
For younger students
miraculously, old, 100, descendants, promised, true, faith, obeyed, Moriah, bound, altar, angel, sacrificing, ram, bushes, pleased, faith

Test
1. c. 2066 B.C.
2. Genesis 21–22
3. Isaac was born.
4. He asked Abraham to sacrifice Isaac.
5. to stop Abraham from sacrificing Isaac

Review
1. He made the people speak different languages and scattered them over the earth.
2. Pharoah Menes (also called Narmer)
3. civil war in Egypt
4. to bless him and make him a great nation
5. God said he would protect them and make Ishmael a great nation.
6. because of their great sin
7. See the master list on page 362.

THE MIDDLE KINGDOM IN EGYPT
Worksheet
1. c. 2050–1800 B.C.
2. Amenemhet
3. Great irrigation projects, trade with Syria and Palestine, and some of the finest hieroglyphics of the age
4. Joseph, Jacob's son, was sold into slavery and came to Egypt.
5. Senwosret III; he gained control of more of Nubia than any prior Egyptian leader.

Project 1—Hieroglyphics
For younger students

Project 2—Gateway of Karnak
For older students

Test
1. c. 2050–1800 B.C.
2. enjoyed peace
3. great irrigation projects, trade with Syria and Palestine, and some of the finest hieroglyphics of the age
4. Joseph, son of Jacob
5. Senwosret III; he gained control of more of Nubia than any prior Egyptian leader.

Review
1. God rested.
2. He murdered his brother Abel.
3. the pyramids
4. leave his home in Ur
5. to bless him and make him a great nation
6. See the master list on page 362.

JOSEPH AS A SLAVE
Worksheet
1. Genesis 37–40
2. c. 1898 B.C.
3. because of his dreams and the beautiful coat his father gave him
4. They put him in a pit and then sold him to Midianite traders.
5. made him head of all he owned and then put him in prison
6. He was falsely accused by Potiphar's wife.
7. He was in charge of all the other prisoners.
8. He interpreted the dreams of Pharaoh's baker and butler.

ANSWERS

Project 1—Dreams Illustration
For younger students

Project 2—Genesis 37 Summary
For both younger and older students

Project 3—Joseph's Grocery Bag of Many Colors
For younger students

Test
1. that his brothers, mother and father would bow down to him as their ruler
2. because of his dreams and the beautiful coat his father gave him
3. They put him in a pit and then sold him to Midianite traders.
4. one of Pharaoh's officers in Egypt
5. Potiphar's wife falsely accused him.
6. Pharaoh's baker and butler
7. Genesis 37–40
8. c. 1898 B.C.

Review
1. Day 1: Day and night
   Day 2: Heaven and earth
   Day 3: The seas and the land
   Day 4: The sun, moon and stars
   Day 5: The creatures of the sky and sea
   Day 6: The creatures of the dry land, and man
   Day 7: Nothing; He rested.
2. He was unable to grow corps and he became a vagabond and a wanderer.
3. build an ark and fill it with a male and female of all species and then put his family in the ark
4. to be the special tombs of the pharaohs, meant to help them on their journey to the afterlife
5. Genesis 15–17
6. See the master list on page 362.

FAMINE IN EGYPT
Worksheet
1. to interpret Pharaoh's dream
2. There would be seven years of plenty in Egypt and then seven years of famine.
3. He made him second-in-command of all of Egypt.
4. He built storehouses for grain during the years of plenty.
5. Joseph's brothers
6. They were reunited, and Joseph's father Jacob brought his whole household to Egypt to live in the land of Goshen.

Project 1—Genesis 41 Summary
For both younger and older students

Project 2—Signet Rings
For both younger and older students

Project 3—Grain Crops
For both younger and older students

Project 4—Winnowing Fork
For younger students

Test
1. to interpret his dreams
2. There would be seven years of plenty in Egypt and then seven years of famine.
3. He was second-in-command of all of Egypt and built storehouses for grain during the years of plenty.
4. Joseph's brothers; they didn't recognize him and didn't know who he was until he told them.
5. They were reunited, and Joseph's father Jacob brought his whole household to Egypt to live in the land of Goshen.

Review
1. She was her maidservant.
2. to bless him and make him a great nation
3. civil war
4. Menes (also called Narmer)
5. See the master list on page 362.

THE TWELVE TRIBES OF ISRAEL
Worksheet
1. that he would cause a great nation to come from his descendants
2. Abraham's son Isaac and then Isaac's son Jacob
3. Abraham, Isaac and Jacob
4. Israel, twelve
5. They each became a tribe. (When they entered the Promised Land, Levi was given no land and Joseph received a double portion in his sons Ephraim and Manasseh.)
6. The twelve tribes of Israel, also known as Israelites or Jews
7. Jews, chosen

Project 1
For both younger and older students
1. Reuben
2. Simeon

Answers

3. Levi
4. Judah
5. Issachar
6. Zebulun
7. Joseph
8. Benjamin
9. Gad
10. Asher
11. Dan
12. Naphtali

Project 2—Abraham's Family Tree
For both younger and older students
See card

Project 3—Fill in the Blank
For younger students
promised, nation, plan, Jacob, Patriarchs, name,
changed, sons, Israel, Jews, chosen, blessed, faithfulness, unfaithful

Test
1. Genesis 29–36, 46–50
2. c. 1860 B.C.
3. that he would cause a great nation to come from
   his descendants
4. Abraham, Isaac and Jacob
5. Abraham, Isaac and Jacob
6. Israel, twelve
7. Reuben, Simeon, Levi, Judah, Issachar, Zebulun,
   Joseph, Benjamin, Gad, Asher, Dan, Naphtali
8. chosen

Review
1. the Tower of Babel
2. Pharaoh Cheops (also known as Khufu)
3. c. 2091 B.C.
4. Ishmael
5. Lot
6. Isaac
7. See the master list on page 362.

SECOND INTERMEDIATE PERIOD IN EGYPT
Worksheet
1. c. 1800–1570 B.C.
2. dynasties thirteen through seventeen
3. weak
4. smaller areas of Egypt
5. major sites in Nubia to the south

Project 1
For both younger and older students
soul
preserved
a dead body turned hard as stone
to gradually decline or rot
a king of ancient Egypt
mummify
a chemical used for embalming
a jar used to preserve the internal organs
a linen cloth
a box or chest for burying a corpse
a stone coffin
the observances held for a dead person, usually
   at his burial
tomb made of brick and stone
huge stone monument

Project 2—Cat Mummy
For both younger and older students

Project 3—Artist of the Old Empires
For both younger and older students

Project 4—Unwrap Your Own Mummy
For both younger and older students

Test
1. c. 1800–1570 B.C.
2. dynasties thirteen through seventeen
3. weak
4. smaller areas of Egypt
5. major sites in Nubia to the south

Review
1. Genesis 3
2. that He would never again destroy the world by
   flood; a rainbow
3. because they were sinfully proud
4. Genesis 12–13
5. To bless him and make him a great nation if he
   would leave his home and follow God.
6. Lot
7. See the master list on page 362.

ANSWERS

CODE OF HAMMURABI
Worksheet
1. c. 1792-1750 B.C.
2. Babylonia
3. the Tigris and Euphrates rivers and the Garden of Eden
4. Hammurabi the Great
5. laws to protect the weak from the strong and rates of pay and rules of trade
6. carved in stone in cuneiform

Project 1—Cuneiform
For both younger and older students

Project 2—Laws
For both younger and older students
Exodus 22:14—246
Exodus 21:15—195
Exodus 21:16—14
Exodus 21:24—196
Exodus 21:36—251

Project 3—Fill in the Blanks
For younger students
Babylonia, Tigris, rivers, Garden of Eden, sixth, armies, laws, weak, trade, punished, first, first, carved, stone, cuneiform, Sumerians, Mesopotamia

Test
1. Hammurabi
2. the Tigris and Euphrates rivers and the Garden of Eden
3. protect the weak from the strong and rates of pay and rules of trade
4. stone
5. c. 1792-1750 B.C.

Review
1. See the master list on page 362.

HYKSOS INVASION OF EGYPT
Worksheet
1. c. 1730-1570 B.C.
2. Asia
3. horses and chariots
4. Avaris, in the Delta
5. more than one hundred and fifty years

Project 1—Coloring Page
For younger students

Project 2—Hyksos Chariot
For both younger and older students

Project 3—Technology Report
For older students
Possible topics might be: chariot, bronze weaponry, composite bow, upright loom, shaduf

Test
1. c. 1730-1570 B.C.
2. They introduced horses and chariots used in battle.
3. It was the capital.
4. more than one hundred and fifty years

Review
1. Genesis 3
2. Man's every intent was wicked and continuously evil.
3. Day 1: Day and night
   Day 2: Heaven and earth
   Day 3: The seas and the land
   Day 4: The sun, moon and stars
   Day 5: The creatures of the sky and sea
   Day 6: The creatures of the dry land, and man
   Day 7: Nothing; He rested.
4. Canaan
5. See the master list on page 362.

EARLY NEW KINGDOM IN EGYPT
Worksheet
1. c. 1570-1300 B.C.
2. the eighteenth dynasty
3. the Hyksos; the use of new weapons (horses and chariots)
4. Thutmose
5. Hatshepsut
6. Hatshepsut; she ruled behind the scenes then declared herself Pharaoh of Egypt.
7. Amenhotep II
8. Amon and Aton and many other gods

Senefer, a Young Genius in Old Egypt
1. An African boy who lived in Egypt.
2. The days were very hot so they wore little clothing.
3. They were on their way to the market to sell dolls.
4. It was the rich soil where they grew their food.
5. Some people payed with loaves of bread.
6. Egyptian numbers.

ANSWERS

7. People who made their living by writing.
8. Because he was able to write and add numbers.
9. He was missing.
10. He was asleep under a white cloth used to cover the bread at their market stand.
11. The scribes school.
12. A beautiful bird, the ibis who was the Egyptian God of the Scribes.
13. They brought two obelisks, made of stone each thirty meters long.
14. The Pharaoh.
15. They were to point the way to the Egyptian Sun god.
16. He became one of Egypt's greatest mathematicians and builders. He designed the greatest temple in all of Egypt.

Project 1—Egyptian Paddle Doll
For younger students

Project 2—Bird Hat
For older students

Test
1. c. 1570–1300 B.C.
2. the eighteenth dynasty
3. Hatshepsut may have adopted and raised him as her son.
4. Hatshepsut
5. Amenhotep II
6. two of the gods of the Egyptians

Review
1. creatures of the sky and sea
2. The serpent, Satan
3. Adam and Eve
4. Pharaoh Menes (also known as Narmer)
5. The great Pyramid of Giza
6. civil war; the country was split into two sections
7. leave his home in Ur, Mesopotamia, and go to Canaan
8. Cast them out into the wilderness of Beersheba
9. See the master list on page 362.

MOSES' BIRTH
Worksheet
1. They were increasing in number.
2. He made the Israelites slaves, and he ordered the Hebrew midwives to kill all Israelite baby boys when they were born.

3. His parents hid him in a floating basket at the edge of the Nile River.
4. Pharaoh's daughter, Hatshepsut, took him to live with her.
5. that he would grow up to defy them

Project 1—Exodus 2 Summary
For both younger and older students
Answers will vary

Project 2—Basket Weaving
For both younger and older students

Project 3—The Princess and the Nile
For both younger and older students
Answers will vary

Test
1. c. 1525 B.C.
2. Exodus 1–2
3. They were increasing in number.
4. kill all the Israelite baby boys when they were born
5. hid him in a basket along the edge of the Nile River
6. the edict of the pharaoh

Review
1. Civil war; nobles grew powerful and country was split into two sections: north and south.
2. to bless him and make him a great nation
3. because she conceived a child and Sarah could not
4. She turned into a pillar of salt, because she looked back.
5. Genesis 21–22
6. See the master list on page 362.

PLAGUES IN EGYPT
Worksheet
1. c. 1446 B.C.
2. Exodus 3–12
3. through a burning bush, free the Israelites from Egyptian slavery
4. ten
5. Many plagues
6. Each plague was a direct attack on a false Egyptian god.

Project 1—Plague Letter
For both younger and older students

ANSWERS

Project 2—False Gods Attack!
For both younger and older students
Nile changed to blood—*Khnum*
Frogs overran the land—*Heqet*
Gnats overran the land—*Set*
Flies infest Egypt—*Re*
Cattle found dead—*Hathor*
Boils infected the Egyptians—*Isis*
Hail destroyed the crops—*Nut*
Locusts consumed the plants—*Osiris*
Darkness covered the land—*Horus*
Egyptian firstborn children died—*Min*

Project 3—Plague of (Oragami) Frogs
For both younger and older students

Test
1. Exodus 3–12
2. c. 1446 B.C.
3. to free the Israelites from Egyptian slavery
4. ten
5. with many plagues
6. Each plague was a direct attack on a false Egyptian god.

Review
1. He rested.
2. Cain brought fruit, Abel brought the firstborn of his flock.
3. Isaac
4. that his brothers, mother and father would bow down to him as their ruler
5. Israel
6. Hatshepsut
7. See the master list on page 362.

THE EXODUS
Worksheet
1. c. 1446 B.C.
2. Exodus 13–15
3. The firstborn of all families and animals of the Egyptians died.
4. They put blood from a perfect lamb on their doorposts.
5. to leave and go quickly
6. God parted the Red Sea and the Israelites walked through on dry land. When the Egyptians followed, God returned the water and drowned many of the Egyptians.

Project 1—Exodus 14 Summary
For both younger and older students
Answers will vary

Project 2—Moses Play
For older students

Test
1. c. 1446 B.C.
2. Exodus 13–15
3. The firstborn of all families and animals of the Egyptians died.
4. by putting blood from a perfect lamb on their doorposts
5. He parted the Red Sea and the Israelites walked through on dry land. When the Egyptians followed, God returned the water, drowning many of the Egyptians.

Review
1. He disobeyed God in the Garden by eating the fruit of the tree of the knowledge of good and evil.
2. Genesis 4
3. The male and female of every species, and Noah's family
4. civil war; the country was split into two sections
5. cuneiform
6. one of Pharaoh's officers in Egypt who bought Joseph as a slave when Joseph was living there; he made Joseph head of all he owned.
7. Twelve. Reuben, Simeon, Levi, Judah, Issachar, Zebulun, Joseph, Benjamin, Gad, Asher, Dan, Naphtali
8. To save him from being killed
9. See the master list on page 362.

TEN COMMANDMENTS
Worksheet
1. Exodus 19–20
2. 1445 B.C.
3. Moses, Mt. Sinai
4. They showed the Israelites, and us, how God wanted them to live.
5. I. You shall have no other gods before me.
II. You shall not make for yourself a carved image.
III. You shall not take the name of the Lord your God in vain.
IV. Remember the Sabbath day, to keep it holy.
V. Honor your father and your mother.
VI. You shall not murder.
VII. You shall not commit adultery.

ANSWERS

VIII. You shall not steal.

IX. You shall not bear false witness against your neighbor.

X. You shall not covet.

Project 1—Memory Game
For younger students

Project 2—Horns of Moses
For older students

Project 3—Tablets of Stone
For younger students

TIRZAH LITERATURE UNIT

Chapter One
1. cutting grass
2. he has a crippled foot
3. beat them and return them half dead to the mines
4. Manetto, an Amorite, runaway slave from the mines
5. Moses
6. bricks demanded by the Pharaoh; the Pharaoh did give them the straw
7. 12
8. Would Oren be made to work for the taskmasters? Would Pharaoh let them go? She would miss her home. Would Oren survive the journey in the desert?
9. write and learn stories; he is going to learn the stories of Thoth the bird god and this would anger Yahweh
10. she is pregnant
11. a beating
12. her uncle
13. 8
14. death to the first born son
Biblical Events:
   the plagues done through Moses; Moses demanding the Israelites leave; Pharaoh taking away the straw to make bricks; Moses commanding the Israelites to sacrifice a perfect lamb

Chapter 2
1. the sun shone in Goshen but it was dark all over Egypt
2. 15
3. the crops are ruined and the cattle are sick
4. Tirzah's friend, beautiful, and better than a sister she never had

5. people were preparing to leave
6. "Yahweh will surely take care of you, and you will carry my bones up from here." Joseph
7. he is Tirzah's mother's brother; he is trouble, he argues with Moses, demanding proofs and blaming Moses for Pharaoh's cruelties
8. a goat skin tent
9. 3 days
10. four gold Ibises inside a carved box; it could be payment for the Israelites' labors for the Egyptians
11. sacrificing the lamb, following Yahweh's instructions
Biblical Events:
   the plague of darkness

Chapter 3
1. by asking him to come into their home that night to be protected. Pasur does not accept this offer because he wants to die in his own home.
2. two golden necklaces with blue stones
3. roast lamb because they were preparing for the Passover
4. deliverance from Egypt
5. she will live in the land of milk and honey and have many children who will be free
6. lamb, bowls of bitter herbs and unleavened bread
7. they are getting ready to leave, it is nighttime
8. Egyptian men and women weeping, dead bodies being carried on litters, people begging the Israelites to leave
9. bows and arrows, swords, knives and spears
Biblical Events:
   the Passover Meal
   lamb's blood on the doorway
   Egyptians giving jewelry and ornaments to the Hebrews
   Egyptians' firstborns dying
   Egyptians begging them to leave
   the Hebrews leaving Egypt

Chapter 4
1. Shobal wants to go a different route toward Canaan while Jeraheel reminds him that Moses is leading and he is the one chosen by God. Shobal says "Listen to reason."
2. "Moses has brought us this far, we must trust in Yahweh's chosen to lead us the rest of the way."
3. His love and concern for Pasur
4. the presence of Yahweh; moved, leading them, going ahead of them. When the cloud moves, they

ANSWERS

move; when it stops, they stop.
5. a burning red-gold column
6. the direction and possible danger Moses is leading them into
7. "No son of mine will question the chosen of God. You have been listening to that donkey of a Shobal."
8. "Surely Yahweh expects us to show reason and good sense. Why should we walk into a trap?"
9. Why was Yahweh leading them south and not east?

Biblical Events:
God directing them with a pillar of cloud and light; God taking them a longer route

Chapter 5
1. Sorry
2. they are discussing doing something about Moses, getting enough men to split the camp; Ram is concerned about what his father will do
3. she was cross—"Not again? Will that brother of mine never stop?"
4. Yahweh is leading us, and this is the way he has chosen for us to go. You must not turn away to your own route or you will be lost. Yahweh will fulfill his promise to lead us to Canaan.
5. "We are with Moses and Yahweh. We follow the Glory." Moses dismissed them to their camps.
6. The Egyptians are coming toward them with chariots, warriors and the Pharaoh.
7. prayed and quickly packed up
8. "The LORD will fight for you. Stand still and watch."
9. cloud of Glory settled behind them blotting out the entire passageway and the army behind it, parts the sea so the Israelites can cross through

Biblical Events:
grumbling against Moses, Egyptians coming, God parting the Red Sea so the Israelites could come through

Chapter 6
1. Oren: he wanted to walk to see what was around him
   Ram: this was a dream, he admitted he had doubted Moses and Yahweh
   Abishur: anguish over how wrong his father was
   Tirzah: tired and stumbling
2. see page 57
3. Moses taught them a song of praise to Yahweh for his deliverance

4. I will sing to the Lord for he is highly exalted. The horse and its rider he has hurled into the sea.
5. write down all that happened

Biblical Events:
Egyptians getting caught in the sea, people rejoicing, Moses teaching them a song, Miriam and the women dancing.

Chapter 7
1. his inability to trust God and Moses
2. he tells him to ask Moses and Aaron for forgiveness
3. with new wonder and respect
4. he, too, had argued with God but God had shown him kindness and patience; know that Yahweh is with his people to bring them into a good land; "be strong for your people and faithful to Yahweh."

Biblical Events:
Moses meeting with Yahweh at the burning bush

Chapter 8
1. crossing th desert and meeting with the wild Bedouin
2. answers will vary; the shoes kept the heat and absorbed the sweat
3. Moses may have been wrong in spite of the miracle at the Red Sea.
4. Merrie is an Egyptian girl—a niece of Passur. When Passur died, Merrie went to Peleg the Hebrew. She said she knew the Hebrew God was stronger than the Egyptian gods. Hanna said Peleg owed her, so she took Merrie.
5. he showed contempt and anger toward all Egyptians
6. she wonders about the roles being reversed. "Poor Merrie," she thinks.

Biblical Events:
Joseph going to Egypt, Moses killing an Egyptian, the angel of death passing over and killing the first born Egyptians

Chapter 9
1. three days
2. water
3. he threw a branch in it
4. if the people would listen carefully to Yahweh's words and do them, He would not bring on them any of the sicknesses He had sent on the Egyptians.
5. they want bread and meat, the leaders are saying

ANSWERS

we might as well have stayed in Egypt than to have starved in the desert.
6. she puts a small dark line on the basket
7. so she can collect the right amount
8. a pillow for the baby
9. hair color is different, Abishur did not have a quick temper (Abishur is following Moses while Jonathan is quick to follow his father Shobal)

Biblical Events:
   people grumbling about water, tasting the bitter water and Moses fixing it with a branch, complaining about bread and water, collecting manna (an omer for each person), the coming of quail.

Chapter 10
1. white frost, thin white flakes, light as a feather, cool to touch, tiny wafers
2. her father ordered it since they would be busy fixing Shobal's cart, Tirzah said it would be all right, but felt a twinge of guilt.
3. delicious bread with the faint taste of honey
4. "I never thought there wouldn't be. Didn't Moses say we would have bread to eat? Didn't he say not to leave any of it overnight?"
5. there was none left, only stinking worms.
6. they are instructed by Moses to gather a two days' supply, it would not go wormy or smell. There would be no manna lying on the desert floor on Sabbath morning.
7. pelted her with small stones, called to her saying "Dirty dirty Egyptian. Go home. Go home."
8. go in the middle of the day when the sun is up and too hot to be out, dress more like the Hebrew women
9. she does not go to draw water even though the well would not have other woman there
10. Do you think Yahweh brings me a child in my old age? one who will be more comfort to me than I can be to her? She reminds Merrie that Yahweh has brought even her safely here.

Biblical Events:
   collecting manna, instructions concerning manna.

Chapter 11
1. see page 88
2. Ram said, "Yahweh watched over his people here, now."
2. People want to stone Moses because there is no water. He says we have to act like men for the

sake of the women and children.
4. "My father and I will defend him to death."
5. "there was no question in his mind—Moses was Yahweh's servant." He knows Yahweh is leading His people through Moses and he trusts this.
6. Caleb
7. Caleb says, "These bellyachers make me sick."
8. the water rushing from the rock when Moses struck it with his rod.
9. "And what if Yahweh wanted to make it clear that he was behind the whole thing, that he was leading us?"

Biblical Events:
   people grumbling and Moses striking the rock to bring water from it.

Chapter 12
1. the Amalekites
2. Tirzah's worry was "What if they lost? What then? It would be the end of them all."
3. when Moses keeps his arms uplifted, the men press forward to victory, when he grows tired and lowers his arms, they have to retreat.
4. "Yahweh is helping us to fight."
5. "By sunset the battle was over. Joshua and the men of Israel raised a cry of victory."
6. Jerioth hummed "I will sing to the LORD, for he has triumphed gloriously" and Tirzah's father said, "Yahweh is good to his people."

Biblical Events:
   Israel fighting the Amalekites, Moses holding up his arms with help from others and being introduced to Joshua.

Chapter 13
1. Moses' wife, two sons and his father-in-law
2. His wife was tall and dark-skinned, straight nose, large, dark eyes and white, even teeth. His sons were dark-skinned with a look of those used to the hard life of the desert. His father-in-law was wearing rich robes, and he looked like a chieftain.
3. Moses ran out to meet them, and he shouted to everyone who they were.
4. answers will vary
5. persuade Shobal to be satisfied with some small restitution for the death of the ox.
6. "She is almost black, a Midianite." "Just think, Moses married to someone like that." Miriam and Aaron were not happy to see Moses' wife. Miriam was disgusted.
7. a flute by Benj

ANSWERS

Biblical Events:
  Moses family coming to Moses; people grumbling— too many cases for Moses and Aaron to judge them alone.

Chapter 14
1. a judge over 50 people
2. answers will vary
3. on the plain before the mountain of Yahweh
4. dense billows of smoke covered the mountain top, yet it seemed to burn with flames beneath the cloud; jagged streaks of lightning lit up the sky; thunderclaps crashed with terrifying loudness
5. "This is Yahweh's promise: You yourselves have seen what I did in Egypt . . ."
6. bringing the bulls to the altar for sacrifice
7. blood
Biblical Events:
  men being chosen to be officials over the people, to serve as judges; God proclaiming his covenant with his people

Chapter 15
1. how many days since Moses had gone up into the mountain of God.
2. Where is Moses? Should they choose a new leader?
3. Manetto took her to his camp. It looks as if the whole camp has gone crazy over this new god.
4. "O help me, Yahweh. Please help me." Ram comes and they run away.
5. after Moled and Ram's father went down to the camp to reason, they found out they were outnumbered by the others, violence began and they had to flee.
6. they could hear shouts and music of celebration; they laid their earrings and necklaces at Aaron's feet and got him to melt them down; the bull calf came out of the fire; they are saying this has brought them out.
7. yes
Biblical Events:
  the Hebrews wanting an idol and the worshipping they did around it.

Chapter 16
1. they are going to meet Moses, who is coming down the mountain
2. her mother was in pain and could not go on
3. her mother goes into labor
4. "Yahweh is good. Whatever he wills is right."
5. cleaning up, brushing Sorry

6. the baby is small and their mother is not doing well
7. Moses is angry, he broke the tables, had the calf ground up and sprinkled powder in the water, made the people drink the bitter water, killing of many rebels against Yahweh.
8. he was put to death at the hand of a Levite neighbor
9. Tirzah's mother was sleeping peacefully as well as the child
Biblical Events:
  Moses coming down from the mountain and the events following that regarding the golden cow

Chapter 17
1. go down to the camp and nurse the sick
2. to not go down or to let Merrie go with her
3. fever and boils, death
4. cool the fevered body with water mixed with fever herbs, clean the sores
5. 7 or more
6. she dies
7. Merrie stays in the sun with Hanna, she gets very sick
8. Tirzah and Jerioth
9. The Promised Land
Biblical Events:
  The plague

Chapter 18
1. the death of his father and thoughts that he could have saved him
2. reminding him that Ram knew about guilt, too; he had once followed Shobal and Jonathan; also reminding him that "only Yahweh knows what might have been; you did what was right before Yahweh."
3. 3 coneys
4. full grown, long, black whiskers, broad nails on each toe for digging, not much longer than a rabbit, hard to catch, black and brown skins
5. for the building of the new tabernacle
6. by bringing him food
7. a fossil of a fish and seashell embedded in the rock
8. awe and peace, "how great Yahweh was"
Biblical Events:
  building of the Tabernacle, Noah's ark

Chapter 19
1. the commandment to not misuse the name of the LORD

ANSWERS

2. the new tabernacle
3. "Everything is changed now. We are a nation now, the People of the Covenant. We have the laws of Yahweh for living rightly. It's a whole new way of life, a good one."
4. the Passover
5. through song
6. weak, she mourned the death of Hannah; some people still slight (snub) her
7. it makes her back stiffen and her voice go unsteady; she does not like the idea, even if Merrie does follow Yahweh.

Biblical Events:
   receiving and learning the Ten Commandments, the Tabernacle and the Passover.

Chapter 20
1. for blaspheming the name of God
2. "... His words are just and must be obeyed."
3. discontent, grumbling; people want meat not manna, they say life was better in Egypt
4. the quail and the plague
5. "People are so cruel ... Can you imagine blaming the girl for being Egyptian? She is more uncomplaining, more faithful to Yahweh, than the one who spurns her."
6. Aaron and Miriam are angry with Moses over his foreign wife.
7. She was put out of the Tent of Meeting, she had become a leper, God was punishing her for speaking against Moses
8. Leah had spoken against Moses' wife, she was guilty of Miriam's sin; she did not want Ram to marry Merrie
9. Ram and Merrie will get married

Biblical Events:
   people grumbling; quail and the plague sent; Miriam getting leporsy for speaking against Moses' wife

Chapter 21
1. a raid, or worse, a mutiny in the camp; some people turn away from following Yahweh over the least hard thing.
2. the men Moses sent to spy out the land; a month
3. a good land, flowing with milk and honey, big and sweet grapes, good soil, well-watered, walled cities, large giant-like people, people too strong
4. "There is no need to fear. Listen to Moses. We can take possession of the land. We are well able to overcome it."

5. women tore their clothes, men shook their fists, some wailed, others shouted in anger, crowds got out of hand, confusion sets in.
6. Tirzah remembers that Yaweh is giving them the land, he is still with them, his cloud was still there. Leah was crying and full of fear. She said Yahweh was angry with them—and she was afraid of Tirzah dying.
7. stone Moses and get a new leader
8. Do not rebel against the LORD. If Yahweh is pleased with us, he will give us this land. Do not be afraid of the people ... the Lord is with us."
9. the cloud of Glory seemed to swell with burning fire at the Tent of Meeting.
10. Yahweh's love and mercy are great. He forgives sin and rebellion, yet he does not leave the guilty unpunished. Only Caleb and Joshua and the children you said would be taken as plunder will enter the Promised Land.
11. he says he and her mother will prepare them for the day that will come when they shall enter the land; they will teach them all they can, as long as Yahweh wills it; Yahweh forgives and He will care for us; although we die here in the desert our lives can be good ones.
12. Tirzah begins to sing the song and Abishur plays his flute while the others join Tirzah in the singing.

Biblical Events:
   Spies in the Promised Land, men returning with the grapes and reporting what they saw, Joshua and Caleb describing all the good, the other ten speaking of the fearful things, people responding in fear and distrust of God, Joshua reminding them that God is with them and the land is theirs, the people about to stone them, God declares that only the children of the Isrealites will enter the land as well as Joshua and Caleb.

Test
1. Mt. Sinai
2. I. You shall have no other gods before me.
   II. You shall not make for yourself a carved image.
   III. You shall not take the name of the Lord your God in vain.
   IV. Remember the Sabbath day, to keep it holy.
   V. Honor your father and your mother.
   VI. You shall not murder.
   VII. You shall not commit adultery.
   VIII. You shall not steal.
   IX. You shall not bear false witness against your

ANSWERS

neighbor.
  X. You shall not covet.
3. See the master list on page 362.

AMENHOTEP IV AND MONOTHEISM
Worksheet
1. c. 1361–1344 B.C.
2. the eighteenth dynasty
3. Nefertiti
4. Aton
5. the belief in only one god
6. to relate himself to the god Aton instead of Amon
7. Akhnaton's mother

Project 1—Coloring Page
For younger students

THE GOLDEN GOBLET LITERATURE UNIT
Chapter One
1. Answers will vary
2. Ranofer
3. working with gold and a crucible
4. that the little ingot he was working on would e part of something splendid
5. He wished he had never heard of Geb. His father died. Gebu is his step-brother.
6. it is during the season of growing, cool air, pleasant wintertime
7. a Babylonian; he is not pleased to see him, he is just barely pleasant, he disliked him
8. Gebu never drank the wine, he poured it on the pavement. This made Ranofer uneasy "it was not healthy"
9. gold in small quantities
10. he has a half-brother Gebu, he is not an apprentice to Rekh, he must hand over his money, he lives with his brother, his father is dead
11. Ibini and Gebu were the ones stealing the gold

Chapter 2
1. mummy-shaped outline of Libyan cliffs, awesome Valley of the Tombs, ancient city on the other side of the gateways, tombs, white washed jumble of workshops, low mud-brick buildings, high-walled garden palace
2. eyelids rimmed with black paint
3. glassmakers, papermakers, weavers, carpenters, potters, sculptors, painters, embalmers, masons, coffin builders; for the tombs
4. noisily jocular, ferociously quiet
5. papyrus

6. May your spirit/soul be happy
7. accusing Gebu, being a part of the crime
8. that he wants to be a goldsmith, to be apprenticed to Zau, but he only works
9. Street of the Crooked Dog
10. to defy Gebu, leave his house, discover gold, make beautiful necklaces for the Pharaoh to buy

Chapter 3
1. The sun
2. "it will quiet your rumblings, as the man said when he tossed his right leg to the crocodile"
3. each worker accepting his portion of gold from Ranofer, then starting their tasks
4. to soothe
5. it is the incident with Merya "You are not striking the metal true" Ranofer shows him how to do this. Also when he makes the gold leaves
6. Make 50 gold leaves for a necklace
7. yes he does; he does not take the wineskin
8. with anger and violence
9. to not work for Rekh and to be an apprentice with Gebu, who is a stonecutter

Chapter 4
1. his father's ba
2. it was a thank you gift for his father
3. he tells the story of how he helped his father tally the mistress's cupboard
4. he wants Heqet to tell Rekh that Ibini is stealing the gold
5. there would be gold in the wineskins and it would take awhile for Ibini to gather more gold
6. roaring good humor
7. "Though it is of small importance now, eh?"
8. copper ring coin
9. knowing Wenamon was looking at him made every hair on his head pricked
10. get food

Chapter 5
1. good humor
2. He was a tomb robber.
3. the ba of the dead pharaoh was starving, destitute in the land of the west
4. Ibini was gone
5. making a few gold leaves for Lady Hatasu's bracelet
6. Gebu lets him go—he no longer is going to use him

Old Testament and Ancient Egypt / 353

ANSWERS

7. he was finished working for Rekh and he would work at the stonecutters shop
8. Ranofer asks to leave Gebu to build a small house, cut down papyrus, he needs him to buy a donkey; Gebu laughs at him

Chapter 6
1. the stonecutter's shop is loud, dust covered and cluttered by stone slabs
2. great sarcophagi were built, carvings were not done
3. an old man who works at the shop cutting stone; warning him of Pai; his right thumb was hacked off at the knuckle
4. he looks like he is made of twisted wire, he looks disdainfully at Ranofer, he is loud
5. answers will vary—"His task was so small, so monotonous, so utterly lacking in interest that he found it almost impossible to keep even part of his mind on it."
6. doesn't want to damage his hands, which he needs to do goldsmith work
7. Gebu takes his wages
8. squeaky door shut cautiously; it reminds him of another night when he thought his father's ba had come to help him
9. he does but eventually they stop

Chapter 7
1. fall: Nile overflowed its banks and spread over the fields; winter: waters withdrew, leaving behind a thick new layer of fertile mud; after winter: crops grew
2. every available man went out into the fields to gather, temple building ceased
3. "well, you're quite a stranger these days, as the capterpillar said to the butterfly."
4. if they met often, in the evening or midday, Heqet could tell Ranofer what he has learned at the gold house
5. he willingly shares his food
6. he wants it but thinks Heqet is pitying him
7. he stops them from fighting over food
8. straggly eyebrows, sharp eye, walks around with his donkey, mild voice, shrill cackle
9. a time with good friends and food

Chapter 8
1. heat swells and river shrinks; they meet as often as they can for instruction in goldwork
2. to be glad to be learning a trade even if he doesn't

like it, so he can have a future; through experience of not learning a trade
3. to go to Zau the Master's place to fetch a stake
4. that he will talk to Zau, Zau will remember him and that Zau will make Gebu release Ranofer to him
5. "it was almost another world" high walls, palms and acacias showing above them, no dust, very quiet, pervading fragrance of flowers and wealth, grand villas, large gardens and vineyards, purple vines
6. he is a well respected goldsmith—Ranofer knew him because his father knew him
7. to come and watch him work
8. he remembers his 20 year friendship with Thurta, Ranofer's father and he remembers the work that Ranofer did; he tells Ranofer he can come learn for free; Ranofer cannot dissolve his apprenticeship
9. "You must reshape our life into some other form. When you have done this, come to me again and I will teach you."
10. He had forgotten his coppers and Gebu was violent with Ranofer

Chapter 9
1. fine head clothes, sandals, expensive ointments
2. he realizes Gebu looks well to-do; he has grown rich very suddenly
3. Ranofer will watch Gebu and see where he goes
4. follow Gebu's companions and spy, too
5. smear a mixture on his shoulders where Gebu beat him
6. do not follow Gebu at night, when full night has fallen
7. he follows Gebu
8. no, Gebu only went to the wine shop and stayed awhile before going home

Chapter 10
1. a voice like a hyena; no
2. Heqet's story was the same as Ranofer's; no
3. a week; "they are lying low—avoiding each other"
4. from a dog and possibly Gebu
5. it is wrinkled
6. because Gebu is behaving so innocently and Wenemon seems very devoted to his wife
7. gold; night time
8. a truncated passage or a small room in a location that does not make sense; with a blow to Ranofer's head and yelling

ANSWERS

9. he is hungry and there is food upstairs in this room
10. a golden goblet of Thutmose; it is over 100 years old; Gebu has stolen it from a tomb
11. Gebu's door had been shut with a seal, Ranofer had broken it and Gebu would realize this

Chapter 11
1. braver then he has been before; wetted clay crumbs with his spit, softened and mixed them with a careful finger; pressed them into a crack and smoothed the edges, used the sliver of a palm fiber off the torch handle for an engraving tool, scratched in the missing bits of the scarab mark
2. drunk; he doesn't see it is a fake seal
3. being free, Gebu hanging, telling people of Gebu's crime, pharaoh thanking him, Zau being ordered to take Ranofer as a student
4. who would he tell? who would listen to him?
5. Setma and Gebu quarreling bitterly; Gebu walking away and saying Setma was finished; gold
6. the goblet wrapped in old clothes; yes; he thinks it is insane
7. he looked all over for the goblet

Chapter 12
1. should he tell Heqet about the goblet; he can not tell anyone about the goblet
2. that Gebu and Wenamon will use the room themselves for hiding the gold they steal
3. Festival—the greatest feast day of year; every one will feast and drink at the Pharaoh's expense
4. he sees Gebu and Wenamon in a shed where pots are dried, he hears Gebu say "a curse on the festival" and "meet me at daybreak beside the broken tree. it is safe enough now", as well as more conversation about Gebu's plan
5. they are going to the valley of the Tombs of the Kings while everyone is feasting
6. How was the crime found out? The tomb robbers were followed into the tomb.
7. no
8. he alone will follow Gebu and Wenamon into the Tombs of the Kings

Chapter 13
1. the stars were still out—it was not full daytime yet
2. no—he is nervous and afraid; (1) he remembers "the chilling knowledge" of what lies ahead; (2) he thinks "the chances are slim he would ever taste

another honey cake"; (3) while he walks across they courtyard "everything in him wants to run the other way; (4) when he opens the gate he is shaking all over, he wishes he were someone else
3. he loved the pharaoh and the gods of Egypt and he wanted to be free
4. digging at something; a crevice opening big enough for one man's body, secret entrance
5. it was a passage not another storage chamber
6. overslept; by Heqet telling Ancient the stories from yesterday; follow after him
7. a great black vulture; Ranofer

Chapter 14
1. it would be too scary with Gebu and Wenemon as company
2. a life-sized wooden statue; so it couldn't stare at the two men while they stole things
3. household furniture, armchairs, beds, honey jars, painted boxes, wicker trunk, perfumed garments, winecups, scent jars, jeweled collars and armbands
4. Huda and Tuda, the parents of the queen of Egypt
5. Ranofer's elbow grazed a table and tilted a vase, it fell and made a noise; he lunged a box at Gebu "with all his might."
6. yes

Chapter 15
1. about Gebu and Wenemon digging the passage long ago, stealing from Rekh and breaking into other tombs
2. guard the place where Gebu and Wenemon are so Ranofer could get help
3. Zau's place; no
4. the palace
5. he is caught
6. no, they think he is a babbling boy
7. Qa-nefer, favorite pet to the queen
8. into the palace of the pharaoh

Chapter 16
1. rug of many colors, chairs made of cedarwood, cushions of fine linen, folded stool with a leopard belt, flowered twined wine jar, blue goblet, basket heaped with fruit
2. the queen
3. "what was the object leaning against the north wall of parents burial chamber?"
4. her father's oaken staff; yes
5. "Fetch soldiers, send them to the valley! Make haste!"

ANSWERS

6. Count Zobek; chief cupbearer to the queen; about the golden goblet, where he could be found
7. his household men; cupboard against the wall in the scroll room
8. to make sure Ranofer is thanked; food, rest, bandaged, oiled and dressed nicely
9. yes; returned to the tomb and put in order
10. beside the queen on a carved table
11. yes
12. a donkey; laughter of surprise and pleasure
13. new sandals, rings for his friends, six fine goldsmith hammers and a good donkey
14. "I have reshaped my life into another form."

Project 2—Senet
For both younger and older students

Project 3—Fill in the Blanks
For younger students
18th, Nefertiti, Akhetaton, Thebes, Aton, Amon, name, Amenhotep, Akhnaton, Aton, Aton, monotheism, decrease, Aton, Amon, Tiy, Nefertiti, mystery, Nefertiti, Tutankhaton, name, Amon

Test
1. c. 1361–1344 B.C.
2. Nefertiti
3. He possibly wanted to decrease the power of the priests of Amon.
4. Akhnaton

Review
1. the creatures of the sky and sea
2. Genesis 3
3. Genesis 11
4. Pharaoh Menes (also known as Narmer)
5. Sarah
6. Lot
7. See the master list on page 362.

REIGN OF TUTANKHAMON
Worksheet
1. c. 1333–1323 B.C.
2. the discovery of Tutankhamon's tomb; Howard Carter
3. Nine
4. nine years
5. eighteen
6. to signify Egypt's change from monotheistic worship of Aton to the worship of Amon and other gods

7. because of the many treasures that were found, which help us better understand Egypt's past

TUT'S MUMMY LOST . . . AND FOUND!
Chapter One
1. eighteen
2. The Land of the Dead is where the Egyptians believed one's spirit went upon death. There the dead person would do all the things they loved to do when they were alive. It was a place of perpetual happiness.
3. They needed to take food, furniture, clothing, jewelry, and games. Anything they used in their earthly life, including, most of all, the body.
4. The spirit cannot move on without its body. Mummies were made to dry out bodies so they would last forever.
5. seventy days.
6. In a secret underground tomb, where grave robbers could break in and steal all the treasures or disturb the body.
7. Look on pages 10 & 12 for examples.
8. to enable the mummy's spirit to speak, see, and hear
9. The Egyptians put their faith in earthly treasure, spending their lives storing up for their death. The Bible teaches just the opposite. All our earthly treasures will rot and decay, but our faith in God never will.

Chapter Two
1. a scientist who digs in the earth to find clues to the past
2. temples, wall paintings, statues of animals and gods, and mummies
3. a valley where many tombs were discovered. They hoped to find Tutankhamon.
4. Howard Carter

Chapter Three
1. Lord Carnarvon
2. Terrible. It was rocky, burning, dry, hot and dusty.
3. Carter begged Carnarvon for one more try.
4. They found a step and then another, until they saw a whole stairway leading to a secret door.
5. Lord Carnarvon, who was in England

Chapter Four
1. Incredible sights! Golden chariots, jeweled chests, couches in the shapes of animals, vases, and statues. Everything glittered with gold!

ANSWERS

2. Sweet from ancient funeral flowers.
3. Treasure, specifically two statues of the king, big as life, and Tutankhamon's golden throne.

Chapter Five
1. It was the greatest treasure ever found.
2. King Tut
3. A huge golden cabinet. Inside the cabinet was a great stone box. In the box were three coffins nested one inside the other.
4. He died from a bad insect bite. The newspapers said it was a mummy's curse. They said Tut was angry because his tomb was opened.

Project 1—King Tut Mask
For both younger and older students

Project 2—King Tut, Tomb of Treasure
For both younger and older students

Test
1. c. 1333-1323 B.C.
2. the tomb of Tutankhamon
3. nine
4. nine years
5. to signify Egypt's change from monotheistic worship of Aton to the worship of Amon and other gods
6. because of the many treasures that were found, which help us better understand Egypt's past

Review
1. He promised to never again destroy the earth with a flood.
2. the building of the pyramids
3. Genesis 15-17
4. He told him to sacrifice his only true son Isaac.
5. Reuben, Simeon, Levi, Judah, Issachar, Zebulun, Joseph, Benjamin, Gad, Asher, Dan, Naphtali
6. the sixth ruler of Babylon, a lawmaker
7. with horses and chariots
8. in Pharaoh's family
9. See the master list on page 362.

LATER NEW KINGDOM IN EGYPT
Worksheet
1. c. 1300-1090 B.C.
2. Egypt regained power and influence in Asia.
3. Ramses I
4. Ramses I, Seti, Ramses II
5. the Battle of Kadesh

6. The temple at Abu Simbel and seven major temples in Nubia

Project 1—Visit to a Temple
For both younger and older students

Project 2—Quest for Eternity
For both younger and older students

Project 3—Travel Brochure
For both younger and older students

Test
1. c. 1300-1090 B.C.
2. It regained its power and influence in Asia.
3. the nineteenth dynasty
4. the Battle of Kadesh
5. Ramses II

Review
1. Reuben, Simeon, Levi, Judah, Issachar, Zebulun, Joseph, Benjamin, Gad, Asher, Dan, Naphtali
2. I. You shall have no other gods before me.
   II. You shall not make for yourself a carved image.
   III. You shall not take the name of the Lord your God in vain.
   IV. Remember the Sabbath day, to keep it holy.
   V. Honor your father and your mother.
   VI. You shall not murder.
   VII. You shall not commit adultery.
   VIII. You shall not steal.
   IX. You shall not bear false witness against your neighbor.
   X. You shall not covet.
Exodus 19-20
3. See the master list on page 362.

DAVIDIC KINGDOM
Worksheet
1. I and II Samuel and I Chronicles
2. c. 1011-971 B.C.
3. Bethlehem
4. David
5. Goliath
6. The people of Israel cheered David more than King Saul.
7. Kill him
8. forty years

ANSWERS

Project 1—Draw David's Life
For both younger and older students

Project 2—I Samuel 16 Summary
For both younger and older students

Project 3—Who Were the Philistines?
For both younger and older students

Test
1. I and II Samuel and I Chronicles
2. c. 1011–971 B.C.
3. David
4. The people of Israel cheered David more than King Saul.
5. A giant Philistine warrior
6. forty years

Review
1. Noah
2. the Ziggurat of Marduk at Babylon
3. tombs for the pharaohs which they thought would help them on their journey into the afterlife
4. Genesis 12–13
5. great irrigation projects began, trade resumed with Syria and Palestine, and great hieroglyphics
6. He invited them to come to Egypt (with their father Jacob) to live.
7. Hatshepsut
8. Honor your father and your mother.
9. See the master list on page 362.

SOLOMON'S REIGN
Worksheet
1. I Kings 1–11, II Chronicles 1–9
2. c. 971–931 B.C.
3. Solomon
4. wisdom
5. to build a temple to worship God
6. the Queen of Sheba
7. He turned from God and became wicked.

Project 1—Building the Temple
For both younger and older students

Project 2—Fill in the Blanks
For younger students
David, king, dream, wisdom, wisdom, riches, wisdom, wisest, peace, plan, temple, gold, artists, Moriah, Covenant, wisdom, distant, temple, Queen, Sheba, questions, blessed, women, wicked, forty, king

Project 3—Art of the Temple
For older students

Test
1. c. 971–931 B.C.
2. I Kings 1–11, II Chronicles 1–9
3. Solomon
4. He asked for wisdom.
5. He turned from God and became wicked.
6. Rehoboam

Review
1. See the master list on page 362.

ALEXANDER THE GREAT CONQUERS EGYPT
Worksheet
1. c. 332 B.C.
2. Cambyses; the local Egyptian deities
3. Alexander
4. because of their hatred of the Persians
5. that the strongest one of them should reign
6. one of Alexander's generals; he became ruler of Egypt.

Project 1—Persians
For older students

Project 2—Alexander the Great Triumphant
For younger students

Project 3—Fill in the Blanks
For younger students
Persian, deities, rebelled, fourth, king, Egypt, hatred, Alexandria, generals, four, Ptolemy I, 250, Ptolemys, Cleopatra

Project 4—Alexandria: A Reading
For older students

Test
1. c. 332 B.C.
2. a Persian ruler who conquered Egypt in 525 B.C.
3. because they hated the Persians who had ruled them brutally
4. Ptolemy I

Review
1. Genesis 1–2
2. because he murdered his brother Abel
3. Narmer

ANSWERS

4. to bless him and make him a great nation
5. God turned her into a pillar of salt.
6. They envied him for the dreams he had and for the beautiful coat his father had given him.
7. He set up storehouses for grain during the years of plenty before the famine.
8. A false Egyptian god
9. when the Israelites left Egypt
10. See the master list on page 362.

EGYPT FALLS TO ROME
Worksheet
1. c. 30 B.C.
2. Julius Caesar
3. Brutus and others, because Julius Caesar had no right to rule the Roman Empire which he had claimed
4. three leaders
5. Mark Antony
6. They lost their kingdom in a war against Octavius.
7. Caesar Augustus
8. They had little power, and their culture gradually disappeared.

Project 1—Caesar and Cleopatra
For both younger and older students

Project 2—Cleopatra's History
For older students

Project 3—Cleopatra's Wig
For both younger students

Project 4—Cleopatra's Necklace
For both younger students

Project 5—Caesar's Breastplate
For both younger students

Test
1. c. 30 B.C.
2. a Roman general who helped Pharoah Cleopatra in an Egyptian civil war
3. Brutus and others, because Julius Caesar had no right to rule the Roman Empire which he had claimed
4. Antony and Cleopatra
5. because they lost their kingdom to Octavius
6. Caesar Augustus

Review
1. to scatter them over the earth because they were sinfully proud of their accomplishments
2. the Old Kingdom
3. Genesis 12-13
4. kill him as a sacrifice
5. interpreted Pharaoh's dreams
6. the Patriarchs
7. his code of laws
8. the use of horses and chariots as weapons of war
9. Amenhotep II
10. See the master list on page 362.

THE PHARAOHS OF ANCIENT EGYPT
The Rediscovery of Ancient Egypt
1. a company of French soldiers from Napoleon Bonaparte's Egyptian Expeditionary Force
2. A chunk of polished stone, 2-feet across and 3-feet high. The flat surface was divided into three sections, each section being engraved with a block of writing. On the top were hieroglyphics, across the bottom was Greek, and in the middle a language unrecognized.
3. It was the key to the lost history of ancient Egypt. Because the message was written in three languages, hieroglyphics were finally able to be translated.
4. The Bible and also Greek and Roman historians, such as Herodotus, spoke of Ancient Egypt.
5. 1. being able to read the language 2. scientific excavation of buried cities and objects
6. When an Italian peasant uncovered an ancient wall that was part of Pompeii, people began to dig for objects.
7. 1. Hieroglyphics 2. Demotic 3. Greek
8. Once we were able to translate the hieroglyphics we were able to learn about Egyptian history. Before this we knew little.

The First Egyptians and Dead Demigods
1. They found that they were small, slender people with dark, wavy hair. They lived by hunting and believed in life after death. They knew this because of what the people buried with them to be used in the next life.
2. flood its banks
3. the rich black river-borne silt that was deposited along the river banks every year
4. It started a chain reaction of causing the people to become more civilized and live in small villages. They no longer spent all their time in

ANSWERS

search of food as they were able to grow more.

5. 1. Delta of Lower Egypt / Bee King 2. Middle Egypt / Reed King 3. Upper Egypt / Hawk King
6. with the first Pharaoh of Ancient Egypt, Menes
7. They believed that life would go on much as it had on earth, as long as one's earthly body was preserved. If not, a man's spirit would wander for eternity. Much care was spent preserving the body before burial.
8. gods

The Good God—Pharaoh Cheops
1. Pharaoh Cheops
2. It took 20 years of 100,000 men laboring constantly.
3. see pages 45-47 for description
4. wigs to shield their heads from the valley's hot sun, and eye paint to protect against the sun's glare
5. the place an army of scribes worked keeping Pharaoh's tax lists. They kept lists of those who paid their taxes and checked incoming payments of produce and livestock
6. hundreds of deities
7. That they are false. There is only one true God.
8. a rectangular flat-topped tomb made of brick
9. Imhotep built a tomb for Pharaoh Zoser.
10. limestone quarried from valley cliffs
11. chisels, copper saws, rope, measuring tapes made of knotted string, sledges and rollers
12. First the huge blocks of stone were unloaded and dragged to the workshops. There they were measured, cut and bound with ropes. Once bound, they were levered up onto rollers or a sledge. A crew of forty men was then harnessed to the ropes, like horses and ordered to pull the stone. Ramps had been built along the side of the pyramid and then men would pull the stones up to the place they needed to be.

I Show Thee a Land Topsy-Turvy...
1. half a dozen ancient papyrus scrolls
2. They described a land in turmoil.
3. They claimed Pharaoh was the Son of Ra and no longer an independent god. As priest they were the earthly representatives of Ra, so they gained influence.
4. They claimed that estates allotted to them by Pharaoh were not just theirs for life. Upon their death, instead of the land reverting to the crown, they began to will it to their heirs.
5. They said that Osiris, god of the dead, had

promised life after death to every worthy man. It no longer depended on whether or not Pharaoh needed their services in the next life.
6. God of the Dead
7. About 400 years after Cheops's death, the defiant nobles grew so strong that the central authority collapsed. There was a period of anarchy, known as the Dark Ages, where little pharaohs were ruling their own domains, causing division in the valley.
8. Pharaoh Amenemhet
9. an obscure race from the regions of the east
10. Prince Ahmise who became the first Pharaoh of the eighteenth dynasty
11. 1. The time of anarchy convinced them of a need for a strong central government, under a Pharaoh whose divine authority must never be questioned. 2. The Hyksos invasion taught them that their isolated valley was not safe from attack. She needed an army.

His Majesty, Herself—Queen Hatshepsut
1. Her little daughter and stepson became Pharaoh and Queen upon her husband's death. After seeming to go along with this, one day she just declared herself Pharaoh.
2. Some of Amon's priests and some nobles and officials were scandalized at the idea of a woman pharaoh.
3. He was banished to the gloomy interior of the temple of Amon. His head was shaved, he was given a simple linen kilt and entered training as an apprentice priest.
4. Hatshepsut's chief architect
5. myrrh gum, living myrrh trees, ebony, pure ivory, green gold, cinnamon wood, incense, eye paint, apes, monkeys, dogs, skins of southern panthers, natives and their children
6. She died. Some believed Thutmose broke free, reseized the throne and murdered Hatshepsut.

The Smiter of the Asiatics —Pharaoh Thutmose the Third
1. Thutmose led his men to fight the Syrians. Thutmose led his men into battle "like a flame of fire." He drove his chariot with force and the Syrians just stood and watched Thutmose and his soldiers. Suddenly the Syrians broke ranks and fled.
2. The Syrian soldiers had fled inside their city, even tying their garments into ropes to climb over the

ANSWERS

locked gate of Megiddo. The soldiers and their families were barricaded behind the walls, so the Egyptians decided to starve their enemy into submission. A few weeks later the Syrians surrendered.

3. 2,000 horses, 924 chariots, 2,000 cattle, 1,921 Asiatic bulls, 20,500 additional animals, 2,000 prisoners of war.
4. He gave Amkon three Syrian towns and the right to their taxes. He also gave other land and cattle from the Syrian herd.
5. his son
6. He was history's first general.
7. by three tomb robbers, one whose name was Abderrassul

The Criminal of Akhetaton—Pharaoh Akhnaton

1. by a peasant woman digging for sebakh, a soil that acts as a fertilizer
2. They opened the door to a little known time period in history, known as the Armana Heresy.
3. Because of all the vast beautiful building projects he had done. He lived a life of luxury and splendor.
4. Queen Tiy
5. Because of gifts given by prior pharaohs, they had enormous wealth.
6. Aton, this new god was the sun itself.
7. It undermined the High Priest of Amon's power.
8. He was a god that could be understood and worshiped by diverse people of vassal states. This god warmed the lands of all people.
9. Aton
10. Nefertiti
11. When he was about 24 years old, three years after his marriage.
12. The "City of the Horizon" that Amenhotep the Third built for Aton.
13. He wanted to be associated with Aton and that meant "He is beneficial of Aton."
14. He was notifying Egypt that Aton had replaced Amon as the crown-supported first god of Egypt.
15. The Amon priesthood was disbanded, Karnak closed and all the temple holders were to revert to the crown. Amon's name was erased from all monuments or temples. He also abandoned the city of Thebes. The City of the Horizon was to be the new capital of Egypt.
16. They became more lifelike, including the pharaoh. No longer was the pharaoh to be painted larger than life, but as he was truly seen.

17. Aton
18. It caused unrest among the people. They were used to worshiping many gods.
19. His mother Tiy came to speak to her son about the unsettledness in Egypt. They argued for days. Tiy won. He fell gravely ill and Nefertiti was banished to live in exile.
20. The nine-year old half-brother of Akhnaton, Tutankhaton.
21. The priest of Amon forced him to change it to Tutankhamon.
22. 18
23. November 29, 1922
24. He may have been one of the least important pharaohs, but this tomb appears to have been untouched. It was filled with treasure beyond compare.

The Beginning of the End— Pharaoh Rameses the Second

1. Pharaoh Haremhab, Rameses was his vizier
2. Seti, Ramses the Second
3. He retook lands lost by prior pharaohs.
4. Rameses was left alone to face 2,500 Hittite charioteers, with only his personal bodyguard to defend him. He tied his reins around his waist to leave his hands free and charged forth. Eventually his men came to his aid and began to fight. The battle ended and Rameses claimed victory even though he had not captured the city.
5. Seven Great Royal wives and untold numbers of secondary wives. His marriage to his Hittite bride sealed a treaty signed 16 years earlier with the Hittites.
6. a new capital he called Tanis
7. 85
8. They invaded the lands and the Egyptians fought for a while and then seemed to give up. Indo-Europeans
9. Egypt suffered a series of disastrously low floods causing famine to be severe.
10. Alexander the Great. Greece.
11. Queen Cleopatra
12. the Arabs in the name of their prophet Mohammed

ANSWERS

OLD TESTAMENT AND ANCIENT EGYPT
HISTORY CARDS *Master List*

Creation | *Genesis 1-2*
The Fall in the Garden | *Genesis 3*
Cain and Abel | *Genesis 4*
The Flood | *Genesis 6-9*
Tower of Babel | *Genesis 11*
Unification of Upper and Lower Egypt
The Old Kingdom in Egypt
First Intermediate Period in Egypt
    | c. 2200-2050 B.C.
Call of Abram | *Genesis 12, 13* | c. 2091 B.C.
God's Covenant with Abraham
    | *Genesis 15-17* | c. 2082 B.C.
Hagar and Ishmael | *Genesis 16, 21* | c. 2080 B.C.
Sodom and Gomorrah | *Genesis 18-19* | c. 2080 B.C.
Birth and Sacrifice of Isaac | *Genesis 21-22*
    | 2066 B.C.
The Middle Kingdom in Egypt | c. 2050-1800 B.C.
Joseph as a Slave | *Genesis 37-40* | c. 1898 B.C.
Famine in Egypt | *Genesis 41-47* | c. 1878-1871 B.C.
The Twelve Tribes of Israel |
Genesis 29-36, 46-50 | c. 1860 B.C.
Second Intermediate Period in Egypt
    | c. 1800-1570 B.C.
Code of Hammurabi | c. 1792-1750 B.C.
Hyksos Invasion of Egypt | c. 1730-1570 B.C.
Early New Kingdom in Egypt | c. 1570-1300 B.C.
Moses' Birth | *Exodus 1-2* | c. 1525 B.C.
Plagues in Egypt | *Exodus 3-12* | c. 1446 B.C.
The Exodus | *Exodus 13-15* | c. 1446 B.C.
Ten Commandments | *Exodus 19-20* | c. 1445 B.C.
Amenhotep IV and Monotheism | c. 1361-1344 B.C.
Reign of Tutankhamon | c. 1333-1323 B.C.
Later New Kingdom in Egypt | c. 1300-1090 B.C.
Davidic Kingdom | *I & II Samuel, I Chronicles*
    | c. 1011-971 B.C.
Solomon's Reign | *I Kings 1-11, II Chronicles 1-9*
    | c. 971-931 B.C.
Alexander the Great Conquers Egypt | c. 332 B.C.
Egypt Falls to Rome | c. 30 B.C.

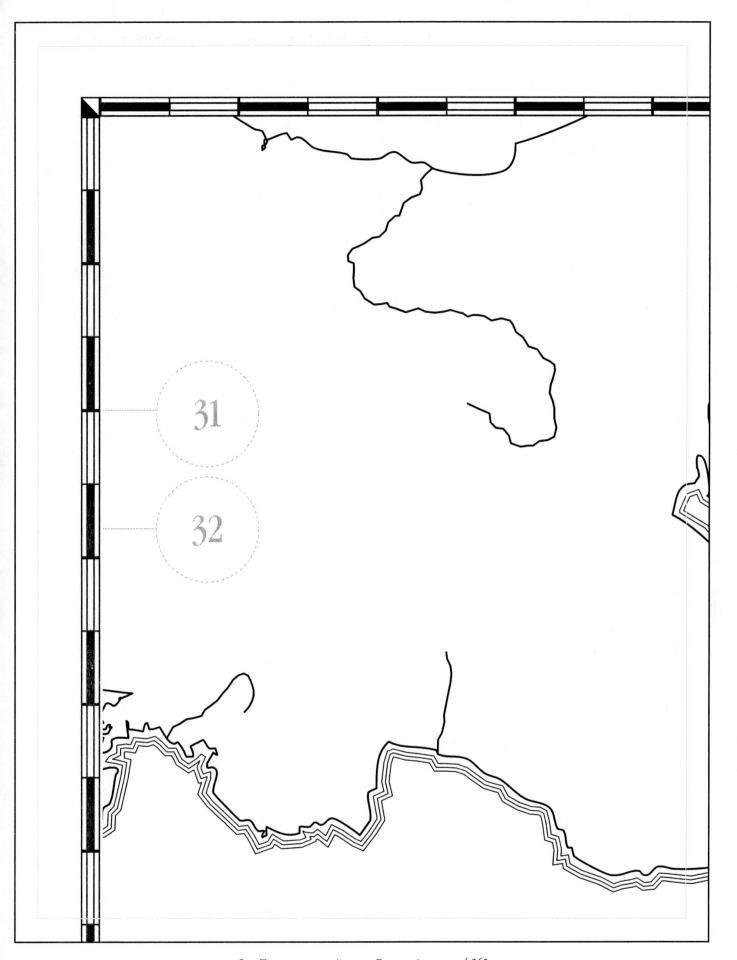

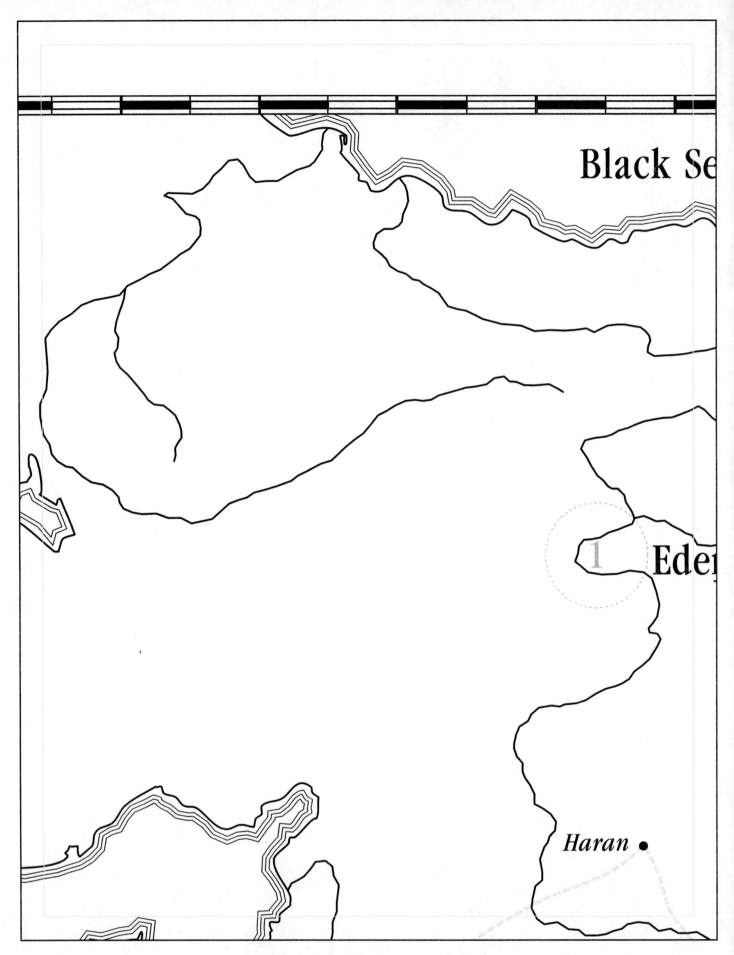

Black Se

1 Eder

Haran •

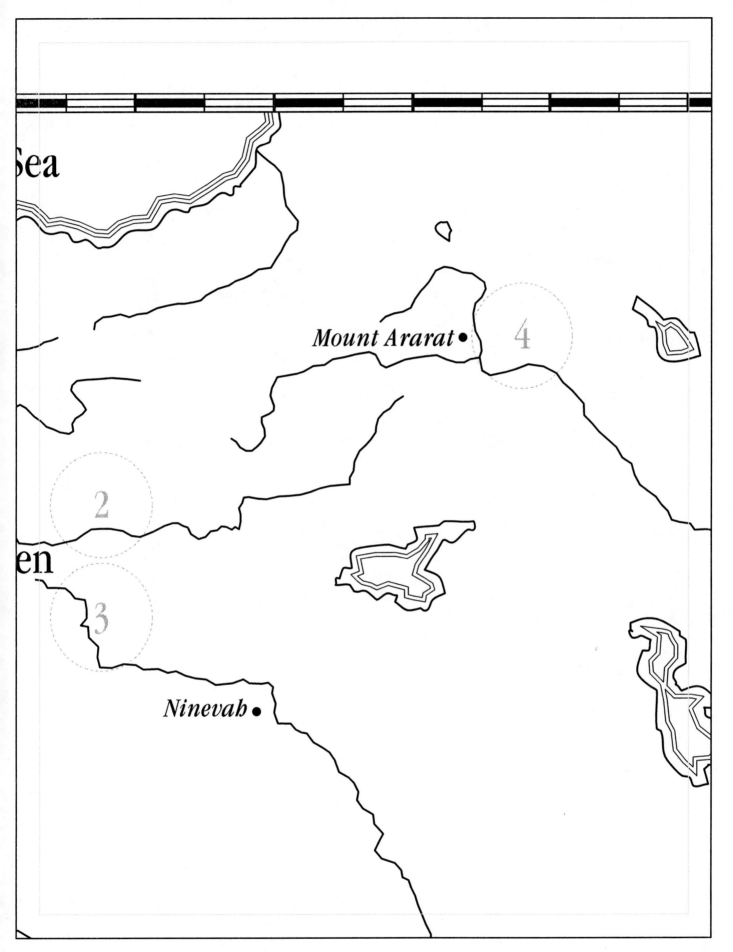

Sea

en

Mount Ararat •

4

2

3

Ninevah •

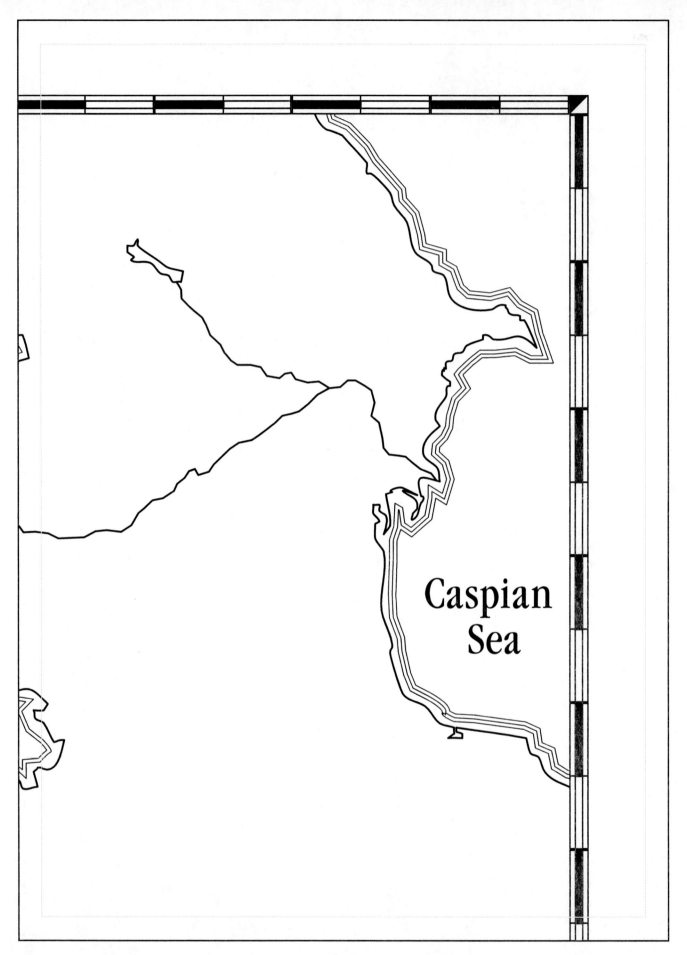

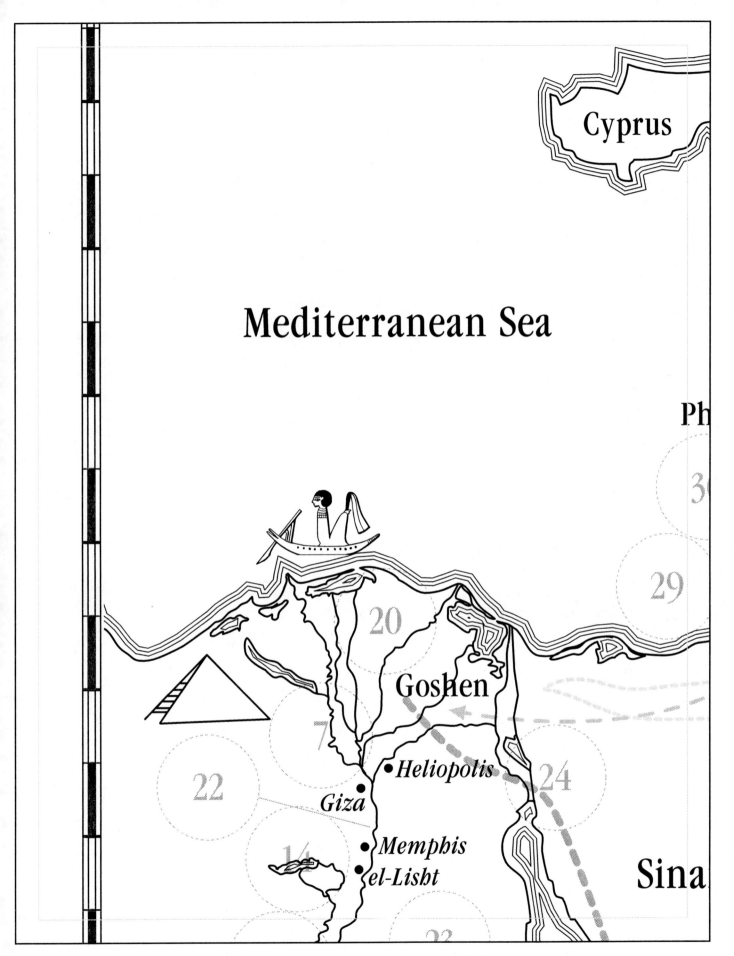

Cyprus

Mediterranean Sea

Ph

20

Goshen

22

7

• Heliopolis

Giza

24

14

• Memphis
• el-Lisht

Sina

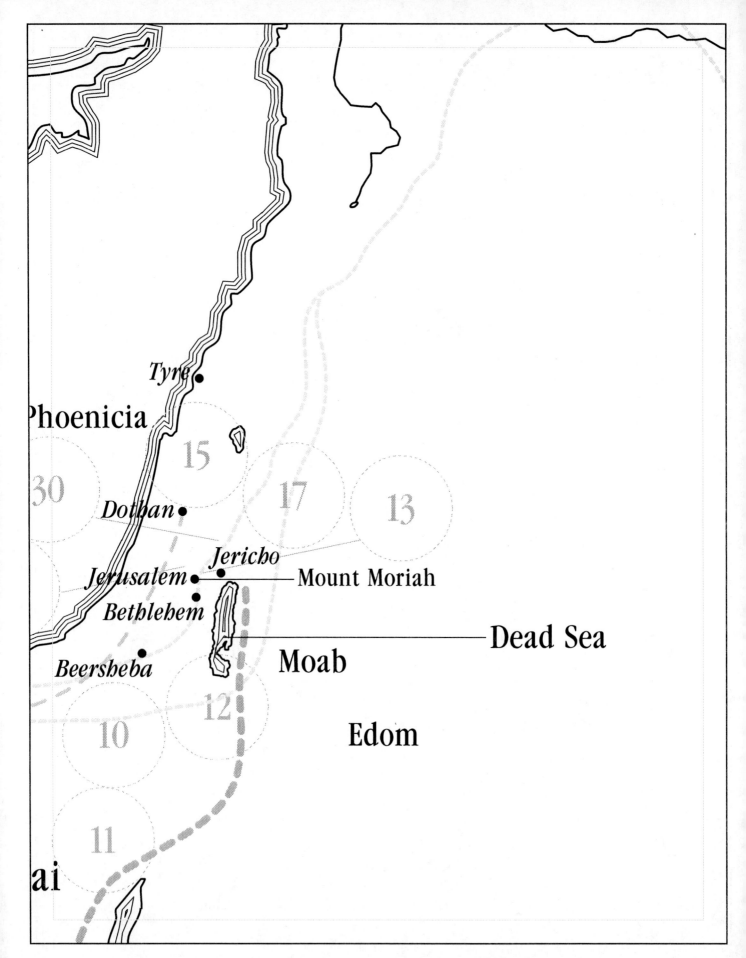

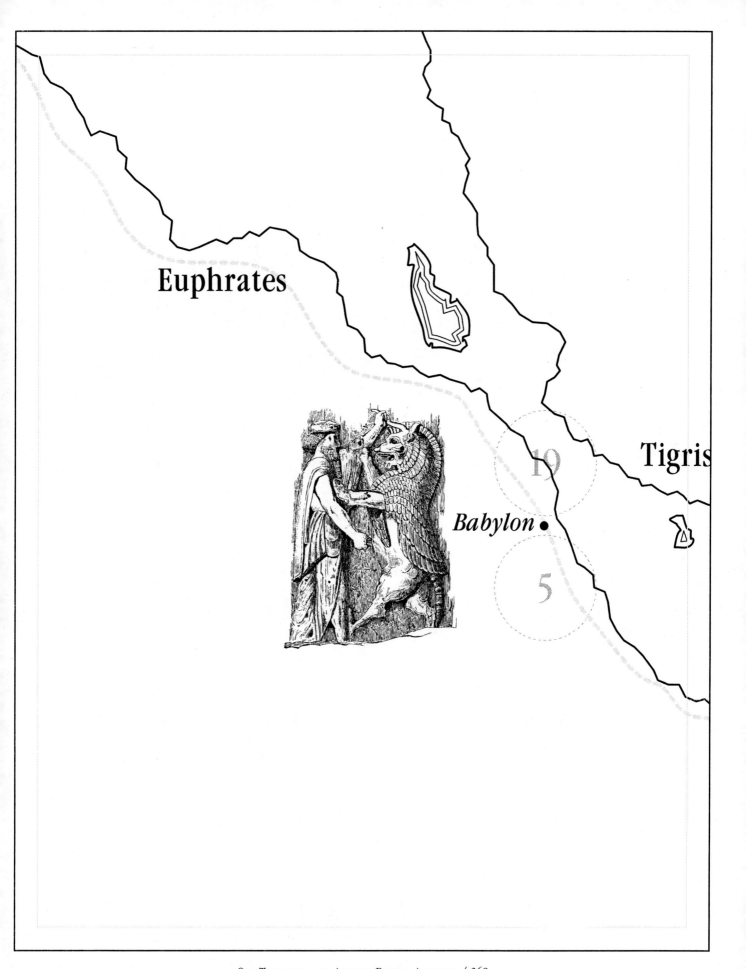

Euphrates

Tigris

Babylon •

19

5

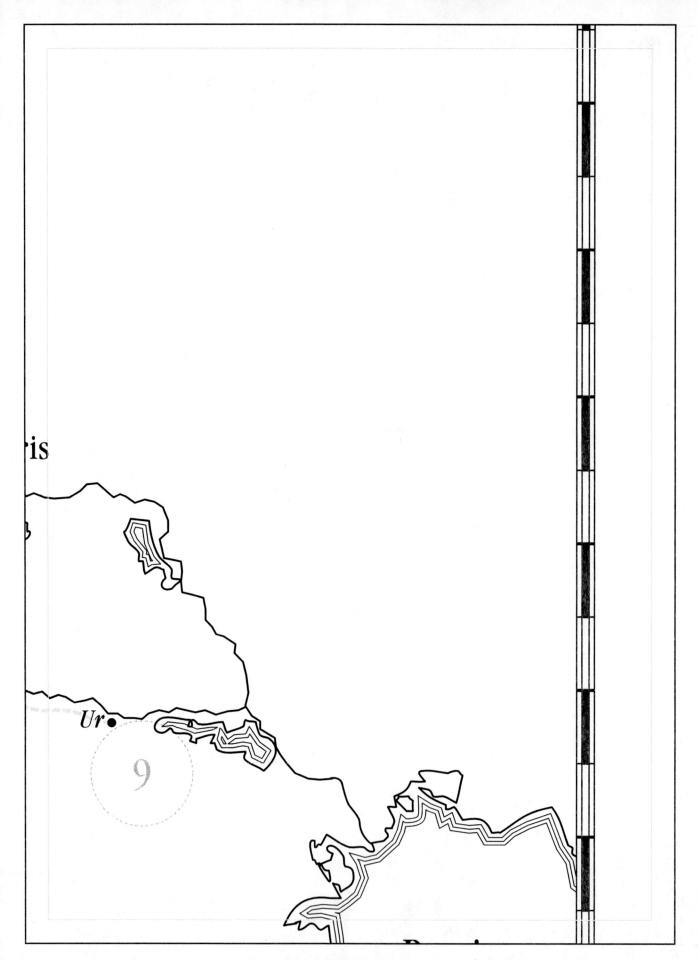

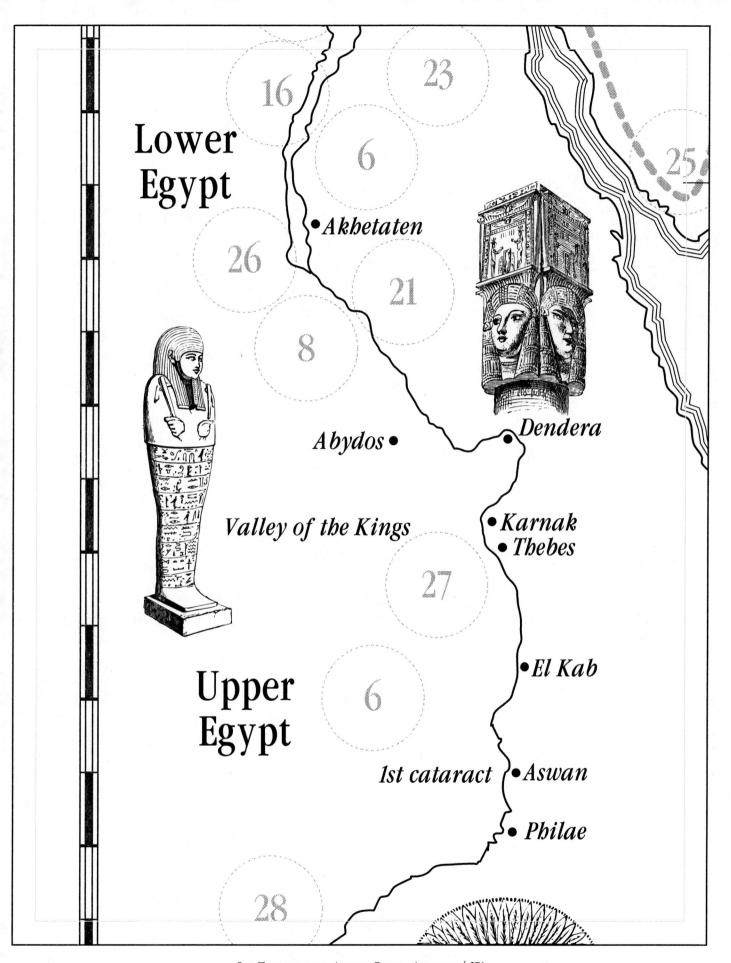

Lower
Egypt

16

23

6

•*Akhetaten*

26

21

8

25

Abydos •

Dendera

Valley of the Kings

27

•*Karnak*
•*Thebes*

Upper
Egypt

6

•*El Kab*

1st cataract •*Aswan*

• *Philae*

28

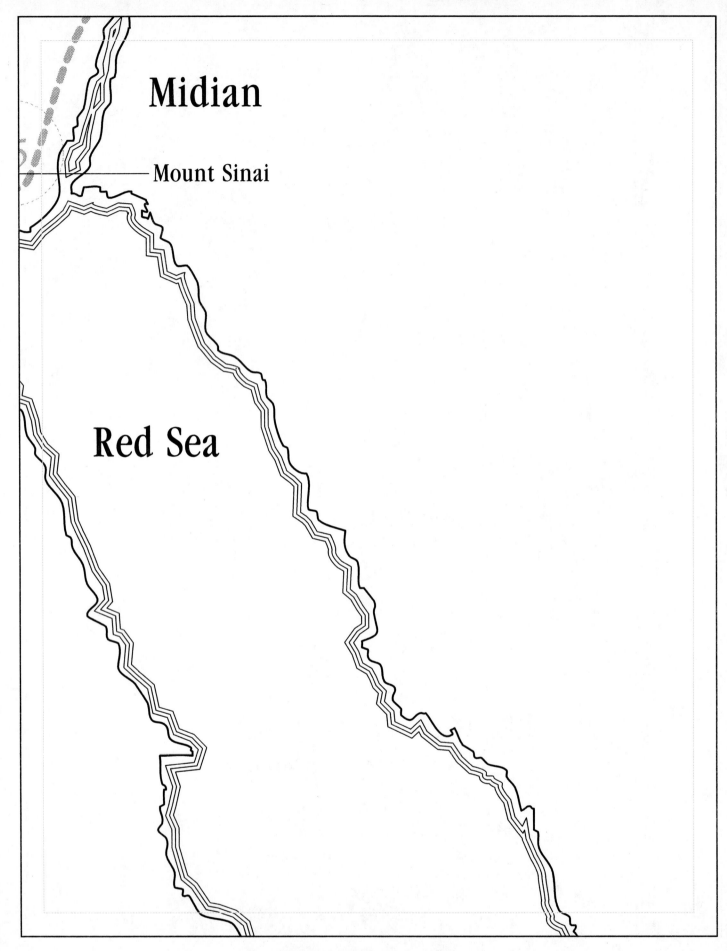

Midian

Mount Sinai

Red Sea

OLD
TESTAMENT
and ANCIENT

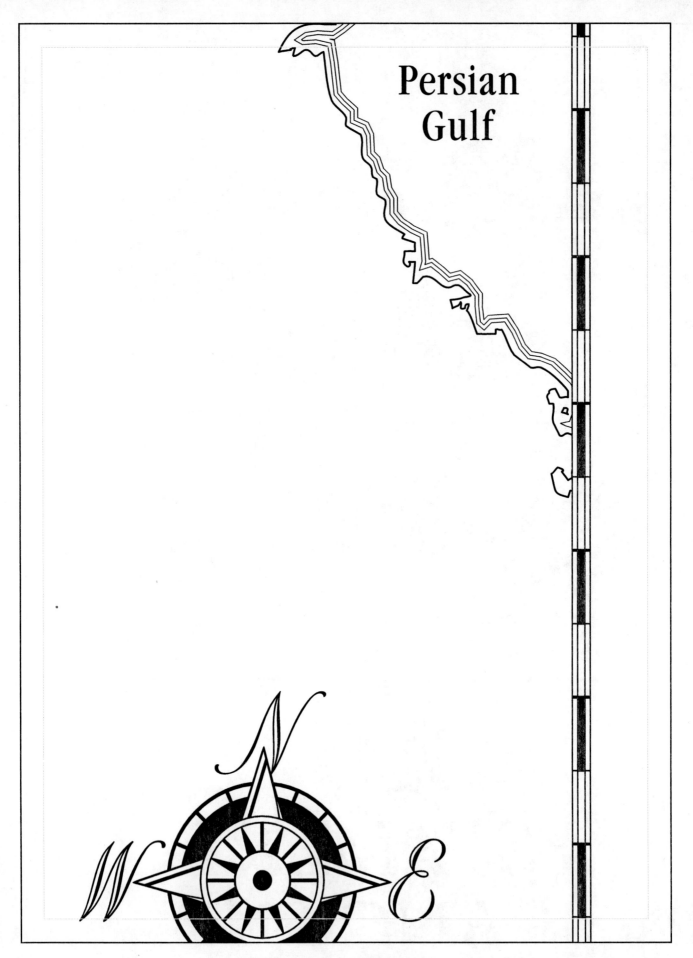

Persian Gulf

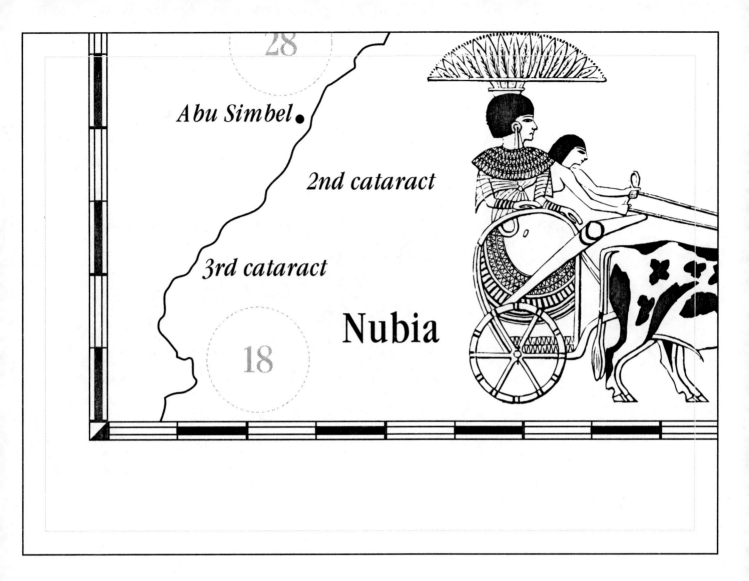

Abu Simbel

2nd cataract

3rd cataract

Nubia

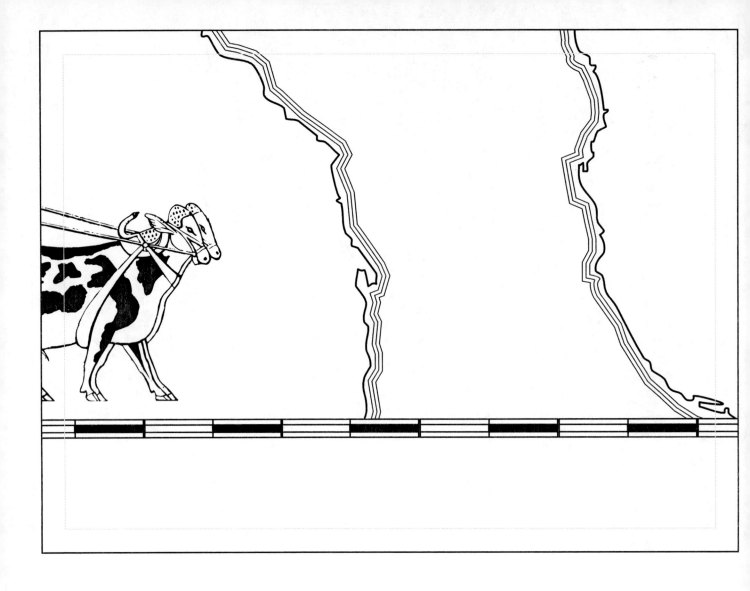

and ANCIENT EGYPT

CREATION

Date: _____

SCRIPTURE REFERENCE: _____

We are beginning a journey that you will never forget. You are going to follow the same path as Adam and Eve, Moses, Abraham, and even King Tut. Remember that God was faithful to His people as He led them on the path. Where did they begin? Start by placing the first history medallion near the source of the Euphrates and the Tigris rivers. It is thought tht Eden was near the source of these rivers which is in the Armenian highlands on modern maps. The text says, "And a river went out of Eden to water the garden; and from thence it was parted, and became into four heads. The name of the first is Pison; that is it which compasseth the whole land of Havilah, where there is gold; And the gold of that land is good; there is bdellium and the onyx stone. And the name of the second river is Gihon: the same it is that compasseth the whole land of Ethiopia. And the name of the third river is Hiddekel [Tigris]: that is it which goeth toward the east of Assyria. And the fourth river is Euphrates" (Genesis 2:10–14)

Other Events

_____
_____
_____
_____
_____
_____
_____

The Arts/Technology

_____
_____
_____
_____
_____
_____
_____

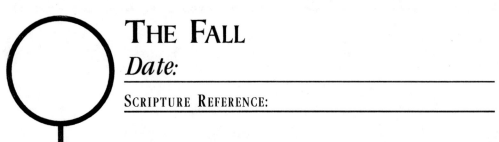

THE FALL

Date: _____

SCRIPTURE REFERENCE: _____

The garden of Eden was a real place. Have you ever seen a gated garden? You walk up to it and peek through the slats of the fence to see the pretty flowers but can't go in because it belongs to someone else. Once Adam and Eve were able to be in that beautiful garden, but because of the sin of Adam, the man and woman were cast out of the garden. Genesis 3:23–24 says, "Therefore the LORD God sent him out of the garden of Eden to till the ground from which he was taken. So he drove out the man; and He placed cherubim at the east of the garden of Eden, and a flaming sword which turned every way, to guard the way to the tree of life." Do you know what cherubim look like? The Bible gives some amazing descriptions of them in Ezekiel, but historically they have often been shown as lion- or eagle-headed winged humans or winged sphinxes. Later on you will study the Egyptian sphinxes that the pharaohs built. Take the history medallion and place it outside of Eden. Remember that Adam and Eve could no longer enter their home as cherubim with a flaming sword stood at the gate to keep them out.

Other Events

_____
_____
_____
_____
_____
_____
_____

The Arts/Technology

_____
_____
_____
_____
_____
_____
_____

CAIN AND ABEL

Date: _____

SCRIPTURE REFERENCE: _____

After the Fall, Adam and Eve began having children. Adam lived 930 years and was the father of many, many children. Two of the sons of Adam and Eve were named Cain and Abel. After the well-known event of Cain's murder of Abel, Cain moved East to the land the Scriptures call Nod—which is east of Eden (Genesis 4:16-17). Cain built the first city, and he called the name of the city after the name of his son—Enoch. Cain's offspring, Jubal, was the father of all those who play the harp and flute and Tubal-Cain was an instructor of bronze and iron craftsmen. Take the next medallion and place it outside of Eden.

Other Events

_____
_____
_____
_____
_____
_____
_____

The Arts/Technology

_____
_____
_____
_____
_____
_____
_____

THE FLOOD

Date: _____

SCRIPTURE REFERENCE: _____

As the cities grew, the wickedness of man grew as well. But Noah found grace in the eyes of the LORD. So God told Noah he was going to flood the earth, so he was to make an ark to save his family and the animals. God's judgment in the Flood is a well known biblical fact which is referred to many times in the Bible (Gen. 7; Isa. 54:9; Luke 17:26–27; Heb. 11:7; 1 Pet. 3:20; 2 Pet. 2:5). We do not know where Noah built the ark, but most scholars maintain that the ark ended up on Mount Ararat, which is now in the country of Turkey. Place the medallion bearing the drawing of an Ark and place it on Mount Ararat.

Other Events

_____
_____
_____
_____
_____
_____
_____

The Arts/Technology

_____
_____
_____
_____
_____
_____
_____

THE TOWER OF BABEL

Date: _____

SCRIPTURE REFERENCE: _____

Following the Flood, Noah had grandchildren and great grandchildren. They had families and wandered for many years, ending up settling on a plain near what would one day be the city of Babylon. Look on the map and see how far away Mount Ararat is from Babylon. They didn't have trains, planes, or mobile homes, so how long do you think that trip would have taken? The Tower of Babel was built on the plain of Shinar (also known as Babylon) in southern Mesopotamia. The descendants of Noah began to build and build and build. They made a giant tower that was probably like a ziggurat. Have you ever seen a skyscraper in a big city? Imagine a skyscaper in the middle of a baseball field and that would be kind of what it was like to look at the Tower of Babel. However, God's city comes down from heaven to earth—it cannot be built from the ground up. Place the history medallion on circle number five.

Other Events

_____
_____
_____
_____
_____
_____
_____

The Arts/Technology

_____
_____
_____
_____
_____
_____
_____

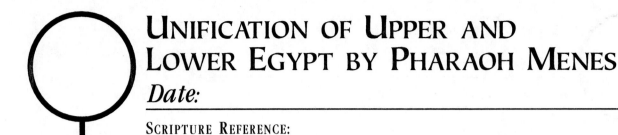

Unification of Upper and Lower Egypt by Pharaoh Menes

Date: _____

Scripture Reference: _____

After the LORD saw the city and the Tower of Babel, He confused their language and scattered them abroad. The Bible follows the children of Shem, but we know that other people were building homes all over the world. The people went north and south and east and west. The people who went south had to cross deserts and other very rough land. You can imagine how happy those travelers, called nomads, were when they reached the lush Nile river. It was a very, very long time between what happened at the Tower of Babel and what happened next in the biblical account. And even then, we do not read about these people living down along the Nile. Yet these people were busy building a new nation. During this time they began to build towns of brick buildings.

Egypt has two lands, the Nile valley of Upper Egypt which is actually in the south, and the delta of Lower Egypt which is located in the north. The delta is the area that fans out near the Mediterranean which was formed of the silt from the Nile. Before this time the upper and lower parts of Egypt were not ruled by the same people. Place the history medallion for this card along the Nile river, above Akhetaten.

Other Events

_____
_____
_____
_____
_____
_____
_____

The Arts/Technology

_____
_____
_____
_____
_____
_____
_____

THE OLD KINGDOM OF EGYPT

Date:

SCRIPTURE REFERENCE:

While the children of Shem were building up the city of Ur in the land of the Sumerians, hundreds and hundreds of miles away, the people in Egypt were building great structures called pyramids. It is believed that during the time of peace in the Old Kingdom of Egypt the great Pyramid at Giza was built. Next we will study Abraham (born at the end of the Old Kingdom during the reign of Pepy II), who would have seen these great wonders as he traveled through Egypt. Place the medallion with the drawing of a pyramid by Giza.

Other Events

The Arts/Technology

FIRST INTERMEDIATE PERIOD IN EGYPT

Date: _____

SCRIPTURE REFERENCE: _____

Egypt is an important land in the Bible, since the Israelites lived there for over 400 years. Also the lives of the Patriarchs of our faith, Abraham, Isaac and Jacob often intersect with Egypt: Genesis 12:10 is the first mention of Egypt in the biblical record, "Now there was a famine in the land, and Abram went down to Egypt to dwell there, for the famine was severe in the land." Place the history medallion for this card above Abydos.

Other Events

_____

_____

_____

_____

_____

_____

_____

The Arts/Technology

_____

_____

_____

_____

_____

_____

_____

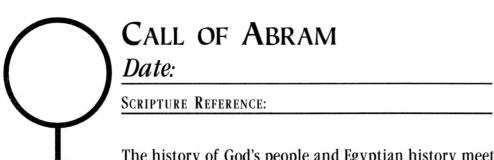

CALL OF ABRAM

Date: _____

SCRIPTURE REFERENCE: _____

The history of God's people and Egyptian history meet each other on this history card. Abram's journey of faith involved over 1,500 miles as he traveled from Ur through Haran, to Canaan and to Egypt. These regions are called the Fertile Crescent. The Fertile Crescent is an arc of land fed by many rivers, making transportation by boat easier and growing food and raising livestock profitable. Place the history medallion for this card at Abram's birthplace—the city of Ur. Glue colored yarn along Abram's route through Haran, Canaan, down to Egypt and back to the land promised to him by God.

Even though the land where Abram lived is called the Fertile Crescent, that doesn't mean that it was always a good place to live. There was a shortage of food that forced Abram to move down to the lush Nile river. While there, he met Pharaoh. Abram introduced his wife, Sarai, as his sister and the pharaoh took her to live in his home. This displeased God, so he sent a series of diseases to Pharaoh's household. When Pharaoh found out that Sarai was Abram's wife, he kicked him out of Egypt.

Other Events

_____
_____
_____
_____
_____
_____
_____

The Arts/Technology

_____
_____
_____
_____
_____
_____
_____

GOD'S COVENANT WITH ABRAHAM

Date: _____

SCRIPTURE REFERENCE: _____

God said to Abraham, "Get out of your country, from your family and from your father's house, to a land that I will show you. I will make you a great nation; I will bless you and make your name great; and you shall be a blessing. I will bless those who bless you, and I will curse him who curses you; and in you all the families of the earth shall be blessed" (Gen. 12:1-3). God "cut" (*berith* in Hebrew) a covenant with Abraham. A covenant involved making an ultimate commitment symbolized by killing an animal (Gen. 21). The dead animal symbolized that death would be the penalty for breaking this bond in blood. The covenant structure which is throughout Scripture was a legal form used by the Hittites and other ancient people of the time of Abraham. Place the history medallion on circle number ten.

Other Events

_____
_____
_____
_____
_____
_____
_____

The Arts/Technology

_____
_____
_____
_____
_____
_____
_____

HAGAR AND ISHMAEL

Date: _____

SCRIPTURE REFERENCE: _____

Remember that Pharaoh had told Abram to leave Egypt. Abram gathered his wife and Lot and went as far as Bethel (Genesis 13:3), to the place where his tent had been in the beginning. Later we learn that he moved his tent by the terebinth trees of Mambre, which is near Hebron. Can you imagine taking your family vacation without getting into your car or a plane, only your legs or an animal to carry you? But that is not the worst part! They carried their entire house with them, as you see Abram and his family were nomads. They lived in tents of patched together animal skins, which stood in place with poles. After Abram had dwelt ten years in the land of Canaan (Genesis 16:3), Sarai took Hagar, her Egyptian maid, and gave her to Abram to be his wife. Hagar had a baby that they named Ishmael. When Abraham was one hundred and Sarah was ninety, they had a son named Isaac. Sarah saw Ishmael scoffing and had Abraham cast Hagar and Ishmael out into the wilderness of Beersheba. Look on your map and place the sticker in this wilderness.

Other Events

_____
_____
_____
_____
_____
_____
_____

The Arts/Technology

_____
_____
_____
_____
_____
_____
_____

SODOM AND GOMORRAH

Date: _____

SCRIPTURE REFERENCE: _____

You have now seen where Abraham and his family traveled. One of the family members was his nephew Lot. After they returned to Canaan there was a quarrel between Abraham's and Lot's herdsmen. They separated and Lot moved to the city of Sodom. We know from Scripture (Genesis 19:27-28) that Abraham could actually see Sodom and Gomorrah from were he had pitched his tent near the great trees of Mamre, near Hebron. Hebron is actually located about 18 miles west of the Dead Sea.

Soon after this Lot was captured by a king that attacked the city of Sodom, but Abraham rescued him. One day angels appeared to Abraham and told him that God was going to destroy Sodom because of its wickedness.

It is commonly thought that the southern part of the Dead Sea covers the place where the cities of Sodom and Gomorrah existed. Place your medallion near the Dead Sea where we believe Sodom and Gomorrah existed.

Other Events

_____
_____
_____
_____
_____
_____
_____

The Arts/Technology

_____
_____
_____
_____
_____
_____
_____

Birth and Sacrifice of Isaac

Date: _____

SCRIPTURE REFERENCE: _____

We keep talking about the fact that Abraham lived for a long time by the terebinth trees of Mamre, near Hebron. Time passed and Abraham moved to Beersheba. Look at your map, find Hebron and with your finger trace where Abraham moved to Beersheba. It was here that Isaac was born to Abraham and Sarah in their old age. After the miraculous birth of Isaac, God told Abraham to leave Beersheba and travel north to the land of Moriah (Genesis 22:2) In the familiar story of the "sacrifice" of Isaac, Abraham called the name of the place, "The Lord will provide." Mt. Moriah is in the area that came to be known as Jerusalem. Find Mt. Moriah on your map and place your history medallion there.

Other Events

_____
_____
_____
_____
_____
_____
_____

The Arts/Technology

_____
_____
_____
_____
_____
_____
_____

MIDDLE KINGDOM IN EGYPT

Date:
_____

SCRIPTURE REFERENCE:
_____

Place your finger where Mt. Moriah is on your map. Look across the map to the west and locate el-Lisht. Less than twenty years had passed since Abraham had taken Isaac to Mt. Moriah to offer him as a sacrifice. While Abraham was on Mt. Moriah, Egypt was in a civil war. That means the Egyptians were fighting one another. During the Middle Kingdom Pharaoh Amenemhet united the kingdom of Egypt. He caused the people to stop fighting. He built a new capital city near el-Lisht, called Itjtawy, and this is where we are going to place our history medallion.

It was during this era that Joseph came to Egypt, after he was sold into slavery.

Other Events

_____

_____

_____

_____

_____

_____

_____

The Arts/Technology

_____

_____

_____

_____

_____

_____

_____

JOSEPH AS A SLAVE

Date: _____

SCRIPTURE REFERENCE: _____

You have found Mt. Moriah on your map. Look over and see where the land of Egypt is. One hundred sixty-eight years had passed since Abraham had taken Isaac up to Mt. Moriah. Isaac grew into a man, and he had a son named Jacob. Jacob would grow into a man and have twelve sons. One of his sons was named Joseph. Joseph's brothers were very jealous of him. In Genesis 37 we read the sad story of Joseph being sold into slavery by his brothers. One day Joseph's father sent him to check on his brothers. He left his home around Hebron and traveled northward to Shechem, about sixty miles. While there he learned his brothers had moved to Dothan another twenty miles to the north, so he traveled on. Dothan was located on a major trade route. Remember back then people did not shop in stores, but traders would bring their wares back and forth to sell. In fact, Joseph's brothers sold him to Ishmaelite traders for twenty shekels of silver.

Joseph was now part of a caravan traveling on a long journey to Egypt. Imagine all that Joseph would have seen as he walked into the land of Egypt. Pyramids, temples, Egyptian people and more. How different this was from the land of his father. He was now in a pagan land. Place the history medallion on circle number fifteen.

Other Events

_____
_____
_____
_____
_____
_____
_____

The Arts/Technology

_____
_____
_____
_____
_____
_____
_____

FAMINE IN EGYPT

Date: _____

SCRIPTURE REFERENCE: _____

Joseph had been living in Egypt for about twenty years when a famine struck the land. He had actually been made governor by Pharaoh. His father and brothers were still living in Canaan. Joseph's father sent his brothers to Egypt in search of grain to purchase. Arriving in Egypt the brothers would have known they were in a different land. The Egyptians lived very differently as they lived in houses in cities, instead of tents in the hills.

Joseph finally revealed himself to his brothers. Pharaoh invited Joseph's father and brothers to come live in the land of Egypt. Place the history medallion on circle number sixteen.

Other Events

_____

_____

_____

_____

_____

_____

_____

The Arts/Technology

_____

_____

_____

_____

_____

_____

_____

The Twelve Tribes of Israel

Date: _____

SCRIPTURE REFERENCE: _____

The brothers of Joseph traveled from Canaan to Egypt. Pharaoh gave them the land of Goshen which was in the eastern section of the Nile River Delta. Look at your map and put your finger on Canaan. Trace with your finger along the coast by the Mediterranean Sea. This was the route Joseph's brothers took to arrive in Goshen.

What is really amazing is God had promised this land to Abraham in Genesis 15: "*To your descendants I have given this land, from the river of Egypt to the great river, the River Euphrates . . .*" Place the history medallion on circle number seventeen.

Other Events

_____
_____
_____
_____
_____
_____
_____

The Arts/Technology

_____
_____
_____
_____
_____
_____
_____

SECOND INTERMEDIATE PERIOD IN EGYPT

Date: _____

SCRIPTURE REFERENCE: _____

The thirteenth through the seventeenth dynasties are known as the Second Intermediate Period. Dynasties are how we divide up the different time periods in Egypt. Look at your map and find Nubia. Now place your history medallion on the spot near Nubia where the nomadic Nubian tribe roamed the deserts near the Nile River. During this period the Egyptians gained control of major Nubian sites.

Other Events

_____
_____
_____
_____
_____
_____
_____

The Arts/Technology

_____
_____
_____
_____
_____
_____
_____

CODE OF HAMMURABI

Date: _____

SCRIPTURE REFERENCE: _____

We have been spending much of our time looking at Egypt. Now look at your map and find the Euphrates River. By the 1700's B.C. Babylon became the center of a kingdom that controlled much of central and southern Mesopotamia. Hammurabi was the most important king of the Old Babylonian Kingdom.

Remember just because we have journeyed to a new land does not mean nothing was going on in Egypt. The Second Intermediate Period was going on.

Babylon and Larsa were the two main cities during the time of Hammurabi, Babylon's sixth king. He defeated the kingdom of Mari in the north. Under him the Old Babylonian Empire was established. Place the history medallion on circle number nineteen.

Other Events

_____
_____
_____
_____
_____
_____
_____

The Arts/Technology

_____
_____
_____
_____
_____
_____
_____

HYKSOS INVASION OF EGYPT

Date: _____

SCRIPTURE REFERENCE: _____

The Hyksos people came from Asia and took Egypt by surprise. They entered through Palestine and settled in the Delta. Look at your map. Can you imagine waking up one day and seeing a strange group of people arriving on horses and chariots and taking over all of your land? Place the history medallion on circle number twenty.

Other Events

_____
_____
_____
_____
_____
_____
_____

The Arts/Technology

_____
_____
_____
_____
_____
_____
_____

EARLY NEW KINGDOM

Date: _____

SCRIPTURE REFERENCE: _____

We have learned that Joseph and his whole family had come to live in Egypt. After the time of Joseph the Israelites continued to live in Egypt, but the new pharaohs had forgotten why Joseph and his family had been given land. They treated the Israelites poorly. During the Early New Kingdom, times got rough for the Israelites. We see that the pharaoh became so hateful that he ordered all Israelite baby boys to be killed. We will learn this on the next card. In the early part of this period Egypt ruled the East and built many monuments all over the land. These included many tombs in the Valley of the Kings. During this period we will see Moses born, the plagues in Egypt, the Exodus, and the Ten Commandments. Place the history medallion on circle number twenty-one.

Other Events

_____

_____

_____

_____

_____

_____

_____

The Arts/Technology

_____

_____

_____

_____

_____

_____

_____

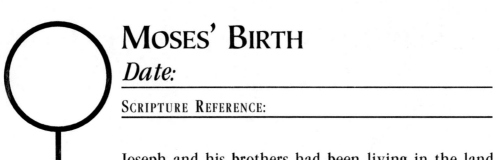

MOSES' BIRTH

Date: _____

SCRIPTURE REFERENCE: _____

Joseph and his brothers had been living in the land of Goshen. Place your finger on Goshen. Remember Joseph and his descendants had been living in Goshen for about 346 years. That would be your great, great, great, great, great, great, great grandfather. Do you remember much from 300 years ago? Probably not. Well, the pharaoh, who may have been Thutmose I, did not know Joseph or remember how he helped to keep the Egyptians alive during seven years of famine. He was scared of the Hebrews, so he ordered all the male babies to be killed.

In the land of Egypt there lived Amram and Jochebed. One day Jochebed had a baby named Moses. She knew that all the baby boys were supposed to be killed, so she placed the baby in a reed basket and put him in the Nile River. Find the Nile River on your map and place the history medallion. Imagine the baby floating in the basket. Pharaoh's daughter, possibly Hatshepsut, had gone to bathe in the Nile. While there she saw the basket and pulled the baby from the river.

Other Events

_____
_____
_____
_____
_____
_____
_____

The Arts/Technology

_____
_____
_____
_____
_____
_____
_____

Plagues in Egypt

Date: _____

Scripture Reference: _____

Remember the baby that Pharaoh's daughter found in a basket in the Nile? He grew up and became a leader of the Hebrew people. Moses had left the land of Egypt after killing an Egyptian who was beating a Hebrew slave. He went to the land of Midian. One day the Lord God appeared to Moses from the middle of a burning bush. God commanded him to go to Egypt and ask Pharaoh for the release of the Israelite people. So Moses journeyed to Egypt and asked Pharaoh, who may have been Amenhotep II to set the Israelites free. Moses returned to Pharaoh ten times and each time he refused. In judgment God sent ten plagues to demonstrate His power over the pagan gods the Egyptians worshipped. The plagues confronted the false gods of the Egyptians. For example, the first plague was turning the Nile into blood. The Nile was a source of life for Egypt. It was also an attack on the god Hapi, the one who brings life-giving water to Egypt. Place the history medallion on circle number twenty-three.

Other Events

_____

_____

_____

_____

_____

_____

_____

The Arts/Technology

_____

_____

_____

_____

_____

_____

_____

THE EXODUS

Date: _____

SCRIPTURE REFERENCE: _____

After the tenth plaque, Pharaoh decided to free the Israelites, so they departed and camped by the Red Sea. Find the Red Sea on your map, and take a close look at it, as you may not believe what was about to happen. While they were there Pharaoh changed his mind, but God parted the sea and the Israelites walked through on dry ground. When the Egyptians tried to follow, God caused the sea to come together, and they all drowned. Although we do not know exactly where they crossed the water, many scholars believe they may have crossed a body of water just north of the red sea. Now look for the dotted line on your map and trace the route the Israelites took to the Promised Land. We know that their journey was not an easy one, but God was faithful and miraculously provided food and water as they wandered in the desert. Place the history medallion on circle number twenty-four.

Other Events

_____
_____
_____
_____
_____
_____
_____

The Arts/Technology

_____
_____
_____
_____
_____
_____
_____

THE TEN COMMANDMENTS

Date:
_____

SCRIPTURE REFERENCE: _____

The Israelites made their way into Sinai and moved toward Canaan. In the heart of the Sinai Peninsula, south of the Wilderness of Shur, is the region called the Wilderness of Sin, in which Dophkah was located (Num. 33:12). This area is thought to have contained the famed copper and turquoise mines of the pharoahs from early dynastic times. The last stop before Mount Sinai was Rephidim (Exodus 17:1), in the southwestern part of the peninsula. This is where Moses first struck the rock to get water (Ex. 17:1-7; 1 Cor. 10:1-4). Place the history medallion on circle number twenty-five.

Other Events

_____
_____
_____
_____
_____
_____
_____

The Arts/Technology

_____
_____
_____
_____
_____
_____
_____

AMENHOTEP IV AND MONOTHEISM

Date: _____

SCRIPTURE REFERENCE: _____

Amenhotep IV was the tenth king of the 18th dynasty, who changed the way he thought about religion. This may be hard to believe, but he decided to establish a cult to worship Aton the sun god. Find Akhetaten on your map. Place your history medallion there. It is here that Amenhotep IV, who now called himself Akhnaton after the god Aton, built a new city. Can you imagine if our president decided that he was going to make-up his own god to worship, then said he could no longer live in the White House, because the god did not like it? After this he would build a new house to live in in another city. What would people think? They would think he was crazy.

Other Events

_____
_____
_____
_____
_____
_____
_____

The Arts/Technology

_____
_____
_____
_____
_____
_____
_____

REIGN OF TUTANKHAMON

Date: _____

SCRIPTURE REFERENCE: _____

Guess what? We do not have to guess where Tutankhamon was buried, because an archeologist discovered his tomb in 1922 with almost everything intact. Find the Valley of the Kings on your map and place your history medallion in the correct place. Tut's tomb was found buried amongst the rubble of Rameses VI's tomb in the Valley of the Kings. Though it had been robbed at least twice before its discovery in 1922, his tomb survived the looting due to its small size and its location. The portion of the history of Israel which overlapped Tutankhamon's reign was during the period of the Judges, specifically, Othniel, who was the nephew of Caleb (Jdg. 1:13-14). "The Spirit of the LORD came upon him, and he judged Israel. He went out to war, and the LORD delivered Cushan-Rishathaim king of Mesopotamia into his hand; and his hand prevailed over Cushan-Rishathaim. So the land had rest for forty years" (Jdg. 3:10-11).

Other Events

_____
_____
_____
_____
_____
_____
_____

The Arts/Technology

_____
_____
_____
_____
_____
_____
_____

LATER NEW KINGDOM

Date: _____

SCRIPTURE REFERENCE: _____

During the resurgence of the Egyptian empire in the Later New Kingdom, many great construction works were added. For example, Seti I launched a major building program, including the great hall of the Temple. Rameses II did everything on a grand scale, and remains of his buildings are at Memphis, Thebes, Abu Simbel, and Aswan. Rameses II was a warrior, and he reestablished the Egyptian Empire in Palestine and Syria after the weakness of the Amarna period. At this time in Israel, the judges Ehud, Deborah, Barak, Gideon, Tolah, and Jair were leading the people. It was also during this time that Naomi and Ruth were living. Place the history medallion on circle number twenty-eight.

Other Events

_____
_____
_____
_____
_____
_____
_____

The Arts/Technology

_____
_____
_____
_____
_____
_____
_____

THE DAVIDIC KINGDOM

Date: _____

SCRIPTURE REFERENCE: _____

We are now going to jump across the desert and find our way back to Bethlehem. Find where Bethlehem is on your map. Is there anything special that you know about Bethlehem that will happen later on in time? The prophet Samuel went to Bethlehem to find the next king of Israel. As he approached Bethlehem he was met by the elders of the city. These were wise men who acted as judges for the people and ran the city's government. They may have met Samuel at the city gate, as they often sat there.

Now we are going to journey over to the Mediterranean Sea. Do you see this sea on your map? During Old Testament times a group of people named the Philistines occupied a strip of coastal land on the Mediterranean, west of Jerusalem, known as Philistia. You are all familiar with the story of David and Goliath. Well Goliath was the best fighter of all the Philistine soldiers, but David defeated him. After this happened David went to live with Saul in his palace. Now look for Jerusalem on the map. King Saul had his palace at Gibeah, which was just north of Jerusalem.

Next we learn that Saul became very jealous of David and tried to kill him. David fled and eventually ended up in Ziklag. David would eventually be crowned king and chose to make Hebron his capital. Place the history medallion on circle number twenty-nine.

Other Events

_____
_____
_____
_____
_____
_____
_____
_____

The Arts/Technology

_____
_____
_____
_____
_____
_____
_____
_____

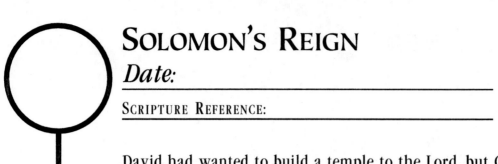

SOLOMON'S REIGN

Date: _____

SCRIPTURE REFERENCE: _____

David had wanted to build a temple to the Lord, but God told him not to do it. Instead his son Solomon would be the one to build it. Look north of Hebron to Mount Moriah and you can see the place where Solomon built his temple. Can you imagine what it would have been like to build a large building in the days before electicity. No electric saws or drills. No trucks to bring the supplies up the mountain. Instead the cedar wood was purchased from King Hiram of Tyre, and the logs were floated down the seacoast to a port city in Israel. Continue north on your map, and you will find the city of Tyre. Place your finger there and trace down to Jerusalem. After the logs came into port they were dragged over the land to Jerusalem. But the temple was not made from just wood, but also stone. Solomon got his stone from quarries in Jerusalem. Just like the Egyptian pyramids, men had to cut the stones by hand and then use a pulley system to bring them up the mountain. Do you think they learned any of this from the Egyptians? Today a building stands on this land, and it is called the Dome of the Rock. Place the history medallion on circle number thirty.

Other Events

_____
_____
_____
_____
_____
_____
_____

The Arts/Technology

_____
_____
_____
_____
_____
_____
_____

ALEXANDER THE GREAT

Date:

SCRIPTURE REFERENCE: _____

Now look across your map to the land of Egypt. We must remember that even though we have been in the land of Israel and time has passed, the Egyptians have still been carrying on with life. Egypt continued to struggle with wars and different rulers. For nearly 200 years the Persians ruled Egypt. These rulers were very cruel to the Egyptian people. You may want to look at another map to see where Persia is. In 332 B.C. however, a man by the name of Alexander the Great, who you will study about when you study ancient Greece, conquered Egypt. Look at your map and find Memphis. This is where Alexander settled into the pharaoh's palace. Soon after settling in he sailed to the mouth of the Nile. Take your finger and find your way to the mouth of the Nile on your map. He decided to found a new city and establish his power. This was a wise place to choose because it had easy access to the trade routes of the Mediterranean. This site would grow into one of the most famous places in the world. Place the history medallion on circle number thirty-one.

Other Events

_____
_____
_____
_____
_____
_____
_____

The Arts/Technology

_____
_____
_____
_____
_____
_____
_____

Egypt Falls to Rome

Date:

<small>Scripture Reference:</small> _____

After Alexander died his four strongest generals divided up his kingdom. Ptolemy I claimed Egypt as his own. For the next 250 years he and his descendants ruled Egypt. The last of the Ptolemys was Cleopatra. We must remember that during this time, one of the things that rulers desired was to conquer other lands for their own. Cleopatra married the Roman general Julius Caesar, and they had a son. Look on another map and find the Roman Empire. These are the people that would rule Egypt for many years. Place the history medallion on circle number thirty-two.

Other Events

_____
_____
_____
_____
_____
_____
_____

The Arts/Technology

_____
_____
_____
_____
_____
_____
_____

UNIFICATION OF EGYPT—EGYPT FALLS TO ROME
The Pharaohs of Ancient Egypt *Literature Unit*

The Pharaohs of Ancient Egypt by Elizabeth Payne is a wonderful overview of Ancient Egypt, starting with Napoleon's campaign in Egypt when the Rosetta Stone was discovered, and ending with Cleopatra and the conquering of Egypt by Rome.

Generally speaking this book can be read independently at the beginning of the year by students in third grade or older and midway through the year by second graders. Because this book is quite useful with many of the Old Testament and Ancient Egyptian History Cards, many of the following chapter headings have been marked with corresponding flash-card numbers.

CHAPTER ONE: "THE REDISCOVERY OF EGYPT"

1. Who discovered the Rosetta Stone?

_____

_____

2. What is the Rosetta Stone?

_____

_____

_____

3. What did the Rosetta Stone do for history?

_____

_____

_____

_____

4. What proof did historians have that Egypt existed?

_____

_____

_____

UNIFICATION OF EGYPT—EGYPT FALLS TO ROME
The Pharaohs of Ancient Egypt, *Page 2*

5. What do historians today say are the only two reliable ways of learning about a long vanished civilization?

_____

_____

_____

6. How was archeology born?

_____

_____

_____

7. What were the three languages of the Rosetta Stone?

_____

_____

_____

8. Why was the Rosetta Stone such an important discovery?

_____

_____

_____

_____

_____

UNIFICATION OF EGYPT—EGYPT FALLS TO ROME
The Pharaohs of Ancient Egypt, *Page 3*

CHAPTER 2: "THE FIRST EGYPTIANS AND THE DEAD DEMIGODS" [Card #6]

1. What did archeologists discover about early Egyptians when they excavated?

   _____

   _____

   _____

2. What does the Nile River do every year?

   _____

   _____

   _____

3. What is kemi?

   _____

   _____

4. What impact did irrigation have on the Egyptians?

   _____

   _____

   _____

5. What were the three Egyptian kingdoms that developed? Who ruled these kingdoms?

   _____

   _____

   _____

   _____

6. Where does Egyptian history officially begin?

   _____

   _____

   _____

7. What did Egyptians believe about life after death? How did this affect their burial?

_____

_____

_____

_____

_____

8. What did the Egyptians consider their pharaohs to be?

_____

_____

_____

CHAPTER THREE: "THE GOOD GOD—PHARAOH CHEOPS" [Card #7]

1. For whom was the great pyramid at Giza built?

_____

_____

_____

2. How long did it take to build the pyramid at Giza? How many men did it take to build it?

_____

_____

_____

UNIFICATION OF EGYPT—EGYPT FALLS TO ROME
The Pharaohs of Ancient Egypt, *Page 5*

3. Draw a picture of what the city of Memphis was like at the time of Pharaoh Cheops.

```
┌────────────────────────────────────────────────────────┐
│                                                        │
│                                                        │
│                                                        │
│                                                        │
│                                                        │
│                                                        │
│                                                        │
│                                                        │
│                                                        │
│                                                        │
│                                                        │
│                                                        │
└────────────────────────────────────────────────────────┘
```

4. Why did Egyptians wear wigs and use eye paint?

_____

_____

_____

5. What was the Great Royal Treasury?

_____

_____

_____

6. Did the Egyptians worship one god or many gods?

_____

_____

7. What does the Bible tell us about Egyptian gods?

_____

_____

_____

8. What was a *mastaba?*

_____

_____

9. Who first used stone to build a pharaoh's tomb?

_____

_____

10. Where did the stone come from that was used to build the tombs?

_____

_____

11. What tools did the pyramid builders possess?

_____

_____

_____

12. What is one theory as to how the stones were raised into place to build the pyramids?

_____

_____

_____

_____

UNIFICATION OF EGYPT—EGYPT FALLS TO ROME
The Pharaohs of Ancient Egypt, Page 7

CHAPTER FOUR: "I SHOW THEE A LAND TOPSY-TURVY..." [Card #8, 14, 18, & 20]

1. What important historical information was found inside a mummified crocodile?

   _____

   _____

   _____

2. What did some of the scrolls say about Egypt not long after Pharaoh Cheop's death?

   _____

   _____

3. After Cheop's death the nobles and priests grew stronger and bolder. What did the priests of Ra do to limit the Pharaoh's power?

   _____

   _____

   _____

   _____

4. What did the Pharaoh's once-devoted nobles do to defy his power?

   _____

   _____

5. What did the nobles begin to say about life after death?

   _____

   _____

   _____

   _____

UNIFICATION OF EGYPT—EGYPT FALLS TO ROME
The Pharaohs of Ancient Egypt, Page 8

6. Who was Osiris?

_____

_____

_____

7. What actually happened to the central authority in Egypt at this time?

_____

_____

_____

8. Who finally brought peace to Egypt once again?

_____

_____

_____

9. Who were the Hyksos?

_____

_____

_____

10. Who took Egypt back from the Hyksos?

_____

_____

11. What two lessons did the valley people learn from the results of the past 1,000 years of history?

_____

_____

_____

UNIFICATION OF EGYPT—EGYPT FALLS TO ROME
The Pharaohs of Ancient Egypt, *Page 9*

CHAPTER FIVE: "HIS MAJESTY, HERSELF—QUEEN HATSHEPSUT" [Card #22]

1. How did Hatshepsut become Pharaoh of Egypt?

   _____

   _____

   _____

2. Was there anyone who was not in favor of Hatshepsut being Pharaoh?

   _____

   _____

3. What happened to Thutmose the Third after Hatshepsut seized the throne?

   _____

   _____

   _____

4. Who was Senmut?

   _____

   _____

5. What was brought back to Egypt from the trading expedition that Hatshepsut organized?

   _____

   _____

   _____

6. What finally happened to Hatshepsut? What part may Thutmose the Third have played in this?

   _____

   _____

   _____

UNIFICATION OF EGYPT—EGYPT FALLS TO ROME
The Pharaohs of Ancient Egypt, *Page 10*

CHAPTER SIX: THE SMITER OF THE ASIATICS—PHARAOH THUTMOSE THE THIRD

1. What was the Battle of Megiddo?

   _____

   _____

   _____

2. How were the Syrians finally taken?

   _____

   _____

   _____

3. What did Thutmose bring home with him that surprised the Egyptians?

   _____

   _____

   _____

   _____

4. What did Thutmose do for Amon the King of the Gods and his priesthood?

   _____

   _____

   _____

5. Who became Pharaoh at Thutmose's death?

   _____

   _____

   _____

6. What is said about Thutmose the Third by historians?

_____

_____

_____

_____

7. How was Thutmose's tomb discovered?

_____

_____

_____

CHAPTER SEVEN: THE CRIMINAL OF AKHETATON—PHARAOH AKHNATON

1. How were the first cuneiform tablets discovered in Egypt?

_____

_____

_____

2. Why were the Tell el Amarna tablets important?

_____

_____

_____

3. Why was Amenhotep the Third called Amenhotep the Magnificent?

_____

_____

_____

_____

UNIFICATION OF EGYPT—EGYPT FALLS TO ROME
The Pharaohs of Ancient Egypt, *Page 12*

4. Who was Amenhotep's wife?

_____

_____

5. Why did the High Priest of Amon have great political power?

_____

_____

_____

6. What new god had risen to prominence at the court of Pharaoh?

_____

_____

_____

7. Why do many archeologists believe Amenhotep encouraged worship of the new god, Aton?

_____

_____

_____

_____

8. What does it mean that Aton was a universal god?

_____

_____

_____

9. Which god did Amenhotep's son, the young Amenhotep, worship?

_____

_____

_____

UNIFICATION OF EGYPT—EGYPT FALLS TO ROME
The Pharaohs of Ancient Egypt, *Page 13*

10. Who was Amenhotep the Third's wife?

_____

_____

11. When was Amenhotep the Third crowned co-regent?

_____

_____

12. What was Akhetaton?

_____

_____

13. Why did Amenhotep the Third change his name to Akhnaton?

_____

_____

_____

14. What was significant about Amenhotep changing his name to Akhnaton?

_____

_____

_____

15. What other changes did Akhnaton make?

_____

_____

_____

16. How did art forms change during Akhnaton's reign?

_____

_____

_____

17. Fill in the blank. From the City of the Horizon a decree went forth to all of Egypt, forbidding worship of any god save _____.

18. What problems did the above decree cause?

_____

_____

_____

19. Describe the end of Akhnaton's reign.

_____

_____

_____

_____

_____

20. Who was the next famous pharaoh?

_____

_____

_____

21. Why did Tutankhaton change his name?

_____

_____

_____

22. How old was Tutankhamon when he died?

_____

_____

_____

UNIFICATION OF EGYPT—EGYPT FALLS TO ROME
The Pharaohs of Ancient Egypt, *Page 15*

23. When was Tutankhamon's tomb discovered?

_____

_____

_____

24. Why was Tutankhamon's tomb such an important archeological find?

_____

_____

_____

CHAPTER EIGHT: "THE BEGINNING OF THE END—PHARAOH RAMESES THE SECOND"
   [Cards #28, 31, & 32]

1. From whom did Rameses the Second inherit the throne of Egypt?

_____

_____

_____

2. Who was Rameses son? Who was his grandson?

_____

_____

_____

3. Egypt's vast empire had disintegrated under Amenhotep IV's (Akhnaton's) rule. What did Rameses the Second do about it?

_____

_____

_____

4. Describe the Battle of Kadesh.

_____

_____

_____

_____

_____

_____

5. How many wives did Rameses the Second have? What was important about his Hittite bride?

_____

_____

_____

6. What did Rameses the Second have built?

_____

_____

_____

7. How old was Rameses the Second at his death?

_____

_____

8. How did the great folk wandering help cause a decline in Egypt? What was another name for the "folk wanderers?"

_____

_____

9. What happened to Egypt after Rameses the Third's death?

_____

_____

_____

10. Who ended the reign of Egypt as an independent country? What country gained control of Egypt?

_____

_____

_____

_____

11. Who ruled Egypt under the Roman Empire?

_____

_____

_____

12. Who seized Egypt in A.D. 641? In whose name did they do this?

_____

_____

_____

_____

OLD TESTAMENT AND ANCIENT EGYPT
Project—History Matching Card Game

Photocopy the artwork on the following pages (back to back) onto card stock and cut apart.

This game is best for three to six players, but it is possible for two to play. The dealer deals five cards to each player (seven each for two players). The remaining cards are placed face down to form a stock.

The player to dealer's left starts. A turn consists of asking a specific player for a specific event. The player who asks must already hold at least one of the cards requested. If the player who was asked has the card requested, he must give it to the player who asked for it. That player then places his matching cards on the table in front of him and gets another turn.

If the person asked does not have any of the card named, he says "Pick a card." The asker must then draw the top card of the undealt stock. If the drawn card is the letter asked for, the asker shows it and gets another turn. If the drawn card is not the one asked for, the asker keeps it, but the turn now passes to the player who said "Pick a card."

The game continues until either someone has no cards left in their hand or the deck runs out. The winner is the player who has the most pairs.

CREATION

Genesis 1-2

THE FALL IN THE GARDEN

Genesis 3

CAIN AND ABEL

Genesis 4

THE FLOOD

Genesis 6-9

TOWER OF BABEL

c. 2200–2050 B.C.

Genesis 11

UNIFICATION OF . . . EGYPT

OLD KINGDOM

FIRST INTERMEDIATE PERIOD

CALL OF ABRAM

c. 2091 B.C.

GOD'S COVENANT WITH ABRAHAM

c. 2082 B.C.

HAGAR AND
ISHMAEL

c. 2080 B.C.

SODOM AND
GOMORRAH

c. 2080 B.C.

BIRTH AND
SACRIFICE OF ISAAC

c. 2066 B.C.

THE MIDDLE
KINGDOM IN EGYPT

c. 2050–1800 B.C.

JOSEPH AS A SLAVE

c. 1898 B.C.

FAMINE IN EGYPT

c. 1878–1871 B.C.

THE 12 TRIBES
OF ISRAEL

c. 1860 B.C.

2ND INTERMEDIATE
PERIOD IN EGYPT

c. 1800–1570 B.C.

CODE OF
HAMMURABI

c. 1792–1750 B.C.

Hyksos Invasion of Egypt

c. 1730–1570 B.C.

Early New Kingdom in Egypt

c. 1570–1300 B.C.

Moses' Birth

c. 1525 B.C.

Plagues in Egypt

c. 1446 B.C.

The Exodus

c. 1446 B.C.

10 COMMANDMENTS

c. 1445 B.C.

AMENHOTEP IV AND MONOTHEISM

c. 1361–1344 B.C.

REIGN OF TUTANKHAMON

c. 1333–1323 B.C.

LATER NEW KINGDOM IN EGYPT

c. 1300–1090 B.C.

DAVIDIC KINGDOM

c. 1011-971 B.C.

SOLOMON'S REIGN

c. 971-931 B.C.

ALEXANDER CONQUERS EGYPT

c. 332 B.C.

EGYPT FALLS TO ROME

c. 30 B.C.

c. 2200-2050 B.C.

UNIFICATION
OF . . . EGYPT

OLD KINGDOM

_____

_____

_____

_____

_____

_____

_____

OLD TESTAMENT AND ANCIENT EGYPT
Project—History Curiosities

Photocopy the artwork on this and the following page back-to-back, then cut apart and staple along the spine, using the artwork below for the cover. Choose an historical event and have the students write and illustrate unusual and interesting facts they find about the event. This project can be used throughout the year (if you copy enough pages) in conjunction with the flashcards' RESOURCES sections.

OLD TESTAMENT AND ANCIENT EGYPT
Project—History Curiosities, Page 2

OLD TESTAMENT AND ANCIENT EGYPT
Sequence Review 1

Event	Date	Reference

OLD TESTAMENT AND ANCIENT EGYPT
Sequence Review 2

Mask out the information the students are supposed to review, then photocopy.

Event	Reference	Date
Creation	Genesis 1-2	
The Fall in the Garden	Genesis 3	
Cain and Abel	Genesis 4	
The Flood	Genesis 6-9	
Tower of Babel	Genesis 11	
Unification of Upper and Lower Egypt by Pharaoh Menes		
The Old Kingdom in Egypt		
First Intermediate Period in Egypt		c. 2200-2050 B.C.
Call of Abram	Genesis 12-13	c. 2091 B.C.
God's Covenant With Abraham	Genesis 15-17	c. 2082 B.C.
Hagar and Ishmael	Genesis 16, 21	c. 2080 B.C.
Sodom and Gomorrah	Genesis 18-19	c. 2080 B.C.
Birth and Sacrifice of Isaac	Genesis 21-22	c. 2066 B.C.
The Middle Kingdom in Egypt		c. 2050-1800 B.C.
Joseph as a Slave	Genesis 37-40	c. 1898 B.C.
Famine in Egypt	Genesis 41-47	c. 1878 - 1871 B.C.

OLD TESTAMENT AND ANCIENT EGYPT
Sequence Review 2, Page 2

Mask out the information the students are supposed to review, then photocopy.

Event	Reference	Date
The Twelve Tribes of Israel	Genesis 29–36, 46–50	c. 1860 B.C.
Second Intermediate Period in Egypt		c. 1800–1570 B.C.
Code of Hammurabi		c. 1792–1750 B.C.
Hyksos Invasion of Egypt		c. 1730–1570 B.C.
Early New Kingdom in Egypt		c. 1570–1300 B.C.
Moses' Birth	Exodus 1–2	c. 1525 B.C.
Plagues in Egypt	Exodus 3–12	c. 1446 B.C.
The Exodus	Exodus 13–15	c. 1446 B.C.
Ten Commandments	Exodus 19–20	c. 1445 B.C.
Amenhotep IV and Monotheism		c. 1361–1344 B.C.
Reign of Tutankhamon		c. 1333–1323 B.C.
Later New Kingdom in Egypt		c. 1300–1090 B.C.
Davidic Kingdom	I & II Sam., I Chron.	c. 1011–971 B.C.
Solomon's Reign	I Kgs. 1–11, II Chron. 1–9	c. 971–931 B.C.
Alexander the Great Conquers Egypt		c. 332 B.C.
Egypt Falls to Rome		c. 30 B.C.

OLD TESTAMENT AND ANCIENT EGYPT
Project—Art History Museum

Create an art museum for your students to visit to reinforce the events studied on the history flashcards.

Building Your Collection

After completing a flashcard, photocopy an image out of the additional readings that represents that event. Color and place the picture in one of the frames below. Hang this artwork in the museum (see next page) to build a collection for that "wing" of your art museum. In the *Veritas Press Phonics Museum* reading program, additional paintings are available that would add color and variety to this project.

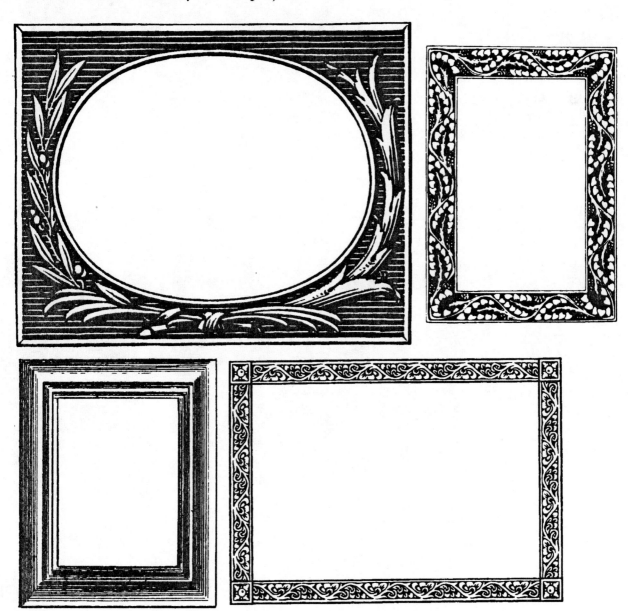

OLD TESTAMENT AND ANCIENT EGYPT

*Project—
Art History
Museum, Page 2*

Building Your Museum

Find a cardboard box and spray paint the inside and the outside white. Artwork is provided on the right that may be photocopied to make "wallpaper" for the exterior of the museum. Or the students can design the outside to their tastes. Seal the box then cut along the top edge of the box, down the adjacent side then back along the bottom to make a "wall" of the museum able to be swung open like a door. Hang your artwork and invite visitors to enjoy it.

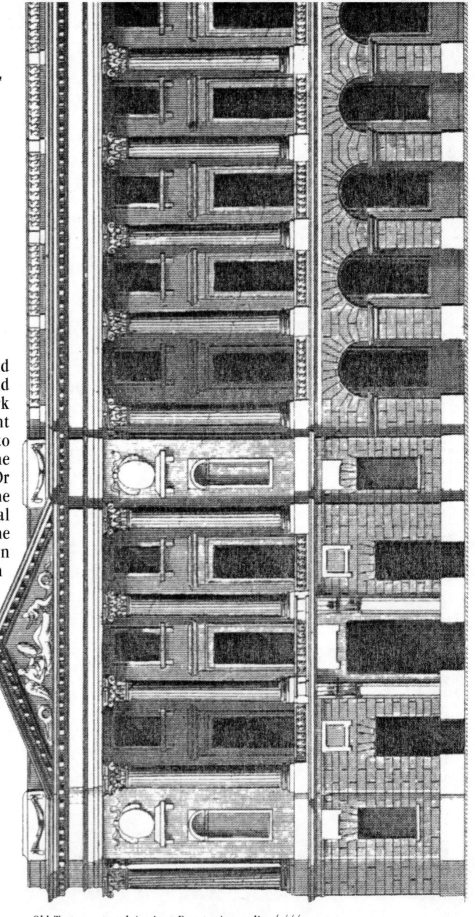

OLD TESTAMENT AND ANCIENT EGYPT
Reference Report

TITLE: _____

AUTHOR: _____

EVENT: _____

_____

_____

_____

_____

_____

_____

_____

_____

_____

_____

_____

_____

_____

_____

_____

_____

_____

OLD TESTAMENT AND ANCIENT EGYPT

Resource Notes—Event

Title of Resource:

_____

Author:

_____

What (is the event?):

_____

_____

_____

_____

Who (was important in the event?):

_____

_____

When (date):

Where (did the event occur?):

_____

_____

_____

_____

Importance:

_____

_____

_____

_____

OLD TESTAMENT AND ANCIENT EGYPT
Resource Notes—Visual Record

Title of Resource:

_____

Author:

_____

Who or What:

_____

_____

Date:

_____

Where:

_____

_____

_____

_____

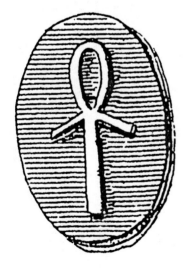

Draw a picture to illustrate what you have studied (turn the page if you need to draw a wide picture instead of a tall picture).

OLD TESTAMENT AND ANCIENT EGYPT
Postage Stamp

In the space provided below, design a class stamp based on an historical event studied or a literature book you have read.

OLD TESTAMENT AND ANCIENT EGYPT
Bookmark

Supplies

One copy of the bookmark on cardstock

markers

glue stick

scissors

hole punch

yarn (4 inches)

Directions

Make a copy of this page onto card stock. Illustrate the person or event you are studying, then color and cut it out. Fold over and glue together. For best results, laminate the bookmark when you are finished to make it last longer. Using a hole punch, punch out a hole at the top of the bookmark. Take pieces of yarn and tie them through the hole.

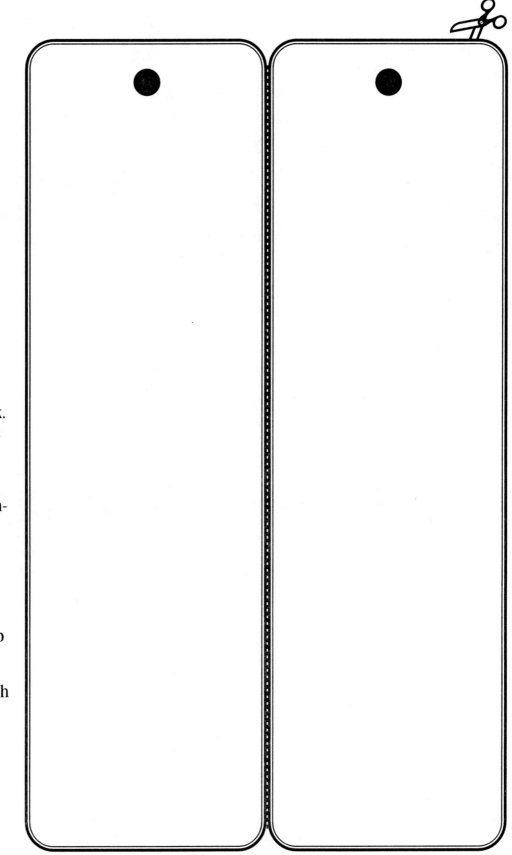

OLD TESTAMENT AND ANCIENT EGYPT
Field Trip Postcard

In the space provided below, make an imaginary postcard based on your field trip. On the front draw a picture of the place, and on the back answer the questions provided.

POSTCARD

Where are you visiting?

What is the favorite thing you have seen?

How does this relate to what you are studying?

Wish you were here!

OLD TESTAMENT AND ANCIENT EGYPT
Timetripper *Board Game*

In this game, the players are trapped in the past and must try to get to the present day by answering questions as they proceed forward in time.

Supplies

scissors

tape

colored pencils

Directions

Make several back-to-back copies of the question cards or glue them together. Cut out all the cards, pocket watch player tokens and the game board. Tape the game board together and then color it. Laminating the board may prove useful, as it will be used throughout the year.

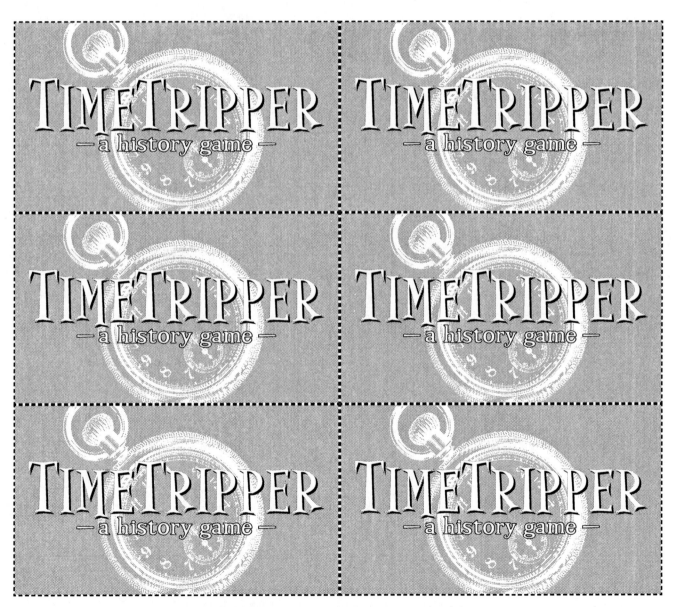

Game Instructions

On each card write out a question and answer based on the history cards studied. To start, each player puts his token on the space marked "The Past." The players then take turns moving forward one space and following the directions on that space. If the player is directed to draw a card, a correct answer to the question entitles him to move ahead two spaces.

Oh, no! You have run into another timetripper going back in time:

SLIDE BACK THREE PLACES

Q:_____

_____

_____

_____

A:_____

_____

Q:_____

_____

_____

A:_____

_____

Q:_____

_____

_____

A:_____

_____

Q:_____

_____

_____

A:_____

_____

Q:_____

_____

_____

A:_____

_____

OLD TESTAMENT AND ANCIENT EGYPT
Accordion Books: Art (front)

Directions

Copy the front and back pages back-to-back or glue them together. Cut out around the outer edges. Holding the book with the front page oriented for reading, lift up the second and third panels and fold over, face down to the left. Now lift the left side of the third panel and fold back over the upside down second panel. Lift and fold the slotted flaps toward the center and "lock" them together. On the other side, illustrate the booklet and give it a title. Then open and unfold to complete the questions inside.

How does the artist use light?

What do you notice first?

Artist:

Title:

Date:

Location Painted:

OLD TESTAMENT AND ANCIENT EGYPT
Accordion Books: Art (back)

What lines can you see (visible and invisible) and where do they lead you in the painting?

Does the painting portray biblical values (ie. Bad is bad and Good is good—not is it a biblical event)?

OLD TESTAMENT AND ANCIENT EGYPT
Accordion Books: Technology (front)

Directions

Copy the front and back pages back-to-back or glue them together. Cut out around the outer edges. Holding the book with the front page oriented for reading, lift up the second and third panels and fold over, face down to the left. Now lift the left side of the third panel and fold back over the upside down second panel. Lift and fold the slotted flaps toward the center and "lock" them together. On the other side, illustrate the booklet and give it a title. Then open and unfold to complete the questions inside.

What does this invention do?

What do you find interesting about this technological advance?

Inventor:

Name of Object:

Date of Development:

Location First Made:

What problem did people have that this device helps solve?

Is this invention still in use?

OLD TESTAMENT AND ANCIENT EGYPT
Accordion Books: Music (front)

Directions

Copy the front and back pages back-to-back or glue them together. Cut out around the outer edges. Holding the book with the front page oriented for reading, lift up the second and third panels and fold over, face down to the left. Now lift the left side of the third panel and fold back over the upside down second panel. Lift and fold the slotted flaps toward the center and "lock" them together. On the other side, illustrate the booklet and give it a title. Then open and unfold to complete the questions inside.

Was it to be performed vocally or instrumentally?

Why was this piece of music written?

Composer:

Musical Era:

Date Written:

Location First Performed:

OLD TESTAMENT AND ANCIENT EGYPT
Accordion Books: Music (back)

What are the composer's most famous works?

Whose music most influenced the composer?

OLD TESTAMENT AND ANCIENT EGYPT
Accordion Books: Other Historical Event (front)

Directions

Copy the front and back pages back-to-back or glue them together. Cut out around the outer edges. Holding the book with the front page oriented for reading, lift up the second and third panels and fold over, face down to the left. Now lift the left side of the third panel and fold back over the upside down second panel. Lift and fold the slotted flaps toward the center and "lock" them together. On the other side, illustrate the booklet and give it a title. Then open and unfold to complete the questions inside.

What do you find interesting about this event?

Describe the event.

Event:

Person(s):

Date:

Location:

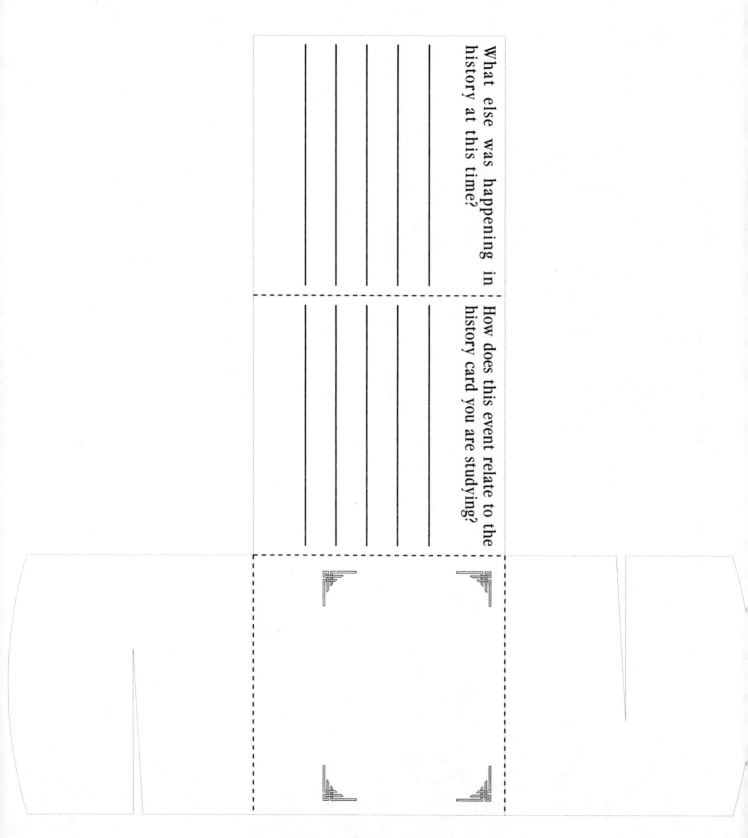

What else was happening in history at this time?

How does this event relate to the history card you are studying?

OLD TESTAMENT AND ANCIENT EGYPT
Diorama Family: Egyptian

Below are paper dolls that can be used in dioramas. After cutting out the figures, fold back the bottom tab at the dashed line below their feet and glue in to the shoebox.

OLD TESTAMENT AND ANCIENT EGYPT
Grading Chart

NUMBER OF PROBLEMS

NUMBER INCORRECT

Inc.	06	07	08	09	10	11	12	13	14	15	16	17	18	19	20	21	22	23	24	25	26	27	28	29	30	31	32	33	34	35	36	37	38	39	40	41	42	43	44	45	46	47	48	49	50
1	83	86	88	89	90	91	92	92	93	93	94	94	94	95	95	95	95	96	96	96	96	96	96	97	97	97	97	97	97	97	97	97	97	97	98	98	98	98	98	98	98	98	98	98	98
2	67	71	75	78	80	82	83	85	86	87	88	88	89	89	90	90	91	91	92	92	92	93	93	93	93	94	94	94	94	94	94	95	95	95	95	95	95	95	95	96	96	96	96	96	96
3	50	57	63	67	70	73	75	77	79	80	81	82	83	84	85	86	86	87	88	88	88	89	89	90	90	90	91	91	91	91	92	92	92	92	93	93	93	93	93	93	93	94	94	94	94
4	33	43	50	56	60	64	67	69	71	73	75	76	78	79	80	81	82	83	83	84	85	85	86	86	87	87	88	88	88	89	89	89	89	90	90	90	90	91	91	91	91	91	92	92	92
5	17	29	38	44	50	55	58	62	64	67	69	71	72	74	75	76	77	78	79	80	81	81	82	83	83	84	84	85	85	86	86	86	87	87	88	88	88	88	89	89	89	89	90	90	90
6		14	25	33	40	45	50	54	57	60	63	65	67	68	70	71	73	74	75	76	77	78	79	79	80	81	81	82	82	83	83	84	84	85	85	85	86	86	86	87	87	87	88	88	88
7			13	22	30	36	42	46	50	53	56	59	61	63	65	67	68	70	71	72	73	74	75	76	77	77	78	79	79	80	81	81	82	82	83	83	83	84	84	84	85	85	85	86	86
8			11	20	27	33	38	43	47	50	53	56	58	60	62	64	65	67	68	69	70	71	72	73	74	75	76	76	77	78	78	79	79	80	80	81	81	82	82	83	83	83	84	84	84
9				10	18	25	31	36	40	44	47	50	53	55	57	59	61	63	64	65	67	68	69	70	71	72	73	74	74	75	76	76	77	78	78	79	79	80	80	80	81	81	82	82	82
10					09	17	23	29	33	38	41	44	47	50	52	55	57	58	60	62	63	64	66	67	68	69	70	71	71	72	73	74	74	75	76	76	77	77	78	78	79	79	80	80	80
11						08	15	21	27	31	35	39	42	45	48	50	52	54	56	58	59	61	62	63	65	66	67	68	69	69	70	71	72	73	73	74	74	75	76	76	77	77	78	78	
12							08	14	20	25	29	33	37	40	43	45	48	50	52	54	56	57	59	60	61	63	64	65	66	67	68	68	69	70	71	71	72	73	73	74	74	75	76	76	
13								07	13	19	24	28	32	35	38	41	43	46	48	50	52	54	55	57	58	59	61	62	63	64	65	66	67	68	68	69	70	70	71	72	72	73	73	74	
14									07	13	18	22	26	30	33	36	39	42	44	46	48	50	52	53	55	56	58	59	60	61	62	63	64	65	66	67	67	68	69	70	70	71	71	72	
15										06	12	17	21	25	29	32	35	38	40	42	44	46	48	50	52	53	55	56	57	58	59	61	62	63	63	64	65	66	67	67	68	69	69	70	
16											06	11	16	20	24	27	30	33	36	38	41	43	45	47	48	50	52	53	54	56	57	58	59	60	61	62	63	64	64	65	66	67	67	68	
17												06	11	15	19	23	26	29	32	35	37	39	41	43	45	47	48	50	51	53	54	55	56	58	59	60	60	61	62	63	64	65	65	66	
18													05	10	14	18	22	25	28	31	33	36	38	40	42	44	45	47	49	50	51	53	54	55	56	57	58	59	60	61	62	63	63	64	
19														05	10	14	17	21	24	27	30	32	34	37	39	41	42	44	46	47	49	50	51	53	54	55	56	57	58	59	60	60	61	62	
20															05	09	13	17	20	23	26	29	31	33	35	38	39	41	43	44	46	47	49	50	51	52	53	55	56	57	57	58	59	60	
21																05	09	13	16	19	22	25	28	30	32	34	36	38	40	42	43	45	46	48	49	50	51	52	53	54	55	56	57	58	
22																	04	08	12	15	19	21	24	27	29	31	33	35	37	39	41	42	44	45	46	48	49	50	51	52	53	54	55	56	
23																		04	08	12	15	18	21	23	26	28	30	32	34	36	38	39	41	43	44	45	47	48	49	50	51	52	53	54	
24																			04	08	11	14	17	20	23	25	27	29	31	33	35	37	38	40	41	43	44	45	47	48	49	50	51	52	
25																				04	07	11	14	17	19	22	24	26	29	31	32	34	36	38	39	40	42	43	44	46	47	48	49	50	
26																					04	07	10	13	16	19	21	24	26	28	30	32	33	35	37	38	40	41	42	43	45	46	47	48	
27																						04	07	10	13	16	18	21	23	25	27	29	31	33	34	36	37	39	40	41	43	44	45	46	
28																							03	07	10	13	15	18	20	22	24	26	28	30	32	33	35	36	38	39	40	42	43	44	
29																								03	06	09	12	15	17	19	22	24	26	28	29	31	33	34	36	37	38	40	41	42	
30																									03	06	09	12	14	17	19	21	23	25	27	29	30	32	33	35	36	38	39	40	

NUMBER OF PROBLEMS

NUMBER INCORRECT

Inc.	51	52	53	54	55	56	57	58	59	60	61	62	63	64	65	66	67	68	69	70	71	72	73	74	75	76	77	78	79	80	81	82	83	84	85	86	87	88	89	90	91	92	93	94	95
1	98	98	98	98	98	98	98	98	98	98	98	98	98	98	98	98	99	99	99	99	99	99	99	99	99	99	99	99	99	99	99	99	99	99	99	99	99	99	99	99	99	99	99	99	99
2	96	96	96	96	96	96	96	97	97	97	97	97	97	97	97	97	97	97	97	97	97	97	97	97	97	97	97	97	97	98	98	98	98	98	98	98	98	98	98	98	98	98	98	98	98
3	94	94	94	94	95	95	95	95	95	95	95	95	95	95	95	95	96	96	96	96	96	96	96	96	96	96	96	96	96	96	96	96	96	96	96	97	97	97	97	97	97	97	97	97	97
4	92	92	92	93	93	93	93	93	93	93	93	94	94	94	94	94	94	94	94	94	94	94	95	95	95	95	95	95	95	95	95	95	95	95	95	95	95	95	96	96	96	96	96	96	96
5	90	90	91	91	91	91	91	91	92	92	92	92	92	92	92	92	93	93	93	93	93	93	93	93	93	93	94	94	94	94	94	94	94	94	94	94	94	94	94	94	95	95	95	95	95
6	88	88	89	89	89	89	89	90	90	90	90	90	90	91	91	91	91	91	91	91	92	92	92	92	92	92	92	92	92	93	93	93	93	93	93	93	93	93	93	93	93	93	94	94	94
7	86	87	87	87	87	88	88	88	88	88	89	89	89	89	89	89	90	90	90	90	90	90	90	91	91	91	91	91	91	91	91	91	92	92	92	92	92	92	92	92	92	92	92	93	93
8	84	85	85	85	85	86	86	86	86	87	87	87	87	88	88	88	88	88	88	89	89	89	89	89	89	89	90	90	90	90	90	90	90	90	91	91	91	91	91	91	91	91	91	91	92
9	82	83	83	83	84	84	84	84	85	85	85	85	86	86	86	86	87	87	87	87	87	88	88	88	88	88	88	88	89	89	89	89	89	89	89	90	90	90	90	90	90	90	90	90	91
10	80	81	81	81	82	82	82	83	83	83	84	84	84	84	85	85	85	85	86	86	86	86	86	86	87	87	87	87	87	88	88	88	88	88	88	88	89	89	89	89	89	89	89	89	89
11	78	79	79	80	80	80	81	81	81	82	82	82	83	83	83	83	84	84	84	84	85	85	85	85	85	86	86	86	86	86	86	87	87	87	87	87	87	88	88	88	88	88	88	88	88
12	76	77	77	78	78	79	79	79	80	80	80	81	81	81	82	82	82	82	83	83	83	83	84	84	84	84	84	85	85	85	85	85	86	86	86	86	86	86	87	87	87	87	87	87	87
13	75	75	75	76	76	77	77	78	78	78	79	79	79	80	80	80	81	81	81	81	82	82	82	82	83	83	83	83	84	84	84	84	84	85	85	85	85	85	85	86	86	86	86	86	86
14	73	73	74	74	75	75	75	76	76	77	77	77	78	78	78	79	79	79	80	80	80	81	81	81	81	82	82	82	82	83	83	83	83	83	84	84	84	84	84	84	85	85	85	85	85
15	71	71	72	72	73	73	74	74	75	75	75	76	76	77	77	77	78	78	78	79	79	79	79	80	80	80	81	81	81	81	81	82	82	82	82	83	83	83	83	83	84	84	84	84	84
16	69	69	70	70	71	71	72	72	73	73	74	74	75	75	75	76	76	76	77	77	77	78	78	78	79	79	79	79	80	80	80	80	81	81	81	81	82	82	82	82	82	83	83	83	83
17	67	67	68	69	69	70	70	71	71	72	72	73	73	73	74	74	75	75	75	76	76	76	77	77	77	78	78	78	78	79	79	79	80	80	80	80	80	81	81	81	81	82	82	82	82
18	65	65	66	67	67	68	68	69	69	70	70	71	71	72	72	73	73	74	74	74	75	75	75	76	76	76	77	77	77	78	78	78	78	79	79	79	79	80	80	80	80	80	81	81	81
19	63	63	64	65	65	66	67	67	68	68	69	69	70	70	71	71	72	72	72	73	73	74	74	74	75	75	75	76	76	76	77	77	77	77	78	78	78	78	79	79	79	79	80	80	80
20	61	62	62	63	64	64	65	66	66	67	67	68	68	69	69	70	70	71	71	71	72	72	73	73	73	74	74	74	75	75	75	76	76	76	76	77	77	77	78	78	78	78	78	79	79
21	59	60	60	61	62	63	63	64	64	65	66	66	67	67	68	68	69	69	70	70	70	71	71	72	72	72	73	73	73	74	74	74	75	75	75	76	76	76	76	77	77	77	77	78	78
22	57	58	58	59	60	61	61	62	63	63	64	65	65	66	66	67	67	68	68	69	69	69	70	70	71	71	71	72	72	73	73	73	73	74	74	74	75	75	75	76	76	76	76	77	77
23	55	56	57	57	58	59	60	60	61	62	62	63	63	64	65	65	66	66	67	67	68	68	68	69	69	70	70	71	71	71	72	72	72	73	73	73	74	74	74	74	75	75	75	76	76
24	53	54	55	56	56	57	58	59	59	60	61	61	62	63	63	64	64	65	65	66	66	67	67	68	68	68	69	69	70	70	70	71	71	71	72	72	72	73	73	73	74	74	74	74	75
25	51	52	53	54	55	55	56	57	58	58	59	60	60	61	62	62	63	63	64	64	65	65	66	66	67	67	68	68	68	69	69	70	70	70	71	71	71	72	72	72	73	73	73	73	74
26	49	50	51	52	53	54	54	55	56	57	57	58	59	59	60	61	61	62	62	63	63	64	64	65	65	66	66	67	67	68	68	68	69	69	69	70	70	70	71	71	71	72	72	72	73
27	47	48	49	50	51	52	53	53	54	55	56	56	57	58	58	59	60	60	61	61	62	63	63	64	64	64	65	65	66	66	67	67	67	68	68	69	69	69	70	70	70	71	71	71	72
28	45	46	47	48	49	50	51	52	53	53	54	55	56	56	57	58	58	59	59	60	61	61	62	62	63	63	64	64	65	65	65	66	66	67	67	67	68	68	69	69	69	70	70	70	71
29	43	44	45	46	47	48	49	50	51	52	52	53	54	55	55	56	57	57	58	59	59	60	60	61	61	62	62	63	63	64	64	65	65	65	66	66	67	67	67	68	68	68	69	69	69
30	41	42	43	44	45	46	47	48	49	50	51	52	52	53	54	55	55	56	57	57	58	58	59	59	60	61	61	62	62	63	63	63	64	64	65	65	66	66	66	67	67	67	68	68	68